Russian People:
Revolutionary Recollections

AMERICANS IN REVOLUTIONARY RUSSIA

Vol. 1
Albert Rhys Williams, *Through the Russian Revolution*,
edited by William Benton Whisenhunt (2016)

Vol. 2
Princess Julia Cantacuzène, Countess Spéransky, née Grant, *Russian People:
Revolutionary Recollections*, edited by Norman E. Saul (2016)

Vol. 3
Ernest Poole, *The Village: Russian Impressions*, edited by Norman E. Saul (2017)

Vol. 4
John Reed, *Ten Days That Shook the World*,
edited by William Benton Whisenhunt (2017)

Series General Editors: Norman E. Saul and William Benton Whisenhunt

Russian People:
Revolutionary Recollections

Princess Cantacuzène
Countess Spéransky
née Grant

Edited and Introduction by
Norman E. Saul

ANTHEM PRESS

Anthem Press
An imprint of Wimbledon Publishing Company
www.anthempress.com

First published by Slavica Publishers, Indiana University, USA, 2016

This edition first published in UK and USA 2026
by ANTHEM PRESS
75–76 Blackfriars Road, London SE1 8HA, UK
or PO Box 9779, London SW19 7ZG, UK
and
244 Madison Ave #116, New York, NY 10016, USA

Copyright © 2026 Norman E. Saul editorial matter and selection;
individual chapters © individual contributors

The moral right of the authors has been asserted.

All rights reserved. Without limiting the rights under copyright reserved above,
no part of this publication may be reproduced, stored or introduced into
a retrieval system, or transmitted, in any form or by any means
(electronic, mechanical, photocopying, recording or otherwise),
without the prior written permission of both the copyright
owner and the above publisher of this book.

British Library Cataloguing-in-Publication Data
A catalogue record for this book is available from the British Library.

Library of Congress Cataloging-in-Publication Data
A catalog record for this book has been requested.

ISBN-13: 978-1-83999-716-7 (Hbk)
ISBN-10: 1-83999-716-8 (Hbk)

ISBN-13: 978-1-83999-717-4 (Pbk)
ISBN-10: 1-83999-717-6 (Pbk)

Cover design: Tracey Theriault

This title is also available as an eBook.

Contents

Norman E. Saul

    Editor's Introduction ix

Russian People

Preface 5

Chapter 1: Proprietors and Peasants 7

Chapter 2: Revolution in the Village 28

Chapter 3: "The Reign of Terror" 54

Chapter 4: The Crimea's Effort—Denikin's Army 76

Chapter 5: The Ukrainian Movement 92

Chapter 6: The New Russian View 111

Chapter 7: Kolchak 115

Chapter 8: Siberian Impressions 137

Chapter 9: Daughters of Russia 158

Index 173

Illustrations

Bouromka .... Frontispiece

Nikita and Lisa, valet and maid at Bouromka .... Figure 1

Lieutenant-General Denikin, Commander-in-Chief of the
South Russian Armies .... Figure 2

Admiral Kolchak .... Figure 3

Catherine the Great .... Figure 4

Catherine Breshkovsky .... Figure 5

Introduction
Norman E. Saul

The author of *Russian People* was uniquely qualified to assess the turmoil in the Russian Empire in the early 20th century. She lived there for eighteen years—from 1899 to 1917—and saw the transition of the country from a mainly rustic and traditional society into one undergoing an uneasy process of modernization. She witnessed the upheavals of war and revolution in both city and country and wrote about them in an educated, yet cautious and tempered manner in this and two other books. Unlike a number of other Americans who came to Russia as journalists and curiosity seekers to write about its travails for the popular press or with specific goals in mind in business or diplomacy, her account was based on an intimate family situation and describes her experiences from the perspective of one who is integrally a part of the scene, not a rambling visitor with an agenda, such as John Reed and many other American visitors who welcomed in various ways the tide of events of 1917 and the civil war that followed.

Russian People is a sequel and expansion of Cantacuzene's *Revolutionary Days*, which concentrates on her observations of the court just prior to and during World War I and the Russian revolution of 1917, published the preceding year.[1] *Revolutionary Days* was a view of the revolution from above, largely from the capital, where the Cantacuzenes had an apartment, while *Russian People* is the view from below, the countryside, and from the Cantacuzene estate in Ukraine, and extends the scope of coverage through the Russian Civil War. This book benefitted from more experience in writing, or perhaps superior editing by Scribner's. Overlapping with these two books is a memoir of early life, dedicated to her children, published in 1921.[2] Parts of

---

[1] Princess Cantacuzene [Kantakuzen in Russian], Countess Speransky, née Grant, *Revolutionary Days: Recollections of Romanoffs and Bolsheviki, 1914–1917* (Boston: Small, Maynard & Company, 1919). It was reprinted in the Lakeside Classics series (no. 97), edited by Terence Emmons with a number of nice color prints and photographs added: Cantacuzene, *Revolutionary Days: Including Passages from My Life Here and There, 1876–1917* (Chicago: R. R. Donnelly & Sons, 1999). The "Historical Introduction" (xvii–lx) by Emmons is an excellent background of Russian history for the period. Unfortunately, there is no indication of what has been deleted nor from which book the material is being produced.

[2] Princess Julia Cantacuzene, *My Life Here and There* (New York: Charles Scribner's Sons, 1921).

all three were published previously in magazines or newspapers, such as the *Saturday Evening Post*. She did not publish another book, such as a more complete memoir that might have set her long life in context.

Julia Dent Grant was born in Washington, D.C., in the White House, on Pennsylvania Avenue, in April 1876, the first grandchild of President Ulysses S. Grant, and was named after her grandmother. Her father, Frederick Dent Grant, was a career army officer who served in the shadow of his famous Civil War general father. Her mother, Ida Honoré Grant, was the daughter of a Chicago merchant and sister of a renowned Chicago socialite and philanthropist, Bertha Honoré Palmer. Bertha and Ida were the daughters of a Louisville merchant who moved north to Chicago in 1855 to found a leading commercial house that would evolve into Marshall Field's. Bertha Honoré (1849–1918) would solidify an aristocratic Chicago connection by marriage in 1870 to Potter Palmer (she was 21, he 44), an entrepreneur best known for establishing the luxury Palmer House as the premier hotel in the city, its first version destroyed in the great fire of 1871.

The pretty young Julia Grant, of modest means, became a protégé of her Aunt Bertha, accompanying her on trips abroad with resulting introductions into European society and into both the Chicago and Florida social scenes, where the Palmers had lavish homes and real estate interests.[3] This Palmer connection would continue in Julia's family through three more generations. The Grant daughter's exposure to European society would increase exponentially after her father was appointed American minister to Austria-Hungary by President Benjamin Harrison in 1889. Frederick Dent Grant remained at the post in Vienna into the second Cleveland administration, thus Julia Grant was in residence in Europe between the ages of 13 and 17. What a glorious time to be growing up in Vienna! Julia's "dark good looks, dancing ability, wit and linguistic aptitude helped her to enjoy the waltzes and gay military uniforms of imperial Vienna."[4]

It was not until several years later, however, that her life turned in a Russian direction. While visiting Rome with her Aunt Bertha, Julia met a young Russian cavalry officer, Michael Cantacuzene,[5] who was attached to the Russian embassy there. They quickly fell in love. Prince Mikhail Mikhailovich Cantacuzene (1875–1955) was a descendant of a Byzantine Greek family (Kantakouzenos), one ancestor being

---

[3] The Palmer Mansion, a Gothic-style castle, was the largest residence in Chicago when completed on Lake Shore Drive in 1885. Later, the Palmers bought considerable property in and around Sarasota, Florida, which would become the base for most of the Cantacuzene family in the 1920s. For more on the Palmer-Grant connections, see Ishbel Ross, *Silhouette in Diamonds: The Life of Mrs. Potter Palmer* (New York: Harper & Brothers, 1960).

[4] "Princess Julia Cantacuzene, 99, Grant's Granddaughter, Dead," *New York Times*, October 7, 1975.

[5] In America, Cantacuzene was pronounced with the accent on the last syllable as "zane." Telephone interview with Julia's grand-nephew, Potter Palmer IV, in Chicago, May 30, 2015.

Byzantine Emperor John VI, who ruled the Roman East with the support of the Ottoman Turks from 1347–54. The princely title derived from the family's political and economic prominence in Romanian Moldavia as "Phanariot Greeks." Mikhail Mikhailovich's great-grandfather, Radu (or Rodion) Cantacuzene joined the Russian service during the Russo-Turkish War of 1768–74, during the reign of Catherine the Great.

Within a generation this branch of the Cantacuzenes had become prosperous merchants in the new port city of Odessa and subsequently acquired a substantial estate of over 80,000 acres in the Poltava province of Ukraine, named Bouromka, described in detail in the first two chapters of this book. Mikhail's mother, Elisabeth Sicard, was from a French Huguenot merchant family in Odessa.[6] An additional title, "Count Speransky," was acquired through his great-grandfather Mikhail Speransky (1772–1839), a Russian reformer and statesman during the reign of Alexander I. As the eldest son, Mikhail Cantacuzene served in the Page Corps at the Romanov court and graduated from the Imperial Alexandrine Lycée in St. Petersburg. A distant cousin, Grigory Kantakuzen (1843–1902), joined the Russian diplomatic corps and served as Russian minister to the United States in the 1890s.

The "Russian" prince and the American president's granddaughter were married in a lavish wedding on September 25, 1899, at Beaulieu, an Astor home in Newport, Rhode Island, that Bertha Palmer, who arranged the whole affair, had leased for the summer.[7] A private Russian Orthodox ceremony at the home preceded the Episcopal Church service, officiated by Bishop Henry Potter of New York. Since the bride's father was engaged in the Philippines dealing with the repercussions of the Spanish-American War, his place was taken by the brother of the bride, Ulysses S. Grant III, then a student at West Point. Others attending were the bride's mother, grandmother Ida Grant, grandfather Henry Honoré, and, apparently, the groom's mother.[8] "The Prince was decked out in a regimental uniform of white with red and silver trimmings, high black boots, and a silver helmet with the Russian imperial crest, while the bride wore a simple gown of white satin."[9]

The reception was notable for the two large second-floor rooms filled with gifts, closely guarded by detectives, and for the spectacular wedding cake prepared by

---

[6] *Wikipedia*, s.v. "Prince Mikhail Cantacuzene," last modified May 15, 2015, https://en.wikipedia.org/wiki/Prince_Mikhail_Cantacuz%C3%A8ne.

[7] Beaulieu was built by a Peruvian merchant (in the guano trade) in 1859 and was subsequently purchased by John Jacob Astor III. By 1911 it belonged to Cornelius Vanderbilt.

[8] Cantacuzene, *My Life Here and There*, 199–205. A Chicago newspaper reported that Mrs. Palmer gave a reception in honor of the prince's mother in Paris at the Ritz Hotel on May 4, 1899, to announce the betrothal ("Reception by Mrs. Palmer," *Chicago Daily Tribune*, May 5, 1899: 8).

[9] Ross, *Silhouette*, 143–44.

Jerome of Sherry's, one of New York City's most celebrated chefs.[10] After a honeymoon cruise from Newport to New York on a private yacht and a trans-Atlantic journey, the couple retired to Bouromka, the Cantacuzene estate in Ukraine, where the American princess added one more dimension to the multinational family. Charming and poised, she was apparently warmly welcomed into the larger family, which included three of her husband's siblings and their families but was clearly dominated by his French mother and a retinue of long-established servants. We can assume that French, in which the new member was fluent, was the main household language—with smatterings of English, German,[11] Ukrainian, and Russian.

Bouromka, as depicted on the frontispiece of the book, was dominated by a neo-Gothic "castle" that housed the family and a number of servants. The estate and its three villages, where most of the peasant workers lived, lacked a convenient railroad connection, the nearest station being in Lubny (in 1897 a town of just over 10,000), located about one hundred miles southeast of Kiev on the northern edge of the Ukrainian steppe, or about halfway between Kiev and the district capital of Poltava. It was a sizeable trip by horse and carriage or troika from Lubny to Bouromka. Julia's first year at Bouromka was not easy, as she succumbed to pneumonia. This brought her mother from Washington for a visit and to assist in her recovery. Ida Grant returned the following year with her husband, General Fred Grant, for a pleasurable trip from St. Petersburg through Moscow and Kiev to Bouromka.[12]

Still, within a year Julia's first child was born, a boy, Mikhail, named after his father. He would be followed by two girls, Varvara or Barbara (usually known as Bertha, after her great-aunt) in 1904 and Zenaida (Ida—after her Grandmother Grant) in 1908.[13] There were no doubt strains in the marriage due to Julia's lengthy visits to her family in the United States (1910, 1911) and to Prince Cantacuzene's frequent absences on military and court business, which often necessitated extended periods of residence in St. Petersburg. He served in the Russo-Japanese War (1904–05) and as aide de camp to Grand Duke Nikolai Nikolaevich, uncle of the tsar, who was to command the Russian army at the beginning of World War I. As an officer in an elite Guard's Regiment, Mikhail Cantacuzene would be among the first to enter combat in World War I. Severely wounded in the first reckless offensive, he was very

---

[10] "Jerome of Sherry's Cuts Wedding Cakes For Two Cantacuzene Princesses," *New York Times*, October 18, 1925, E1.

[11] There were several "frauleins" on the staff.

[12] "Mrs. F. D. Grant Starts Home," *Chicago Daily Tribune*, April 5, 1900, 3. A photograph of Julia, her father, and son Mikhail (age one), at Bouromka, is in *Revolutionary Days* (1999), 111, from the collection of Rodion Cantacuzene in Chicago, Julia's grandson.

[13] The repetition of names can be confusing, especially with three Mikhail Mikhailovich Cantacuzenes in direct line, but also of Idas, Berthas, and Potters in the Palmer family and Ulysses Grants (Julia's brother, uncle, and grandfather).

fortunate to survive a difficult transport back from the front and a long recuperation.[14] Restored to health and promoted to the rank of general, he commanded a cavalry regiment in what has been claimed to be the last major cavalry charge against a fortified position (1915).[15]

Despite Bouromka's distance from the railroad and Russia's industrial centers, life on the estate would not remain untouched by the turmoil of the Russo-Japanese War and the 1905 revolution. Sadness and loss brought the war home. Julia's Russian brother-in-law Boris, an officer in the navy, served aboard the Second Russian Pacific squadron (Baltic Fleet) enroute to the catastrophic Battle of Tsushima in May 1905, though he never reached Tsushima, succumbing to "tropical fever" enroute. The 1905 revolution reached Bouromka in the pillaging of shops in town while Julia and the children were away, first in St. Petersburg and then in England and Europe. In 1906, hoping to keep Mikhail and Bertha out of harm's way, Julia sent them to visit family in the United States.

By this time, Julia Grant had settled into the life of a Russian noblewoman, attended by servants and nurses, and would proudly carry her titles of Princess Cantacuzene/Countess Speransky somewhat awkwardly to the end of her life and well after she divorced her husband in 1934. Reading *Russian People*, one feels the aristocratic milieu depicted through an authorial lens tinted with nostalgia for her life of privilege, since by the time of writing the world of Bouromka was no more, except in memory. No doubt nostalgia underlies her sentimental and perhaps overly idyllic picture of the "Russian" countryside on the eve of war and revolution: the growth in peasant ownership of land due to the reforms instituted by Prime Minister Petr Stolypin (assassinated in 1911), new schools, pride in progress and prosperity. But Cantacuzene also notes the inroads made by "travelers" carrying revolutionary ideas, ideas that found fertile soil among villagers increasingly dissatisfied with ineffectual government leadership and the hardships and human losses brought by the seemingly endless and senseless First World War. The princess is perhaps overly optimistic about Russia's divine destiny—if only the Allies will recompense Russia for the sacrifices that allowed them to win the war.

Isolated from Allied support due to the closure of the Baltic and Black Sea ports, by 1917 Russia had run short of the supplies crucial to waging total war. The strains on rail transportation are revealed in the author's descriptions of wartime trips back to Bouromka. The Provisional Government created after the revolution of

---

[14] This is described in Cantacuzene's first book, *Revolutionary Days: Recollections of Romanoffs and Bolsheviks, 1914–1917* (Boston: Small, Maynard & Company 1919), 38–46.

[15] Noted in several later newspaper articles; it cannot be verified by American experts on Russia in World War I.

February–March 1917[16] and the abdication of Nicholas II was powerless to stop the deterioration of conditions within the Russian Empire and the increasingly vociferous opposition to the war. In the spring of 1917, Julia Grant Cantacuzene traveled from Bouromka to Petrograd,[17] where she took up residence in the family apartment at the Evropeiskaya (Hotel Europe). Her chief motivation was to check on family interests, especially son Mikhail who, at sixteen, was a student in the Imperial Alexandrine Lycée. The teenager's main complaint about the revolution was the disruption of his school classes. Prince Cantacuzene had reached Petrograd earlier, just a week after the tsar's abdication, on previously scheduled business, and was forced to carry his bags from the station to his club, the Yacht Club, on the Neva, then to suffer the indignity of arrest and abuse before being released and allowed to complete his assignment.

The Cantacuzenes, frustrated by the lack of adequate leadership at the top and blaming the nefarious influences of the empress and a "German clique," supported this revolution. At first, they welcomed the Provisional Government and hoped that the Constituent Assembly would produce a new leader with vision and experience. Grand Duke Nikolai Mikhailovich (1859–1919), a cousin of the tsar and respected historian and estate manager who promoted education, had support in the Duma, and was favored by the dowager empress.[18] But the economic situation and the war effort continued to deteriorate throughout 1917. The Cantacuzene family escaped most of the rest of the revolutionary year by taking residence in Kiev, where Mikhail's regiment was stationed to maintain order. Since the city was comparatively calm, Mikhail saw further action on the Southwestern Front, participating at the head of his unit in the "Kerensky Offensive."

Julia felt that "Kiev seemed enchanting after the capital, with its gay streets and gardens, its charming, luxurious homes, and the great, splendid, picturesque piles of ancient monasteries and churches, crowned by their numerous golden domes."[19] Their home, conveniently located near the military headquarters, had a balcony that

---

[16] Russia at this time was officially on the older Julian calendar, while most European countries adhered to the newer Gregorian. In the twentieth century the difference was 13 days, thus February 28 in Petrograd was March 13 in London.

[17] At the beginning of World War I, the unbecomingly "German"-sounding St. Petersburg was renamed Petrograd; after the death of Vladimir Lenin in 1924, the city became Leningrad. Many Russians, however referred to the city as "Piter" throughout. The original name of St. Petersburg was restored in 1990.

[18] Cantacuzene, *Revolutionary Days*, 174–76. The grand duke, after a period of exile in Vologda in 1918 would be executed the following year in Petrograd, along with two of his cousins. For an excellent biography of this lost opportunity for Russia, see Jamie H. Cockfield, *White Crow: The Life and Times of Grand Duke Nicholas Mikhailovich Romanov, 1859–1919* (Westport, CT: Praeger, 2002).

[19] Cantacuzene, *Revolutionary Days*, 228.

overlooked a small garden for entertaining. "One had the impression of a wild festival in every class."[20] She did comment on some problems: the horde of Polish and Jewish refugees from the Eastern Front and the granting of privileges to Ukrainians in the form of a *rada*, or parliament. "Committees became an epidemic everywhere"[21]—a common complaint of all administrators.

She even managed to spend a couple of weeks at her mother-in-law's villa on the Crimean coast, awaiting the children's planned departure for America. Having received word of the arrangements completed through American ambassador David Francis, she succeeded in shepherding the children by train to Petrograd (the Cantacuzenes did a lot of traveling during the war and revolution!), arriving on July 14 in the middle of the "July Crisis," a rather bloody uprising that began with an armed demonstration by radical forces on Nevsky Prospect. Despite this—and being lodged at the Evropeiskaya nearby—she managed to process visas and passports for the children, then ages 16, 12, and 8, and an accompanying nurse to leave with a party of Americans on the Trans-Siberian.[22] Having dispatched the children on their long and hazardous journey, Julia returned to Kiev to wait out more revolutionary turmoil, especially the Kornilov Affair.[23]

Long established radical movements in Russia, especially the "Bolsheviks" led by Vladimir Lenin and Leon Trotsky, took advantage of the situation to gain control of central authority in key cities, such as Petrograd and Moscow, through their leadership of workers' and peasants' councils (Soviets) and their national union in an All-Russian Congress of Soviets in October–November 1917 (the October Revolution).[24] Large portions of rural Russia, especially in Ukraine, remained outside of central control and in opposition to Bolshevik rule. Hence the situation was ripe for civil war. A major factor in the success of the Bolsheviks was the weakness of Alexander Kerensky, now styled "minister-president," and rapidly diminishing trust in his leadership. For her part, Cantacuzene endorses the German conspiracy theory, that the

---

[20] Ibid., 230.

[21] Ibid., 234.

[22] Ibid., 213–19.

[23] The Kornilov Affair in August–September 1917 is symptomatic of the confusion of the time. It resulted from a policy conflict between the head of the Provisional Government and the commander in chief of the Russian army over the measures necessary to curb the rising Bolshevik menace. Kornilov believed that re-establishing discipline and martial law in cities in turmoil, such as Petrograd, was essential. Kerensky saw this as a usurpation of power and attempt to establish a military dictatorship. The confusion was augmented by British involvement, with the Foreign Office supporting Kerensky, while the War Office urged on Kornilov. See my "British Involvement in the Kornilov Affair," *Rocky Mountain Social Science Journal* 10, 1 (January 1973): 43–51.

[24] The literature on the Russian Revolution is enormous. A good brief summary is that by Sheila Fitzpatrick, *The Russian Revolution* (Oxford: Oxford University Press, 1982).

revolution in Russia was plotted and funded by agents in Germany, even down to the level of villages in Ukraine.

After the Bolshevik Revolution, the Cantacuzenes proceeded with plans to leave Russia and rejoin their children in America. It would take some time. In October, on the eve of the Bolshevik seizure of power, Julia, accompanied by her faithful maid, Elena, had undertaken another trip to Petrograd to make preliminary arrangements, including settling some banking affairs, selling and storing furniture, and establishing useful contacts. Returning to Kiev, Julia encountered additional complications: Mikhail had difficulty obtaining the dismissal papers he should have been issued after being wounded in 1914; the couple undertook a harrowing journey back to the villa in Crimea to bid farewell to their family; luggage had to be sorted and jewels sewn into clothing, etc. Finally, in December, they set out for the last time for Petrograd, now under Soviet authority.

Throughout these journeys the Cantacuzenes were fortunate to have faithful servants, sympathetic fellow travelers, and, as Julia claimed, a good luck charm, a small owl carved from Siberian stone in the Faberge workshop in St. Petersburg. Probably more important was that the name Cantacuzene denoted to Russian officials the sacrifice of a "wounded warrior," a liberal and tolerant stance, and a family in need. The final hurdle was passing through passport control at Torneo on the Swedish border in January 1918.[25] There Julia looked back to bid farewell to her second homeland: "Mysterious as always, Russia stretched out her great plains towards the light, and that was all we could see of her."[26]

Julia Cantacuzene tells her family's story of survival and escape from Russia through her and her husband's February 1918 arrival in the United States. Mikhail Cantacuzene, however, would return to Russia as a volunteer in the White (anti-Bolshevik) army of Admiral Alexander Kolchak during the Civil War.[27] For Cantacuzene this involved an arduous (and expensive) trip via the Pacific Ocean through Tokyo to Siberia, where he spent six futile, exhausting months with the Kolchak army. In the meantime, back in the United States, Julia, as organizer and chairwoman of the American Central Committee for Russian Relief, devoted herself to Russian efforts to assist those fleeing Bolshevik rule, and campaigned for American support for Kolchak. These activities shaped the strong anti-Bolshevik and anti-German tone of *Russian People*, which she was writing at this time.

Julia Grant Cantacuzene used her name in the United States and experience in Russia to solicit donations to the American Central Committee for Russian Relief, gaining endorsements from a number of prominent Americans, including John R. Mott, executive secretary of the YMCA; Cyrus McCormick, a Chicago industri-

---

[25] The story is told in *Revolutionary Days*, 291 and passim.

[26] Ibid., 367.

[27] "Cantacuzene Urges Help for Kolchak," *New York Times*, December 24, 1919, 6.

alist with interests in Russia; and Charles Eliot, president of Harvard, who was the committee's honorary president. By highlighting the need to support Russians with American connections, she succeeded in collecting over one million dollars, including a $50,000 donation from the Carnegie Endowment for International Peace.[28] The American Central Committee for Russian Relief experienced difficulties in coordinating with similar European relief efforts, other American relief organizations such as those focusing on Near Eastern and Armenian assistance, and especially the American Relief Administration (ARA), directed by Secretary of Commerce Herbert Hoover. In 1921, Julia's committee provided nearly $200,000 in relief to Russian refugees, many of them the remnants of White armies, with a quarter of that sum going to Constantinople, and nearly as much to Poland. By that time Congress had committed $20,000,000 to the ARA; the following year it would distribute over $60,000,000 in aid donated by a variety of organizations, including the Red Cross, ultimately saving over 10,000,000 lives. The Cantacuzenes strongly opposed the ARA, believing that its work was strengthening the Bolshevik regime at the expense of the anti-Bolshevik refugees who represented the true Russia. In July 1922, Julia called an end to the American Central Committee for Russian Relief "on the grounds that Americans are no longer interested in contributions toward the relief of Russia."[29]

Unlike most refugees from the Russian Revolution, the Cantacuzenes were well-off, enjoying the support of the Palmer family and the comforts of their summer estate near Sarasota, Florida, where Julia wrote about her experiences for this book. Though they lost all their property in Ukraine—it was pillaged and burned during the Russian Civil War—they managed to smuggle out jewels and art work that they preserved for many years in the United States. Julia displayed these frequently at social occasions. Unlike many emigre nobles, the Cantacuzenes would not need to resort to the proverbial driving of taxis in Paris.

Russian People was preceded by *Revolutionary Days*, which tells Julia's story more from "the top," from Petrograd and the center of Russian politics. *Russian People* is a sequel of sorts, but focuses on the countryside rather than the city. The follow-up chapters on the Civil War are impressions of the Denikin and Kolchak campaigns as recounted by others, especially her husband's experiences with Kolchak. The book went to press early in 1920, certainly before the middle of February, when Kolchak was executed by the Bolsheviks, since this is not mentioned in the book.

In regard to Julia's political views, she was a supporter of the moderate progressive faction led by representatives of the old nobility and a believer in strong central government, while quite critical of the nefarious elements at work in St. Petersburg,

---

[28] "Carnegie Fund Aids Russia," *New York Times,* June 28, 1920, 32.

[29] "Would End Russian Relief," *New York Times,* July 20, 1922, 31. For the full story of the ARA and its complications, see Bertrand M. Patenaude, *The Big Show in Bololand: The American Relief Expedition to Soviet Russia in the Famine of 1921* (Stanford, CA: Stanford University Press, 2002).

especially the notoriously corrupt Rasputin clique around the empress.[30] She admired Sergei Witte (1849–1915), minister of finance (1892–1905), and his modernization policies but found him socially backward. Surprisingly, she had a personal fondness for Minister of Interior (1902–04) Viacheslav Plehve, despite his reputation as a ruthless ultraconservative.[31]

Princess Cantacuzene supported the February Revolution that brought an end to the reign of Nicholas II but hoped for the return of a more moderate and capable leadership, possibly under the Romanov dynasty. She had little use for Alexander Kerensky, "that demagogue," but almost uncontrolled praise for Alexander Kolchak, who led the last valiant attempt to overthrow the Bolsheviks but received much criticism from other sources. For what went wrong in Russia, she blames first the "German gold" flowing to the Bolsheviks and then the Allies for not aiding Kolchak's and other anti-Bolshevik efforts.

In America, the Cantacuzene family largely melded into the Palmer family, especially the children of Bertha Palmer, Julia's cousins, who had been central to Julia's life before her marriage. Life centered around the early Palmer investments in Florida, with occasional sojourns in Chicago. Prince Cantacuzene became manager of the 1,500-acre "Hyde Park" citrus grove and an officer in the Palmer Bank in Sarasota, which was active in real estate development in the region. In a 1920 article in the *Washington Post*, he voiced at length his opposition to the Bolshevik Revolution and predicted a new world war involving an alliance of Germany and Japan against Russia and the West, an accurate prognosis.[32]

Ironically, Julia was much more active in support of the Russian relief effort and more strongly anti-Bolshevik than her husband. She had some independent financial support, having shared with her brother a $375,000 inheritance from their mother.[33] While Mikhail's business activities were centered in Florida, Julia's interests drew her more to Washington and New York, where there were still Grant relatives and memorialists (mainly Civil War veterans). This diverence of interests may have contributed to their divorce in 1934 on grounds of desertion and "failure to show interest in matrimonial duties." The divorce was processed quickly in Sarasota, and a month later Mikhail married Jeannette Draper, a clerk in the Sarasota bank. He became known for his leadership in local civic organizations such as the American Legion, Kiwanis,

---

[30] Grigory Rasputin (1872–1916) was a Siberian peasant and "holy man" who gained influence over Empress Alexandra in 1905 with his apparent ability to stop her hemophiliac son's bleeding through hypnosis. His opposition to the war and generally nefarious character led to his assassination in late 1916.

[31] Cantacuzene, *My Life Here and There*, 266–74.

[32] "Prince Cantacuzene Prophesies a New World War," *Washington Post*, February 22, 1920, 49.

[33] "Mrs. Grant Left $375,000," *Washington Post*, October 16, 1930, 20.

Elks, and Chamber of Commerce. The children would continue their father's orientation to the Palmer connections in Florida and Chicago—with mixed results.[34]

Julia, now restyled as Princess Julia Cantacuzene Grant, resided mainly in Washington, with occasional visits to Chicago and Bar Harbor, and she became a leading Republican Party activist in the Women's National Republican Club. She campaigned for the election of Alf Landon in 1936—in strong opposition to President Franklin Roosevelt's support for diplomatic recognition of the USSR. In an effort to win the French Canadian vote in Maine, she addressed a large crowd in Lewiston—in French![35] She continued to spend winters in Florida, where she impressed younger members of the Palmer family with her elegant teas, served in English and/or Russian styles.[36]

In 1937 she joined President Roosevelt in a special tribute at the Lincoln Memorial on the occasion of Abraham Lincoln's 128th birthday, reading excerpts from the Grant-Lincoln correspondence. She was also a special guest at Roosevelt's 1937 reception for King George VI and Queen Elizabeth of England. As the granddaughter of President Ulysses S. Grant, she was naturally supportive of his legacy; she attended the rededication of Grant's Tomb in New York on his 117th birthday in 1939.[37]

In her later years Julia was a leading member of the Sulgrave Club in Washington, a generous hostess for visiting Russian émigrés, and an active lecturer in support of old Russian and new Republican causes. Afflicted with blindness in her 80s, her movements in society were more limited, though she did recover some vision during her last years: "My sight is better than it was five years ago, but not as good as it was six months ago, it comes and goes," she reflected on her birthday in 1970.[38] In 1975 she died at age 99 in her apartment on Connecticut Avenue only a few blocks from the White House.

---

[34] Daughter Bertha (1904–91) married Donald Macintosh, a cashier at the Palmer Bank in Sarasota, a few months later, after divorcing her first husband, Bruce Smith ("Bertha Cantacuzene to be wed March 27," *New York Times*, October 19, 1934, 28). Son Mikhail (1900–72) followed Potter Palmer in establishing a real estate business and residence in Chicago with his wife, the former Clarissa Curtis of Boston, with whom he had two children. After their divorce in 1935, he had two more marriages. Daughter Ida (1908–84) more successfully married the son of Sir John Hanbury-Williams, British military attaché in Russia during the war and revolution; the ceremony in Washington was attended by President Calvin Coolidge ("President Sees Princess Married," *New York Times*, November 2, 1928).

[35] Dudley Harmon, "Mme. Cantacuzene-Grant Off to Speak for Landon," *Washington Post*, September 28, 1936, X10.

[36] Telephone interview with Potter Palmer IV, a grand-nephew, May 30, 2015, who had fond memories of his "Aunt Julia."

[37] "New Grant's Tomb Opens on Birthday," *New York Times*, April 28, 1939, 27.

[38] Marie Smith, "Princess at 94," *Washington Post*, June 8, 1970, 32.

The title *Russian People* may seem to be a misnomer, since the book concerns the experiences of a multinational family in Ukraine, but Cantacuzene is using "Russian" not in the sense of *russkii* (a person of Russian ethnicity) but rather in the sense of *rossiiskii* (subject of the Russian Empire), denoting loyalty to the tsar and including a wide variety of non-Russian nationalities. In fact, only about half of the population of the Russian Empire was ethnically Russian; the remainder included a variety of Turkic and Caucasian peoples, as well as non-Russian Slavs (Ukrainians, Poles, Belorussians), native Baltic Germans, and a number of immigrant settlers of German, Dutch, and Greek background. The Cantacuzene family itself was non-Russian, and the family language at home was French, owing both to the prevalence of that language in aristocratic circles and the French ethnicity of the prince's mother. Though the author does not discuss the rise of national movements in detail, it was an important factor shaping events, especially in Ukraine. The destruction of the Cantacuzene estate, described in chapter 2, may have been motivated as much by national (Ukrainian vs. non-Slav) as by class (have-nots vs. haves) animosities. Princess Cantacuzene did not witness the end of Bouromka firsthand but learned about it from other sources; she sees its destruction, and unrest in the countryside in general, as the work of outsiders, specifically a "German conspiracy" to exploit Russia's rich agricultural and human resources by bankrolling the Bolshevik Revolution.[39]

Cantacuzene has interesting observations about the Ukrainian independence movement, which she and the family observed (chapter 5), and skillfully conveys her husband's experience of the complicated situation in Siberia during the Russian Civil War (chapter 7). Especially informative is her description of the changing role of Russian women in the course of war and revolution, in particular their role in combat (chapter 9). Despite her revulsion at the destruction of old Russia's upper classes, and some obvious elements of exaggeration and hyperbole, her account of the Russian people in war and revolution rings true in all its tragic complexity.

---

[39] This belief, common at the time, has been largely discredited by modern scholarship. Evidence from both Russian and German archives supports assertions that in 1917 some monetary assistance was provided not only to the Bolsheviks but to other radical revolutionary parties as well. This suggests a much more extensive conspiracy, for which there is much less proof.

Suggested Additional Reading

Bisher, Jamie. *White Terror: Cossack Warlords of the Trans-Siberian.* London: Routledge, 2005.

Cantacuzene, Countess Speransky, Julia Grant. *Revolutionary Days: Recollections of Romanoffs and Bolsheviks, 1914–1917.* Boston: Small, Maynard & Company, 1919.

———. *Revolutionary Days: My Life Here and There, 1876–1917.* Edited by Terence Emmons. Chicago: R. R. Donnelly & Sons, 1999.

Cockfield, Jamie. *White Crow: The Life and Times of the Grand Duke Nicholas Mikhailovich Romanov. 1859–1919.* Westport, CT: Greenwood Press, 2002.

Figes, Orlando. *A People's Tragedy: The Russian Revolution, 1891–1924.* London: Oxford University Press, 1996.

Fitzpatrick, Sheila. *The Russian Revolution.* Oxford: Oxford University Press, 1982.

Francis, David R. *Russia from the American Embassy, April, 1916–November, 1918.* New York: Charles Scribner's Sons, 1921.

Hoyt, Edwin P. *The Army Without a Country.* New York: Macmillan, 1967.

Ignatieff, Michael. *The Russian Album.* New York: Viking, 1987.

Jackson, George, ed. *Dictionary of the Russian Revolution.* New York: Greenwood Press, 1989.

Katkov, George. *Russia 1917, the Kornilov Affair: Kerensky and the Break-up of the Russian Army.* London: Longman, 1980.

Lieven, Dominic. *The End of Tsarist Russia: The March to World War I and Revolution.* New York: Viking, 2015.

———. *Russia's Rulers Under the Old Regime.* New Haven: Yale University Press, 1989.

Lincoln, W. Bruce. *Passage Through Armageddon: The Russians in War and Revolution, 1914–1918.* New York: Oxford University Press, 1994.

Luckett, Richard. *The White Generals: An Account of the White Movement and the Russian Civil War.* New York: Viking Press, 1971.

McMeekin, Sean. *History's Greatest Heist: The Looting of Russia by the Bolsheviks.* New Haven: Yale University Press, 2009.

Palij, Michael. *The Ukrainian-Polish Defensive Alliance, 1919–1921: An Aspect of the Ukrainian Revolution.* Edmonton: Canadian Institute of Ukrainian Studies Press, 1995.

Pipes, Richard, ed. *Revolutionary Russia.* Cambridge, MA: Harvard University Press, 1968.

Plokhy, Serhii. *The Gates of Europe: A History of Ukraine*. New York: Basic Books, 2015.

Poole, Ernest. *The Village: Russian Impressions*. New York: Macmillan, 1919.

Rabinowitch, Alexander. *The Bolsheviks Come to Power: The Revolution of 1917 in Petrograd*. New York: W. W. Norton, 1976.

Ross, Ishbel. *Silhouette in Diamonds: The Life of Mrs. Potter Palmer*. New York: Harper, 1960.

Sanborn, Joshua A. *Imperial Apocalypse: The Great War and the Destruction of the Russian Empire*. Oxford: Oxford University Press, 2014.

Saul, Norman E. *War and Revolution: The United States and Russia, 1914–1921*. Lawrence: University Press of Kansas, 2001.

Smele, Jonathan D. *Civil War in Siberia: The Anti-Bolshevik Government of Admiral Kolchak, 1918–1920*. Cambridge: Cambridge University Press, 1996.

Smith, Douglas. *Former People: The Final Days of the Russian Aristocracy*. New York: Farrar, Straus, and Giroux, 2012.

Thompson, John M. *Russia, Bolshevism, and the Versailles Peace*. Princeton, NJ: Princeton University Press, 1967.

Unterberger, Betty Miller. *America's Siberian Expedition, 1918–1920: A Study of National Policy*. Durham, NC: Duke University Press, 1956.

———. *The United States, Revolutionary Russia, and the Rise of Czechoslovakia*. Chapel Hill: University of North Carolina Press, 1989.

Wade, Rex. *The Russian Revolution, 1917*. 2nd ed. New York: Cambridge University Press, 2005.

Ward, Colonel John. *With the "Die-Hards" in Siberia*. New York: George H. Doran, 1920.

Weeks, Charles J., Jr. *An American Naval Diplomat in Revolutionary Russia: The Life and Times of Vice Admiral Newton A. McCully*. Annapolis: Naval Institute Press, 1993.

White, Dmitri. Fedotoff. *Survival Through War and Revolution in Russia*. Philadelphia: University of Pennsylvania Press, 1939.

Wildman, Allan K. *The End of the Russian Imperial Army*. 2 vols. Princeton, NJ: Princeton University Press, 1980–87.

Zeman, Z. A. B. *Germany and the Revolution in Russia, 1915–1918: Documents from the Archives of the German Foreign Minister*. London: Oxford University Press, 1958.

Editorial Notes

This republication of *Russian People* is complete as originally published without any omissions and following the chapter series, though some redundancy and duplication may occur. A number of alterations have been made in regard to modern style and usage. This is especially the case for names and places. For example, "Trotsky" replaces "Trotzky" and "Lenin" instead of "Lenine" and "f" or "ffs" ending by a "v" as in "Kiev" rather than "Kief" or the more modern "Kyiv." Other similar changes are to substitute "Czechs" in place of "Tcheques," "Tatars" for "Tartars," and "Irkutsk" for "Irkoutsk." And there are arbitrary alterations, as with the frequently appearing "Bolsheviki" being changed to "Bolsheviks," and changes in names (e.g., the Czech officer Gaida or Geydl becomes Gajda). Modern forms of spelling have been adopted as well. In general, the Library of Congress transliteration system has been employed for conversion of Russian to English with exceptions for common usage.

Another problem in the original was a number of short, one-sentence paragraphs, as well as long multipage paragraphs, which have been combined or separated into normal length paragraphs. Similarly, long, embedded quotations were reformed to an indented form.

Simple, short clarifications, usually dealing with people, places, and dates, are in brackets in the text, while longer annotations, or editorial supplements to the text, appear in footnotes at the bottom of the relevant pages.

RUSSIAN PEOPLE
REVOLUTIONARY RECOLLECTIONS

BY

PRINCESS CANTACUZÈNE
COUNTESS SPÉRANSKY
NÉE GRANT

WITH ILLUSTRATIONS AND MAPS

NEW YORK
CHARLES SCRIBNER'S SONS
1920

Frontispiece. Bouromka

This little volume is dedicated to the men
who have so nobly worked and fought
for Russia in the past five years.

—Julia Cantacuzène Spéransky, née Grant

Preface

Encouraged by the kindly reception given to my first book, *Revolutionary Days*, I venture herein, with the kind permission of *The Saturday Evening Post*, which first published them, to present to the public some further tales of the varied and amazing currents of our Russian developments.

The facts are offered as I observed them, or learned of them at first hand, and I have tried to be truthful and unprejudiced. Otherwise these pages claim no merit, but only the indulgence of a public, which has shown me much sympathy and understanding, and to whom I owe sincere gratitude.

Julia Cantacuzène Spéransky, née Grant
New York, January 1920

I
Proprietors and Peasants

Christmas 1915, we spent in the country. I rejoiced on the long trip, to go away from Petrograd's December darkness, toward the southern sun. I had finished my Christmas shopping, and attended to various business—my own personally, our regiment's, and some for the Red Cross branch in which I was interested—and I left town with a good conscience. I met my husband at Kiev on the way home. He had just come from the trenches on our Polish front, and had a ten days' holiday leave. We were to be a large family party at Bouromka [the Cantacuzène estate in the Ukraine] this year, and we anticipated infinite pleasure in the reunion.

Forty-eight hours on the train and we landed, at 5 a.m., at our station, Lubny. There Lukantchik—or little Lucas, who is twenty-seven years old and six feet tall, but having grown up in the house remains "little" in distinction to Old Lucas, who has cleaned the château lamps as his unique occupation for forty years or more—met us, with welcoming grins and hand-kisses. He seized our baggage, helped us out of the train, and while he and his colleague, faithful Davidka, who had been my husband's valet since their extreme youth, struggled with trunks, we seated ourselves in the station dining-room, with the comfortable provision-basket sent us from home.

By the time we had eaten and felt refreshed, the winter's sun was rising, and Lukantchik announced that the carriages "were served"—one for us, another for Davidka and my maid Elène, with a wagon for our impressive piles of baggage. The servants ate, then packed our dishes quickly with many gay phrases, Lukantchik giving us the Bouromka news: "Her Highness the Princess is well... Their Highnesses the children are also well and happy; awaiting your arrival and their presents with great excitement... The young Prince has already hunted with his aunt and uncle... Old Grandmother Anna-Vladimirovna"—my husband's ex-nurse and present housekeeper—"has many goodies prepared already for the Christmas dinner." Though his chatter was so animated, it was not at all familiar; for Lukantchik's is the touching devotion coming from generations of good relations between the château and village, such as I have seen in nearly every Russian household I have entered during twenty years.

Finally, all being ready, we go to the station door, and our traveling carriages—since the snow is not deep enough for sleighing—clatter up, to the edification of the gaping, crowding idlers, mainly peasants or quaint village Jews. We travel in a "berline de voyage," which belonged to my grandmother-in-law. She drove it from

Bouromka to St. Petersburg in the old days, before the time of railroads. It is well built on low, heavy lines, large and well-cushioned inside, swinging luxurious and strong over its iron-bound wheels. Dimenti, most perfect and vast of coachmen, with a reputation, when sober, of being one of the best "troika" drivers in all Russia, and when drunk of being quite the best, sits on our box-seat, spreading over most of it, holding his glossy black horses back upon their haunches without the least apparent effort.

The large red ball of the rising sun makes a good background for the equipage, with its brass-studded, red-tasseled harness, scarlet knit-silk reins, and the gold-painted "douga" arching high above the central horse. Dimenti's silhouette is magnificent, with his long hair and beard, the head crowned by the small, round hat of the classic troika driver, trimmed with a gay wreath of standing peacock feathers. His clothes are elaborate and numerous. First, a scarlet blouse, over which is a black velvet sleeveless garment or dress, buckled and belted with silver. On his breast he wears our shield on red enameled ground, the arms traced on it in gold. Over all this finery is thrown a great coat of black wool-plush homespun, fur-lined, with a high collar, and held in place by a nail-studded belt of leather.

Dimenti's well-booted legs are thrust into homespun, loose, felt "walinki" against the cold, while ice is caked already on both his mustache and his beard. Little Lucas wraps himself in a twin cloak to Dimenti's, and it entirely covers his smart blue Cossack costume with the scarlet sash. Even his face and his high astrakhan-trimmed scarlet cap are lost to sight. Then he tucks fur robes about us, and we lean back cozily and prepare for our sixty-versts' [c. 30 miles] drive in a temperature of twenty below freezing!

The carriage steps are raised, doors slammed and locked, and the horses plunge forward as Little Lucas reaches his perch and Dimenti relaxes the reins. We go like the wind through the town and out over a vaguely marked road stretching across the steppes. These are slightly rolling and white with snow, upon which the radiant sun shines, and here and there a few trees or a tiny village of much "hatas" [peasant huts] nestling in the hollows of the great plains, break the flat monotony. Occasionally a man or woman, in a great sheepskin cloak, passes us and bows low, bending from the hips in Oriental fashion, or a child stares round-eyed at Dimenti's and his horses' glory. We alarm chickens and dogs with our clatter, sometimes, but generally we fly rapidly over the white silence, lulled by the silvery ringing of the bells on our "douga."

I doze through the hours, rousing myself only at the two relay stations, where horses and stablemen from Bouromka have come to meet our cavalcade. We don't feel the cold inside our furs, and at last quite suddenly I awaken to the fact that the sun is already very high, and we have swung into the home village, with its lovely church on the hilltop and its crystal lake below. So transparent is the ice on the latter that the children seem to be skating on a water surface, while their homes round the lake are reflected in the natural mirror. Peasant women are washing clothes at a square-cut hole in the ice. These clothes are wet, then pulled out of the water and trampled with heavy-booted feet, and afterward rinsed again and again till they are clean!

The people with their animals are all concentrated in the village at this season, and the place seems crowded, alive, and prosperous. It has six thousand "souls" (inhabitants), and last month forty-five thousand roubles were deposited in the post-office savings-bank! On all sides I see smiles of welcome and bows from the hips, always dignified and graceful. We turn into the park gates at a gallop and go full tilt up to the great doors of the house where the horses stop short, jerked back on their haunches in Dimenti's most approved fashion. Our horses are not tired, for they are blooded stock, bred and trained to their work on the estates and, besides, we have had relays of three each for our carriage, and of four for each of the other traps, making a total of thirty-three animals for the trip from the train homeward.

The park seems beautiful with its splendor of ancient trees in winter garb, and the château looms up, larger than ever—a very mountain of comfort. It has grown with the generations into a luxurious salad of various peoples' tastes—Empire, Hochdeutsch, Gothic, and even English styles. Parts of the house are two stories high, and parts are only one, with a tower containing five stories at one end; and on the other side of the house some columns trim a great terrace in the style of 1830. But, in spite of mixed, incongruous lines, it has a most sympathetic and inviting air.

There is a great bustling as we draw up in front of the wide-swung double doors. Shouts in children's voices, full of joy. The Princess, my mother-in-law, who is French, shows great enthusiasm and excitement, giving many orders. The servants are quiet but smiling, and so numerous that they seem to crowd one another, even in this great space. They all precipitate themselves to help me, and I am lifted almost bodily from the carriage, as they tear out wraps and baggage with deft hands, and rush everything into the house, sweeping along Davidka and Elène in their midst.

News of the front and of the capital is asked for, for Bouromka is far away and mails are slow these days. The head men kiss my hands and ask, with kindly, genuine expressions, after my health. There is old Moses-Kouzmich, nearly ninety years old, born a serf in the great Speransky's [Mikhail Speransky] time, who has served in the house since he was ten years old. He still calls my mother-in-law the "Young Princess," and considers her somewhat unlearned in the traditions of the family. He no longer works, but he insists on appearing to serve dinner on occasions which he judges important, making great difficulties then for the young butler of sixty-five, whom the Princess brought from France, and whom the elder man considers a "childish outsider," after years of careful observation.

August, who came from Dresden in his youth with my grandfather-in-law, as valet, is house-steward now, with the special function of spoiling the children. He is also a friend of mine who has rendered me many services since the day when he came to meet us at the frontier, with our special car, at the time of our marriage. Then he traveled back with us to Bouromka, for my first entrance into its halls, and always since he has been my ally.

There are a number more of the head servants—Old Lucas, who has cleaned lamps for thirty or forty years, Tiechon and Simeon, in Cossack clothes; Kyril, the children's best friend, who can carve fish and birds and spoons in wood with his penknife, and who sings and plays the "balalaika" with true Russian talent and versatility. The children themselves, an avalanche of arms and curls and noise, rush upon us, asking, all at once and breathless: Whether I have all those Christmas things I promised? And am I well? Where are the trunks? And did I remember all their special errands? How nice I have arrived! And isn't the weather fine?

After hugs and kisses I go up the three steps of the anteroom to the Princess, who, with artistic instinct as to her proper place in the picture, has become immobilized on the top step, and is already embracing my husband. I kiss her hand and am kissed upon the cheek in return, and she asks after my health and the comfort of our trip, and whether I have her letters and newspapers from town? And are her errands done? I compliment her mien and the beauty of Bouromka in its winter garb, and I satisfy her as to the letters and the rest.

Then I pass on to the two dear sisters-in-law—one tall and blonde, the other dainty, small, and dark, with lovely black sparkling eyes. Warm devotion has been our relation always, and I am glad to have their affectionate welcome, also that of the two charming men who are their husbands and my almost-brothers. Beyond in a group of nephews and nieces, stand a number of governesses (misses and mademoiselles and frauleins), and at the rear our children's nurse, who has been by own special tyrant for seventeen years past. Finally the enormous proportions of "Grandmother Anna-Vladimirovna," who, in her best cap, surrounded by a number of little housemaids, ends the reception line.

Everywhere there are wood-fires in open grates or in vast stoves, with the smell of burning green pine, and through huge windows the sun comes streaming gayly. One sees views that are romantic and tranquil over the lake and wooded valley, which form the park. Great rooms there are, rich in priceless books and paintings, while treasures collected through three hundred years fill cabinets scattered about. Old wood-paneled walls carved in Bouromka by our own people, as are also the marvelously fine inlaid floors, with ancient furniture, used by many generations, worn, but still luxuriously comfortable; splendid old porcelains, silver, and bronzes complete the house, itself built by our serfs of home-made bricks. Carpets and laces woven by peasant women's hands add a dainty note here and there to the picture.

Everything is the slow growth of centuries of family life, and an atmosphere of delightful civilization pervades all. The village people who work in the château partake of its tone and air. From generation to generation they have belonged to us and to it, and their pride is in their service, which is intelligent and willing. They speak of everything as "ours," and, taking part in our lives, they expect us to enter into theirs. It is all a typically Russian scene, and this whole frame of life lacks completely cold or classic style, but is brimming over instead with sentiment. It is rich in kindliness and in patriarchal hospitality built on generous lines.

With Christmas Eve, excitement in the château culminates. Guests arrive, our neighbors, coming from their estates, the frontiers of which touch ours next door—meaning fifteen miles or so away. They look and act as if they had just stepped from one of Gogol's novels. One is General Paul-Karlovich Lang, who was an aide-de-camp years ago to the old Grand Duke Mikhail Nikolaevich, in the gay days when the latter was Viceroy of the Caucasus (about 1870). He was decorated for bravery on the field during the Turkish War; and now at the age of seventy-five, though a little bent and slow of movement, Paul-Karlovich's eyes twinkle merrily behind his big spectacles, and his florid round face is most agreeable still. He is courteous, accomplished, and altogether willing to add to the general fun, and one readily understands the rumor that his road through life has been strewn with broken hearts.

His widowed sister, who came with him, is rolling in fat, and wears a round skirt, loose jacket, flat shoes with silver buckles, and heavy white woollen stockings. Nothing on her is stiff or tight, and the children adore her and go to her naturally—she is so maternal. In fact, we all love her almost as much as they do, for her charm is as potent as her brother's, and they are both simple and sincere. They have come to us with children and grandchildren, and an English governess, to reinforce our large group, and the house is full now with gay talk, and songs, and laughter, and little running feet. The guests join in trimming the rooms with green branches, brought in fresh-picked from the forest, and in arranging the gifts on the Christmas tree. There is great gaiety in unpacking all my purchases, choosing the various presents and doing up the bundles; and, as usual in such cases, everything is lost and found many times over, to be finally, by the united efforts of the crowd, put each in its right place for the fête.

In all this the guests are as busy as we are, and just as interested; and old Paul-Karlovich and his sister tell us how they came to play at Bouromka when they were babies, with their parents, who visited my husband's grandmother. The phonograph alternates with the piano. Of course lessons are tabooed, and the children play a pantomime and dance a ballet for us; and, complimented duly, they are feeling most proud of their success.

The tree is finally ready, and all the vast household pours into the great hall that it lights up so well. The servants are a joy to see with their radiant faces; especially the dozen or so young under housemaids, who are dressed in pretty national costumes and look like lovely dolls. Red, blue, and green-flowered skirts, full-sleeved, hand-embroidered blouses they wear, with necklaces of varied beads hanging from chin to bosom in masses, colored ribbons tying these behind at their necks. They wear flowers in large crowns about smooth-brushed heads, and, with their young, fresh faces, are as decorative as the tree itself.

"Grandmother Anna-Vladimirovna" sits regally presiding, with a huge clothes-basket full of cakes on her left, and a pendant basket on her right, which is filled with multi-colored boxes of sweets for all the retainers. Presents for the children are scattered about in piles, and for us grown-ups a large table groans under its load of them. It is the reign of music and good cheer, song, dance, and light. Our men are all here from the trenches, and the boys are back from their city schools. Every one has been working through the hard long year of 1915 to help the army win the war, and all have suffered; so now we feel we have a right to these few days of rest and plenty; and we enjoy them to the full, forgetting the past strain. Tomorrow we must again take up our burdens; but we shall then have at least the memory of this glowing family fête to help us live.

Christmas Day there is a beautiful religious service in the church, where from our loge we look down on all the peasants gathered there, devoutly praying. Then there is a feast at table, with the priest and the intendants invited—the bigwigs of our estate. After that, for a few days there are dancing, riding, sleighing, skating, skiing, and hunting in the old classic Russian manner, with low sledges and the borzoi-hounds. The older people set about the house, playing bridge or talking endlessly, and with a brilliancy no other race could put into its conversation—anecdotes and experiences covering three or four reigns, quotations from the best literature of two or three languages, sallies of wit, gay, light-hearted laughter, with no effort or ceremony at all.

Only too quickly it came to an end and the party scattered! Our neighbors went back to their home interests, our men to the three fronts, where each had his service—my husband commanding the Cuirassiers on the Polish front, one brother-in-law to staff work in Galicia, and the other joining the brigade he was attached to on the Persian frontier. The boys returned to their schools in the capital, and we women were left to take up our quiet round of duties and anxieties again—the Princess, my sisters-in-law, and I, with our younger children only.

I lingered on through several months that year, perhaps with the instinctive feeling that this would be my last stay of any length in the old family home. My mother-in-law had decided to spend her entire winter at Bouromka for the war work she had begun, and we younger members of the family kept her company in turn for what time we could. Our group included also the family doctor—a kindly woman, very fat, but as intelligent as she was big, who helped us make the talk entirely cheerful about the hearth in the Princess's small, red-brocaded salon, were we sat during the long, cold winter evenings. In spite of the war, it seemed to me, I never before felt our country so rich and prosperous, and I was greatly interested in comparing this Russia of 1916 with the Russia of 1899 I had found on my arrival as a bride.

In the old days the village had miserable huts, or "hatas," composed of mud, and built on crooked lines, with tiny holes for windows, and crumbling roofs of straw or reeds, which were badly thatched, and were disturbed by every wind. The people fifteen years before looked white and thin, and were never sufficiently covered; and, though there were masses of children, mortality was very great among them, and many were deformed or scrofulous. One's heart ached to see their poor pinched faces and meager little bodies.

The peasants were all in debt also in the olden days, and were more or less sodden with "vodka," which was the only consolation for their misery, and incidentally was the greatest source of revenue in our government's budget. Every man cultivated just enough of the "commune's" land to pay his debt to Rabinovich, the usurer, and to have a little poor grain left over, barely enough to keep the family alive. They were a gentle people always, but sad, inert, and dull from drink and poverty; and they were without a care for the morrow only because fighting to-day's difficulties took all their strength.

When I first saw Bouromka village I was filled with pity, in spite of the charming scenery and its picturesque traditions. Even in the fields, in 1899, the people seemed entirely helpless to dominate Nature, or to draw her riches from her. They were armed with the most primitive wooden ploughs, and with other instruments which looked biblical in epoch, and which were really not fit tools for use in the greatest agricultural district of the world. Sad and hopeless these people seemed, though whenever they moved from the surroundings of their village, they made good at once, and would awake and shake themselves. Those who were in our house or employed on the estate, for instance, rapidly grew alert and clever, nearly always made and saved money, enjoyed life, and sang over their duties, doing us service and showing us a devotion such as in all my wanderings in many countries I had never seen before.

In time I attributed our peasantry's faults (and their woes) to three things—the long generations of serfage, the parasite money-lenders, and the vodka plague. Yet, even at the lowest ebb, the Little Russians were kindly folks, full of sentiment and the love of beautiful things—music especially; only they had no energy or will power, and were so childish that despair overcame one's patience in trying to do them good.

The first step forward I saw them take was at the time of the Russian-Japanese War, when the mobilization orders called out the first reservists, and Bouromka's contingent of one hundred men or so left us. I accompanied my mother-in-law to the village square the day these soldiers were collected and marched off. We drove to the tumble-down little town hall and stood on its balcony while the priest said a mass for the departing men. Naturally they were the pick of the village, fine young fellows, who had kept something of the well-set-up look due to their military training. As they stood listening to the service with bared heads, their sobbing women clinging to them and their babies in their arms, one felt the fine primitive strength and beauty and the possible real value in this race. I think most of them had no notion of the war's reasons or conditions, save only that they were going very far to serve their Little Father, the Czar. Where anything was understood, the war was unpopular; but our Bouromka people, as I saw them, were only unhappy to go away, while perfectly docile, as always, to do a vague master's bidding.

After the religious ceremony the soldiers came toward us, and my mother-in-law and I put about the neck of each man a red cord, upon which hung a small silver "icon" to protect him from danger. As we did this, each one kissed his medal and our hands before hiding the present in his shirt. I saw one remove his and hang it round the neck of the pretty curly-headed child he was handing back into its mother's arms. Then there were hurried, sad good-bys; the women wept, and the men, as always were dignified, quiet, and full of gentleness. Finally they were lined up and marched off down the dusty highroad, following a row of peasant carts which carried the small square bundles of their baggage, as much as the law would allow each man.

After this mobilization our village settled back into its lethargy; but as times grew bad from the war, the elders among our peasants made up a committee to look after those women who had no protectors or workers to supply them with food and fuel. They named my mother-in-law "president," and the meetings, held in the château dining-room, were intensely interesting to me. The strange simplicity and the extreme common sense these men displayed were remarkable, both in discovering and aiding real misery, and in showing up imposture of any sort. The assembled group, as they sat, looked like one of Holbein's paintings.

The Japanese War certainly drew us nearer to our people than the château had been since the days of the serfs, and my husband's grandmother; for, in admiration of the effort the village was making, our estate doubled the funds raised by the committee, and the Princess also helped the people in small ways, sending milk to ill babies and giving flour or other provisions to the women or the older elements who were in need. Good feeling became noticeable, and it was then I had my first impression of the population of Bouromka as a mass of thinking humanity.

By 1905 and 1906 this awakening had partly worn off. The revolutionary movement was slow in reaching us, for we were far from factory centers and from railroads; and our peasants were only roused at last by a group of student-propagandists, who came and settled in the village, made inflammatory speeches, and finally spread the news that the Emperor was imprisoned by the bureaucrats in St. Petersburg, and that he begged his people to come and liberate him! This started demonstrations and disorder. Our intendant took fright and fled, abandoning the estates; but even then nothing was really done in the way of anarchy, save the burning of some haystacks. There were meetings though; and noisy crowds, half drunk, were threatening the estate with destruction. We asked for government protection and obtained twenty-five Cossacks, who came and settled down in our stable courtyards to do guard and police work at our order and expense, and on our responsibility.

The family all went to Bouromka as usual that year—1905—relaying one another through the summer months. We gave out that everything should be as heretofore, and that we would give our peasants work through the harvest time at the usual wages. The Princess had them also informed that the Emperor was safe and not in prison, and that the propagandists who had told these lies were paid to make trouble in the land. As we had always kept up good relations with the village, and had lived among our people, she said we meant to go on the same old way; but my mother-in-law added, though she greatly respected the village always, if, after all she had done and said, there were still those among the peasantry who did us harm, and who burned or injured our property, the Cossacks were here to execute justice; and she would, if necessary, fire the village to revenge any attack on the château!

It sounded very ferocious. For a time we did not go outside the park gates without armed outriders to accompany us; and always we kept our revolvers in our pockets, while sentinels stood at various points in and about the house. The people looked somewhat surly at first, and made sullen accusations against the old intendant, whom they had hated, it appeared. I was glad the children had not been brought with us into what might become a hornet's nest. But time passed and village workmen came to their usual work in our fields and shops, the house servants remained loyal all through the difficulty, and gradually we saw the leaders of the revolutionary movement relaxing their hold, and our childish peasantry resuming old, quiet ways.

The Cossacks stayed with us about six months, and after the first third of that time they were purely ornamental; became, in fact, vastly popular guests in the village, where half a dozen of them settled down definitely and married girls from our own place. Within two years some few of the most revolutionary spirits were made our head machinists or aid intendants, and they espoused our side of most questions thereafter, recognizing that it was the right one as against outside propaganda. So the first revolution died down in our province without ever having caused us more than passing inconvenience; and it left us a closer understanding with our peasantry than had existed for a long time.

I talked with many others among the big landowners in our part of Russia, and nearly all told me a tale of experiences similar to ours. Those near railroads or in factory districts suffered more, however, than we did; and where the administration of estates had been left entirely to superintendents, and there were no personal relations between the proprietor and his dependents in the village, there invariably had been serious trouble, and a certain amount of destruction as well, hard to forget or forgive.

Soon after this, perhaps with the return of the soldiers from Manchuria, there was a further stirring of our people's mental faculties. It was like a breath of fresh air let into a room where heaviness had reigned before. A new school was built in the village, so that there was one now belonging to the church, and another under the direction of the Ministry of Education. Later a new priest replaced our old one, who had died or moved elsewhere, and a new doctor came. Which of these innovations brought the change I cannot say, but it came on through the years from 1907 to 1914.

My brother-in-law and my husband took over the administration of the estates about then, and improvements were introduced, with an intensive cultivation, better machinery, finer results and larger wages; and outside, round us in the peasant fields, one saw a reflection of our efforts. Their land was better worked also, and the "mujiki" [male peasants] came and bought from us at lowered prices the metal ploughs we were selling off with also other farming instruments.

Instead of threshing by hand, they bought in common for the village, first a horse-worked threshing-machine, and then they made the proud acquisition of a steam threshing-machine, which was soon followed by two more of the same kind! The furrows made by the new methods grew deeper, while crops became heavier with intelligent fertilizing. They purchased grain for sowing from us and took the best we had. Then they brought their wheat to our motor-run mill, leaving their primitive windmills as ornamental notes in the landscape. The village itself looked more civilized. New houses were being built on straighter lines, and these grew gay with carved wooden trimmings, such as windows with frames and even shutters on them, or gayly painted doors with tiny balconies.

A number of very advanced people even put tin roofs on their homes, buying the materials from our shops at cost prices, and painting them green or red. Now and then the hatas grew quite large, with two rooms, or even three; while the village cattle were sleek, and many a yard boasted trees, which were offered free of charge by the château nurseries. It was the dawn of a new epoch, and into their songs, which had been so sad before, the peasantry introduced the gayer notes of soldier melodies, brought back from Siberian bivouac or camp.

Bouromka seemed to me much more livable in its atmosphere from then on. I liked the awakened feeling. It made one want to help people who were trying so hard to find their way. Under Stolypin's [Petr Stolypin, 1862–1911] guidance came the land reforms, which made the reputation of the young Minister of Agriculture Krivaschene [Alexander Krivoshein, 1858–1923]. These were not yet carried out all over Russia, but our province of Poltava was one of those that chiefly benefitted.

By the new arrangement, instead of owning the land in common and working it together—so the worthless cultivator of the soil drew on the energy of his stronger brother—each peasant individually owned his own field now, and it received the full advantage of his personal efforts. This scheme worked like magic. At once the people awoke to their possibilities. They came and studied our methods and went home to copy us. Their crops were better and better, while, of course, they grew rich apace. They had reserve of grain put by, and it soon required close care to recognize where our fields ended and the fine ones of the peasantry began.

The Princess gradually became interested in her people and helped them in many ways, the best of which was in founding a small free pharmacy. In the hands of our house doctor—a recent graduate of the Pasteur Institute in Paris—it gave most excellent results. She—the doctor—was a Russian by birth and devoted to her country, and she was glad also to have such an opportunity for experience. She grappled most successfully with the various evils to which our poor population was heir, and the villagers for miles round adored fat, comforting Olga-Ivanovna, with her intelligent face and healing hands. She did immense good, and loved her patients dearly after a few months of residence among us, and soon they were bringing her all their troubles, mental and moral as well as physical.

By the time the great war came (in 1914) our village of Bouromka had grown beyond recognition. The population was doubled and lived in coquettish homes, real ornaments to the lovely landscape, while smiling faces were constantly seen, and there were round rosy babies everywhere. Money was saved, and, best of all, only one of the vampire village usurers remained, the others having moved to more profitable spheres, leaving the business of three or four shops, recently sprung up, in the hands of our own Russians. It was hard to say just how the change had come, but certainly it was a very marked one. Though there was still vodka, it was much less felt than before, and the faces about us were no longer inert or sodden.

Every one hated the Germans, so this war was popular, and the mobilization was not so sad as in 1904. The front was not far off, as in the old war, and the men would be able to write, and perhaps even come back on leave occasionally. Large groups of reserves and recruits were gathered in, who went off singing to the frontier, while the old committee reformed, my mother-in-law presiding over its meetings as before. This time it was much easier for them to arrange matters, as the peasants had grown rich. First, in their own right, the women had means, for the government was paying every soldier's wife a small pension in the absence of her natural supporter, and this allowance increased in rising proportion according to the number of her children.

Then the land of all these women was pooled and was cultivated for them by those men remaining in the village, or by Austrian prisoners who were hired out to help. This arrangement brought more money than usual to the small-proprietor peasantry, and suddenly our village matrons found themselves, for the first time in the history of Holy Russia, independent, managing their own homes and lands almost as they saw fit. With new clothes, and boots, and ribbons, they made a splendid show at church and in the market-place, but even with all their extravagance of finery, they still had large savings in the bank.

In spite of the sorrows we had suffered during the spring and summer—1915— with the retreat of our armies, and in spite also of our keen anxiety as to the future possibilities in the political situation fast darkening, the atmosphere in our province during the spring of 1916 raised my hopes and made me believe that all might yet be well. Never had our peoples seemed so gay, so prosperous, and so full of energy. For eighteen months vodka had not existed, health was renewed and spirits were high. It was a question to me, as I watched them, whether all the matrons of Bouromka were not growing too large in their own estimation and their new-found power, whether when their spouses reappeared on the horizon and claimed ancient rights and privileges, almost Oriental, these might not meet with refusal of obedience and of the old traditional service? How would our soldier-men put up with new ideas? Would they give way to the rule of these unconscious suffragettes? Or would they prove themselves masters in their homes by brute force?

The women, in the men's absence, were doing all sorts of masculine work, both in the village and on our estates. Young Amazons cleaned and fed the horses in our stables, under the orders of two or three head coachmen, too old to be mobilized, who were all that remained of the usual staff. Women, with small boys to help, had brought in the harvest for two years now, and had been paid men's wages for their work. Dressed in trousers and heavily booted, they even went that winter into the forests with our sleds, to bring the cut fuel-wood and the building lumber out, and they managed their teams with consummate skill. They had tided us over two years of war, and kept the country in our parts of Russia at its maximum power of production, so the armies could be fed.

On our estate about eighty Austrian prisoners—and in the village about fifty more—did special work, as builders, machinists, and so on. We had no Germans, for, having tried them, after endless difficulties we had sent them away. Those of the southern enemy's country, on the contrary, fraternized with our own people easily, and were polite, good-natured, and grateful. Paid much less than other workmen, but fed, housed, and clothed comfortably, their coming among us was a wise solution of the government's problem to take care of so many captured men; also it solved the problem of carrying on the nation's life agriculturally.

It seemed strange after months of war, to find the southern villages working, living, and singing with more intensity than ever before! I was so interested in the phenomena that I studied our provincial frame with great curiosity, and I went into details as if the place had been in my own hands for administration. Not only were the women awake and working for themselves, but in the Princess's lace and carpet school the attendance was much better than heretofore. Then the older men of the town had organized the general provisioning so intelligently that they held extra grain to sell. Children in the schools showed themselves excellent pupils as compared with ancient times. And they had learned pieces and games for their celebration of the Christmas festival, which we attended, as if they had been cultivated and progressive for generations past.

The priest came to see us one day, and during a long talk I discovered he had in his care twelve thousand roubles, the savings of the villagers, while thirty-five thousand more reposed at the post-office. Also, he said there was an effort on foot to replace the public vodka shop with a sort of people's amusement hall, and he wanted us to give the land and building for this use, the village to contribute to the work of installation. It was to be used for theatricals, played by the villagers, and for concerts and lectures, or a traveling movie show now and again! Of course we entered heartily into his scheme, and soon I began to realize that this priest, who had come to us full of zeal only two years or so before, was the worker of many miracles I had witnessed.

Instead of being the browbeaten, miserable creature the Russian village priest generally was, this one was a man of great energy and faith, who had used the events of the moment to draw his people to him, and into a path of progress, in which he rightly saw their only chance of development. He and his wife lived among their flock in mind and soul as well as body, and they preached more by their example than in words. His services in church were as short as the law allowed, and were better attended than those of olden days had been. On January 6, for the "Feast of the Three Kings," when all over Russia waters are blessed, he had made every one of the villagers take an interested part in the ceremonies. A great crystal house of ice was sparkling on the village lake for days, which had been built as a chapel by willing hands, amid laughter and singing, under the father's eye.

He told me of two cases where a "mauvais sujet" of the village has been reformed by war. The dangers on the firing-line had sobered these men and made them think, said "Batioushka" ("Little Father," the title used in speaking to our Russian priests), and they had come back to confession at their first leave from the front. One, who had money, had even bought two new banners for the church processionals, and with these he had come humbly one day to the altar during the Sunday mass, saying he wished to make public avowal of his sins and reparation to the church before going out to fight again. Till now he drank and spent his money as he should not have done, he said, and he offered these banners as a gauge of reform! "No, Highness; this war is our great opportunity; it has suppressed our worst enemy—the drink; it has awakened our people and made them think; it has given the women work and independence, and brought us riches through the wise financial arrangements of the government, and suddenly we are civilized!"

And it was really true, but not many villages had as their pastor a man so capable of leading them. I was enchanted with what I discovered, and I took great pleasure in writing to one or two Cabinet ministers the impressions of their work which one got when one stood far off. The echo of their efforts rang clear in our province... I discovered they felt very grateful for the news I gave them, and one of them even asked me for details as to special facts connected with the people's need.

In the midst of their discouragements in the capital, where they were at war with the hideous occult propaganda, already flourishing at court, such patriots as were our liberal-minded ministers in 1916 were glad to know that some group was aided by their thought and care, and that from all their planting, somewhere fruits were grown. Each one of them complained to me of the terrible and radical difficulty in a scheme of government so centralized that much of their labor was not necessarily lost. Never could they see results or divine needs, and, at best, they were in the hands of provincial officials who might be good, bad, or indifferent, truthful or not in their efforts.

Once, toward the winter's end, I had a most delightfully interesting experience. I had gone to Kiev, spending two days with my husband, who, being sent there on military business, from the front, had wired me to meet him. The day before I was to return to Bouromka, a telegram from my mother-in-law told me that the usual road from our railroad station to the château was impracticable, as a bridge had broken down. Would I, therefore, instead of the habitual express-train to Lubny, take the more roundabout and complicated route from Kiev to a small station called Palmyra? Of course I had to do it, and I started at five o'clock (before daylight) the following day, hoping to dine at home that evening.

It was cold, and heavy snow covered the ground, but a clear sky promised for a later cheerful, sunny day... About two in the afternoon I reached the small junction where I must change trains, and I found the station building overflowing with refugees from Poland, mostly Israelites, and—judging by their aspects—fairly prosperous ones. Probably the unhappy creatures came from the small provincial towns fallen recently into the enemy's hands. They all had large families, and seemed to have ready money in their pockets, but there were such numbers that they and their effects were piled up everywhere, and the countless children scrambled over furniture, trunks, bags, and bundles, even in the first-class waiting-room. Everything had been eaten from the food counter of the small restaurant. As the baggage-carrier put down our dressing-cases a mass of youngsters, delighting in the new experience, crawled over my things like flies, and took possession.

The station rooms were dreadfully close, and the smell of varied unwashed humanity, with flavors of boots, onions, and sour milk lingered in the over-heated atmosphere, which was thick with the smoke from many cigarettes. My train for home was to stop at this junction—according to the time-table—in an hour; so, ordering tea, I drew out a book and resigned myself to discomfort, since it was inevitable. My maid went out to walk, unable to make up her mind to endure our surroundings, and in a few moments she returned to me with a worried face, saying: "Highness, there is no train for our destination to-day. The one we counted on has been removed as a war measure, and they say we must remain till to-morrow noon before we can go farther."

It was a serious matter, as I had expected to reach home at least in time to sleep there, and the Bouromka horses must be already awaiting me at Palmyra. I sent for the station-master, and he invited me into his private office where we discussed possibilities...

I was but forty versts [20 miles] from my destination, yet entirely unable to get there, and a night in the company of the poor refugees, spent seated on an upright chair and without food, promised to be most disagreeable. The tiny village had no horses for hire, or I might have driven, and since the war began it had been impossible, of course, to get a locomotive with a special car attached, as one could have done of old. In answer to all my questions I found the station-master full of apologies and negatives.

Seeing my disappointment, and because I said I would do almost anything rather than spend the night in such hideous surroundings, he came to me shortly afterward with an original proposal. He said he had just received the signal of a freight-train going in my direction, and to which was attached a warm car—"tepliouchka." Probably there would be occupants in it—peasants and soldiers, but an officer who was anxious to push on had asked to use this means of travel, and a little peasant woman was going too. Would I, with my maid, care to take this means to advance upon our road? It was the best he could offer us till to-morrow's train went through, and he was profuse in his repeated excuses. After a moment's hesitation I accepted, asking him what sort of people usually traveled in these parts in such conveyances? He answered he thought I would find them quiet and well-behaved; so, I thought it seemed rather an adventure, I thanked the man for his kindness and accepted his invitation.

About six-thirty, with the evening already dark, the train came rolling slowly in, and the station-master escorted Elène and me to our new-style railroad-carriage. He and others helped us up to the great side door of the freight-car, where I stood still a moment to get my bearings by the dim light of a small lantern which contained a single burning candle-end. I found myself in a car where the center of the floor was covered by a sheet of tin, nailed down, on which stood a small red-hot iron stove; its pipe ran upward through a hole in the roof cut to fit it. A pile of wood was near, and warm dry ashes covered the tin flooring—a comfortable cushion to put cold feet into! Round this stood half-a-dozen boxes in lieu of seats.

All this arrangement took up somewhat over a third of the interior floor space of the car, while at each end were built two rough, deep shelves of pine-wood—one knee-high, one shoulder-high—where men could sleep, making their berths lengthwise into the depths, with their feet, or their heads, optionally, toward the fire and their baggage piled beyond them against the end walls. Soldiers usually traveled in these cars—forty or more, for ten men were counted to each shelf-bed—and lately the government has used these same conveyances to house the refugees, but it was my first sight of the interior of one.

My bags and Elène were hoisted in after me, and the station-master said in a loud voice: "Please behave yourselves, children, and be careful of the lady. She must go to Palmyra, and I have said she should be comfortable here. Don't smoke." I thanked him in my best words, added to a banknote, with which he seemed pleased, and then I turned toward my new companions. "Good evening!" I said. "The station-master is mistaken, for I don't mind smoke, and I will join you with a cigarette." And I drew one from my bag and lighted it.

Scattered around on the shelf-beds were some dozen men in sheepskin cloaks and heavy boots, peasants evidently, dirty from their toil and all heavily bearded. They were either asleep or drowsily watching the fire with contented faces. A few soldiers were among them, resting, too, but strikingly spick and span in comparison with their uncouth neighbors. About the fire, beside the officer (who had been equally in a hurry with me to leave the junction), my Elène, myself, and the young village matron, were gathered two brakemen of our train, who were off duty, and three soldiers, wide-awake and eating some provisions, which they divided with two elderly peasants.

The head brake-man, full of zeal, saw to our baggage, piling it in a corner, and then he gave me a narrow bench he had been sitting on himself near the fire. He probably guessed I was visiting such surroundings for the first time, and with amiable good-will he set out to make me feel at home. All the men who were awake had replied quietly to my greeting, and as I seated myself and looked about I felt in a most congenial atmosphere of hospitality, tempered with curiosity. But I was inquisitive and I looked forward to having a very interesting trip.

I first inquired how long it would be before we reached my station. "There is one other before yours, Barina (lady), where we shall stop a while; then we go on. And as we have a good engine to-day we shall soon reach Palmyra." There was a smell of leather in the car, and the cheap tobacco of the peasants was very strong, but the man who made me his special care opened the door a crack for air, saying: "So the Barina shall not find it too much." He also gave me his big sheepskin-lined coat, folding it up for me to sit on like a cushion, and he drew my seat nearer to the stove, so I could have my feet on the warm ashes. Then asking permission politely, he sat down next me, and I prepared for conversation.

Elène, on my left, was established on our bags, quite silent, evidently much less pleased with our adventure than I. Next to her was the little village matron, very quaint and dignified, well dressed and with a charming rosy face. I began to talk to her and soon she was telling us all of her trip to the great city of Kiev, where she had visited her husband, a wounded soldier in one of the hospitals there. It had been good to see him again. He was well cared for and would soon recover, and then he was to come home to the village for his convalescence. She hoped this might be by Easter time. Meantime she was bringing apples and toys to the children, of whom she had two, aged two and three years.

I was duly sympathetic, and told her my husband was a soldier also, and had been wounded early in the war, but he was now well again and back under fire; I had also been to Kiev to see him and to spend two days there. I was also going back with some toys for my children, who were much older, however, than were hers. One of the soldiers, touching his fur cap, joined in to ask on what front my husband served and where he had been wounded. I gave details of the wound, but only said he was now commanding a cavalry regiment which had been dismounted and put into the trenches recently on the Polish front.

I neglected to mention Cantacuzène's name and actual rank, as it might have impressed the little company sufficiently to keep them silent, which I should have regretted deeply, as we were just beginning to get on famously. Anyhow, Cantacuzène's part of the battle-line and the soldier's were not the same, so the latter went on to tell us of his own unit's advance through Galicia, and of the difficulties our men from the steppes found climbing high mountains and fighting above the snow line, remaining there for long months without ever having had previous training in high altitudes.

He said the retreat of a year ago had been tiresome—"skoutchno" [boring]—but he did not think of complaining about our armies lacking arms and ammunition during that time. He said they held on, of course, as much as they could, "because the Grand Duke said they must." Then he looked troubled and said: "Now the Grand Duke is not longer at the staff?"

"No; now he is in the Caucasus, and the Emperor is commanding all the armies and living at the staff."

I replied: "Yes; now it is the Emperor..." But the soldier's voice and face lacked enthusiasm, I thought, and the subject was dropped without further comment.

Then the next soldier joined in the conversation. "I have a newspaper here, and it tells of the fall of Erzeroum and the Grand Duke's capture of that fortress," he stated. The others knew only that the great Turkish town had fallen; so his story was listened to with renewed animation, and the owner of the news sheet was given our only lantern to read by. Slowly and haltingly he spelled out and gave us the details of the old chief's latest victory; and even the peasants were immediately absorbed and followed the reading attentively in an effort to understand. It was complicated for them, however, since they spoke only the Little Russian [Ukrainian] dialect, and the paper was in the northern language. However, the soldiers not only could read Russian, but spoke the other also; and the villagers were so keen that doubtless they took on faith what they could not fully comprehend of the exciting recital.

One of them, an old peasant, volunteered some remarks on his own account afterward. He had heard much of the war and of politics these days... "Now it was not as in the old times, when one did not know what was happening in the world..." For instance, he had heard there were great changes in the capital, which he did not understand... "Why did the Czar go away to the staff?... And why was there so much trouble about politics?..."

I plunged into explanations, in my turn, and tried to tell him, how there had been a mix-up among the ministers, and that the Prime Minister, Gorymekine [Ivan Goremykin, 1839–1917] had left because he did not want the people's Duma to take part in the government; but that the Emperor had wished for the Duma, and had presently called it together again, going in person to its inauguration. His Majesty had also named a new minister, Sturmer [Boris Sturmer, 1848–1917] who every one thought would be liberal and would push the war by helping our troops at the front in every way.

My Russian, at best, is very sketchy, and I scarcely speak Little Russian at all; but the soldiers helped me, and after a long time the picturesque old creature I was addressing looked illuminated. "It is I who am starost (elder or mayor) of my village," he said, "and if I desire to do and decide all myself, I am like that old minister; while if I desire to ask advice of others I am like the new man. But sometimes, when things are in this last manner, the others wish to give too much advice... And then what can one do, Barina?"

He was altogether delightful in his naïveté, and as he had evidently seized the point so well, we went on to other topics, less difficult. He informed me that the peasants in the car were "hlopsi" (fellows) who were going down to Cherkass, on the Dnieper River, to dig tranches against the German invasion. "And this was very fine profitable work, as men were paid one rouble and a half a day there; when at home in the village eighty kopecks—or at most a rouble—was all one could earn in a day."

In a corner of the upper berth on our right, a company of four men had awakened, and, producing a candle and a greasy pack of cards, they began to play some game, while various others scrambled up about them and looked on, absorbed by the changing luck. One big fellow was losing and complaining of it, and finally, when the game ended, it turned out he had played expecting only to win, and that he had no kopecks to pay his debt of honor. The group was indignant with him and their voices grew louder. My friend the brakeman, and also the officer, glanced up anxiously, as the culprit suddenly said something—evidently a taunt—in a half tone. The answer rang out in indignation, and it was: "If the Barina were not here I would tell thee what I think of thee!" Then there was silence and the game went on, the delicate question being left to later settlement. I had never received a compliment which pleased me better, and I felt quite comfortable for the rest of our trip, and rather ashamed of having transferred my revolver from my dressing-case to my pocket before starting out with this company of chivalrous gentlemen.

As conversation lagged I said I would sleep, and at once my little bench was moved back for me nearer the wall, so I might have something against which to lean. Using my muff for a pillow, I rested with comparative comfort, and watched my companions through half-closed eyes. I saw my brakeman turn the lantern till its light was off my face, and then he made up the fire, murmuring that it would last a long time and I should, therefore, be undisturbed. The regular noise of the car and the lowered voices of my companions lulled me into a doze, and I forgot them for a while…

When I awoke they were all sitting in the same places, save the officer and the little peasant woman, who were leaving the train, which had stopped. We stayed at this station some time, and the brake-man offered to bring me tea… Then we moved on for another hour or so, and the men asked me discreet questions, in order to identify me if they could. I told them I was a proprietor of the district, and owned a small place not far from Palmyra. Then someone volunteered that the country about there was pretty and rich. I agreed, whereupon he said: "All that part of the province is good, and there are many large estates belonging to great people…"

For instance, he had heard of Bouromka and the Cantacuzène Princes there… I said: "I know the Bouromka village from having driven through it; indeed, it is very fine and big." Whereupon he looked disappointed and evidently thought he had guessed wrongly, though he did not mention this fact. When they heard me say our horses were waiting for me, they all looked quite excited and childishly interested. How many would there be? And were they mine?…

The tickets were gathered up just before we reached Palmyra, and every one was enchanted when I gave ours, for they were for first-class places, and my new friends decided that such had never been seen in a car like this before. As time passed the tone of our company remained quiet and dignified, and to the end all these men of the people were full of care and kindness, both for my maid and for me. We were their guests, and with their beautiful Oriental ideas of hospitality they gave us every respectful attention.

At last we reached Palmyra, about midnight, having taken five hours to do forty versts. We drew up far beyond the platform of the tiny station, and I looked out. It was a fine moonlit night, but near the car the snow seemed knee-deep or more, and, though I had on rather heavy boots, to jump into that appeared a discouraging prospect. I drew back into the car. "Will some of you go down and take our bags? Then I can jump to them," I said.

I made it a general suggestion, and I was immediately answered by my special brakeman, who was fastening on his heavy coat. "One moment, and I will arrange everything," he said. "You soldiers take those bags and carry them to the station platform," he continued, and the military element at once let themselves down to the ground, took our things, which the brakeman handed out, and marched off to the station, tramping a path for us, while our bags were not even touched by the snow.

Then the brakeman himself went down and his comrade followed him. The train-master also came out to see. Turning toward me, my friend said: "Please jump now, Barina, and I will catch you." I jumped, blindly obedient, and he caught me easily, never allowing my feet to get wet, and he carried me like a small child all the way to the station. Naturally I began to protest, saying I could walk without damage to my heavy boots. "Are those little things heavy boots, I should like to know?" he answered amiably. "They would be spoiled, and you would then feel cold, so I shall carry you, Barina, for I am well protected and used to this rough life."

On leaving the train I had said good-by and thank you to all my companions, who had replied with enthusiasm, telling me I had been welcome! Now, I had to thank the soldiers and the brakeman who had taken care of us and our possessions, and had made such a success of the trip. To these I gave some bills, large enough, I hoped, to prove to them my very real gratitude, and I told them quite sincerely that I had never had a more interesting or agreeable trip.

In turn, they all thanked me politely, and wished me good luck on my further journey. My special friend, the brakeman, even went to see whether the wife of the station-master could lend me her "samovar," so Elène might make our tea. Incidentally he had evidently investigated about the carriage and horses, and had found out my name, for when he returned to me he gave me my title instead of the impersonal "Barina" he had used till then.

Finally he hastened off to his train, and as I drank my tea I heard it depart, and wondered whether those in the car were all learning who I was, and were feeling as pleased with the money I had sent them as I was feeling enchanted with them and their sociable qualities. Later, when the horses had been harnessed amid a great to-do—for the coachman and his aid had not expected me to arrive on a freight-train, and had settled down for the night—I drove home with Elène through the dawn and reached Bouromka before its household was out of bed.

The Princess was greatly shocked at my escapade—thought it had been most dangerous, and she "only hoped I had told whose wife I was before starting—to protect myself!...." That I had not done so, but had preferred being the guest and friend of my companions, was "incomprehensible!...." Though she tried to see the joke, she never admitted that with our gentle people I was quite safe or could have been comfortable, and she always called the story "an example of American folly!"

As to the old nurse, her indignation was equally intense, and she insisted that both Elène and I should have baths and wash our hair, changing everything we wore, before we approached "her" children! Of course the latter were delighted with the exciting tale of my adventure, and only too sorry they had missed the party, which had been such fun. "When may we travel in a tepliouchka, mama?" they begged… The rest of the family also seemed to approve and to enjoy my experience vastly.

Soon spring was on us and the steppes lay under a broad sheet of water as the snow melted down. It made a splendid sight. It was as if the château and park and the forests stood up, fairy islands in a great calm sea. The sky was blue, the air soft, and a few birds and blossoms began to appear.

I can't describe the charm of the yearly awakening of earth and people in our provinces of Little Russia, which are quite especially beautiful at that season.

Yet, just then I was obliged to leave and go northward. My boy, who had fallen ill, claimed me, and from that time on I was so tied down by the care his ill health necessitated, and by my Red Cross work, I never did get back to the country again, except in passing. In 1917 came the great revolution. Our people, after most moderate behavior during the first eight months, received the special visit of a committee which came to live among them and to direct the political and economic movements of Bouromka.

The village was fed up on vodka and fiery propaganda for a time, until the peasants were guided to the committing of wild excesses… Our farm-buildings were all burned with their contents of implements, and all our blooded stock was divided among the participants in these disorders, or killed outright, or was simply scattered over the broad plains. Then the distillery and the house cellars were broken into, and finally the château itself was burned one night. The whole place became desolate finally.

The frame of the old life is gone and we exiles have no news now save what reaches us indirectly. Our intendants have been banished to the district town, but, strangely enough, two of the worst revolutionaries of 1905 are trying to represent our interests at Bouromka, and to gather the scattered stock and property. They even re-established relations with the intendants, their ex-chiefs, this past autumn, 1918, but, though apparently full of zeal, in the general chaos, of course they have little power and no plans.

The village, having lost the advantage of its labor on the estate, at wages which meant a yearly income of over one hundred and fifty thousand roubles per season to the workmen employed, is not utterly poor in money and provisions, while the charities, care, and pensions which our family used to give the ill or old (and which have, of course, automatically ceased) are sadly missed.

The fields lie fallow, since the peasants lack organization, knowledge, and the implements to till them. All this has been wantonly destroyed. Twenty-five thousand acres can mean nothing without cultivation, so distress and famine roam our land, and no one knows what plague the next season may bring.

Russian proprietors admit that the patriarchal system has ended as completely as did the feudal days of France in her revolution, yet few among our nobility have lost faith in the future. All those I know seem ready to work out our great problems and to begin national life anew, with fresh understanding and good-will to build upon.

I am glad, for my part—whatever the future may be—that I lived in a time to know the old conditions and the ancient frame of our existence as it was, with its soft charm. Also, I rejoice that I spent those last months of a war winter among our picturesque people, and that I felt their care! Such memories help one to forgive and to forget the worst of what has passed and is still happening, and to recall only the beauty and the best of our ancient, "Holy Russia."

II
Revolution in the Village

It was Easter Eve 1916. All the village of Bouromka was assembled in the church or in the latter's garden on the hilltop. The people listened to the chanted service, then bowed in prayer low to the ground, following their ancient rites with respect and devotion which war had renewed and strengthened. The three great doorways were left wide open, as were all the windows, admitting the fragrance of damp earth, fresh leaves, and spring blossoms, to rival that of the incense. A starry soft night it was, long to be remembered in the annals of this quaint corner of the world, which had been passed over by modern civilization and lived still in the ways of long ago.

The "seigneurs" from the castle were present, in their own "loge," high above the multitude enthroned in feudal power; the handsome elderly Princess, with her well-drawn French features, unmistakable Paris coiffure, and the smart dress of pearl gray, stood in the center of the group, surrounded by her children and grandchildren. Between the genuflexions, which she exaggerated by way of example always, her attention wandered and she gently beat time to the measure of the chant and gazed about at her peasantry. She noted with undisguised pride the splendor of the church decorations she had given, the richness of the priest's robes and of the ceremonial, as well as the prosperous air of the congregation at her feet. She was taking great credit to herself for their progress in such branches of science as she had willed, and for the well-being her encouragement had caused to be introduced.

At midnight the "Halleluia Chant," most beautiful of all those in the Orthodox ceremonials, began. The priest intoned his "Christ has risen," and the thrilling, vibrating chorus of melodious Slav voices followed his with the reply: "In verity He has risen!" Repeated, it soared up and up, until the magnificent rejoicing reached the zenith of its volume and broke against the church's high-domed roof. In every hand appeared a tiny lighted taper at this moment, and the procession formed to march around the church garden, the priest leading, with his deacons spreading incense, the Princess and her children following him; then came our intendants and retainers; after them the village elders and all the general congregation, down to the last poor mendicant, fell in line.

It was a wonderful sight in the perfumed night of Little Russia, which the twinkling stars gazed down upon. When the procession ended and all returned to their places once more, there was still the solemn mass, with its tale of death overcome and vanquished for the saving of the world. The tapers were extinguished, and all was quiet save for the voice of our young priest intoning slowly and impressively. Tiring of the lengthy service, my twelve-year-old girl turned her gaze out through the doorway, over the crowd's heads, toward the château's park and to the ancient grass-grown "gorodok," or fortress, which had been of old a stronghold of the Cossacks against attacking forces from the plains.

Little Bertha's soft, big brown eyes suddenly lost their dreaminess and she grew intense. She leaned toward her uncle and spoke in a vibrant whisper: "Uncle Guishka, do look... Over there on the gorodok, see what is happening." He too glanced up sharply, and with a muttered exclamation he disappeared from the back of the loge, dragging with him out of the church our head intendant, whose aids followed. The village chief of police went as well. They held a short consultation, and my brother-in-law pointed toward the park. Then six men seized their horses, and with click of spurs jumped onto these and were gone. Guishka returned to the loge and every eye was on him. All the family, who by this time had been informed of little Bertha's discovery, were staring with anxious expressions in the direction of the overgrown fortress.

"What an idea!" said the old Princess, audibly disdainful, and then she put up her lorgnon and she turned pale. The churchgoers were naturally distracted from their devotions, and with open-eyed amazement they looked out into the night, while Batioushka finished the mass lamely, said a hasty benediction, took off his gay-flowered robes of brocade, and joined his flock.

"What is it, my children?"

"Eh, Batioushka, see; it is the signal; a great catastrophe threatens; over there the fire dances, and we all know what that portends. Tell about it, Diadia Ivan." And Uncle Ivan stepped forward, leaning on his stick, and told how in the times almost forgotten the Cossacks had robbed and tortured, then murdered, some innocent victims here in their fortress, and how in memory of the crime the souls of these returned from time to time through the ages as dancing torches of flame, and visited the spot of their martyrdom.

The last time it occurred had been at midnight on Easter of the year when the Princess Marie-Alexandrovna died. Her death had been a terrible blow to Bouromka, and: "Who knows what calamity menaces us at present, with the war still going on? See, Batioushka, there dance the torches now, several of them over above the gorodok; I heard his Highness telling Michael-Pètrovich and the other intendants, as well as the police, to go fetch the miscreants who would invent such a masquerade and frighten us all to-night. True, Batioushka, it means disaster, unless it is a game of the youngsters, for never has the miracle been seen without fore-shadowing great trouble to our people."

The apparition of the torches had somewhat dampened the spirit of revelry appropriate to Russian Easter. Probably their gaiety returned, however, after the peasants scattered to their spreads of Easter dishes, with which tradition and the church bade them break their three days' fast. At the château the Princess tried at first to overcome the weight of anxiety among her guests with her Western scepticism and Gallic wit, brought to bear on the flames, but, seeing faces still preoccupied around her, she finally changed her subject of conversation, till by an effort supper became cheerful again...

Later the police returned, reporting they had gone over every foot of the old earthworks, and not a soul was found there, nor was the phenomenon of torches visible to them as they stood on the spot, though it was seen by them and every one else once outside the boundaries. Their tale was merely treated as "interesting" by the Princess, while the rest of the family remained cast down, with a premonition of trouble. The grandchildren were delighted, however, to have "seen a fairy-tale." Each one of the group wondered what would be the outcome? The old Princess finally decided, and announced laughingly, it must mean her death within the year.

But the war went on and neither the Princess nor her soldier sons died. Nor did any scourge strike Bouromka village and its inhabitants. On the contrary, after eleven months came news of the revolution, in March 1917, and that all men were grown free and equal. The people immediately began to prepare for the millennium. Were not the magic words of "land to be given away" part of each motto, announcement, or speech made by the new government? And to our peasants this was always synonymous with progress, riches, and happiness, though of late years their needs and troubles had been less felt with their acquisition of small individual holdings. So, with hearts full of hope, Bouromka inhabitants embraced the new ideals of the revolution, as they understood them...

Time passed, the revolution was eighteen months old, and it was the autumn of 1918, the season when the Slav peasants like to think of a long peaceful winter ahead and to sleep with a well-mended roof covering them, a high pile of fire-wood near the door, and with grain and other food in their barns to be used for fattening cattle, as well as men. All this had seemed good in days before the revolution, and there had been also then a share of comfortable ready money in each man's pocket, which came to him from the château nearby for harvest work... Now things were very different, however, after a year and a half of independence. In spite of the new liberty, life was dreadfully hard—worse even than when as serfs on this place the people had lived under absolute masters, for here the latter were kind and paternal always.

Those who among the peasantry had had to do with the great household had been treated like children of her house by the old Princess Marie-Alexandrovna. She had loved them and felt responsible for their happiness. Her own grandfather's mother had been a peasant woman, married to the village priest, and had lived in poverty until her son became Prime Minister [Mikhail Speransky]. Then he and she were made vastly rich by his sovereign's gratitude. Among the family portraits at Bouromka hung that of this old peasant woman, in her national dress, with a pleased smile upon her face; perhaps because she found herself thus placed among the great lords in uniform, and the fine ladies in court dress.

Old Moses-Kouzmich and Uncle Peter, who were still respectively the retired butler and the eldest gardener, dimly remembered Speransky himself, when in their childhood they had served his daughter, as they had later his granddaughter, the Princess Marie-Alexandrovna Cantacuzène. This second woman was the one they all had adored, for she had cared for her peasantry with her own hands during the cholera epidemic of the sixties, when all over the province the people had died like flies, save only on the fair domains of Bouromka. There she had built a great hospital. She herself had stayed in it for many weeks among the ailing, giving them drops and pills, which helped to cure the scourge. They had refused to take remedies from the government doctors, because rumor told these men were sent to give the poor serfs poison, so even if they escaped the cholera, they would die of something else.

Memory held many anecdotes of Princess Marie-Alexandrovna. She had allowed her peasants to marry as they liked, and had treated them always gently, as no one had ever done before. All those who had served her were devoted to the house. She had lived at Bouromka through her whole lifetime, save when now and then she made a short trip to Italy or Odessa, and once or twice had gone to court at St. Petersburg. The money drawn from her lands had been mainly spent on them. Her boy, and only child, had been brought up at Bouromka, and he had loved the place and studied the people and their needs like his mother. Before he went off to Odessa's university, the old Princess had asked the Emperor to allow him to bear the name and title of her own grandfather, Speransky (who had been the priest's son, and became the greatest man of his time). This favor was granted by imperial decree, and the young Prince Cantacuzène became Count Speransky also. He went out into the world then to study, married and had children, while Bouromka's vast steppe lands, its forests and its three large villages were still administered by his mother till her death.

She faced many complications at the abolition of the serfage, also the problems which had come up as results therefrom. Heavy taxes and the freed peasant's work in house and field must be paid for, but the brave old woman had not despaired. She had labored on, using the small sums of which she could dispose for improvements on the place, and for her boy; also to help her people still, though she no longer owned them, except in their voluntary allegiance.

In the eighties the old lady died, and was deeply mourned by a devoted people, who ever since venerated her memory. After her death the young Prince with his French wife came back to reign in Bouromka, but he himself was of fragile health and lived only a few years. His share in the estate's development consisted mainly of some handsome additions to the château, and of farm-buildings put up on the newest lines. The people were fond of him mainly for their remembrance of his youth, which had been spent among them at his mother's side, so they spoke of him and his kindly ways, and wept sincerely when he was laid near Marie-Alexandrovna, on the hilltop by the picturesque church which the two had put together. Both these people had managed to avoid the fate which overtook most Russian proprietors after the emancipation. In spite of the necessity of paying heavily for labor, they had kept clear of debt. It had been but small compensation the government gave for the serfs' value, and for the property given these (which for us consisted of half Bouromka's land). The change meant a great loss in acres and in "souls" to the ex-masters, but by careful living the Prince, like his mother, left to his heirs estates free of all mortgages, with a contented populace, full of affectionate gratitude, living upon them.

The French Princess brought many theories from her country with her, and also immense energy. With conviction she took hold and pressed upon her Russian people reforms and developments such as she had seen in her own land. Under her direction much was done and with great effort, to bring the peasants forward. New instruments and seeds, new plants and trees, new blooded cattle, new buildings, much new machinery, a distillery, and a mill marked her road through life. The servants coming from the village to work in the château were introduced for the first time to real beds, with sheets and pillow-cases, instead of sleeping on the stoves or under the tables in kitchen and pantry. They were taught to do work regularly, methodically, thoroughly, and all together, as an organized machine, and to keep the great house really clean, while the lands were cultivated as they had never been before, and, though the national costumes almost disappeared, and perhaps also the villagers loved the château somewhat less and drifted away from the intimate patriarchal relations of the past, there was real progress about one, and a new stirring, and, as the Princess would proudly say: "Bouromka was more civilized and almost like abroad."

In the village the inhabitants remained truly Russian, happy-go-lucky and casual, almost to the point of tragedy. The usurer exploited them, and they were lazy and helpless both in their fields and homes. They felt it was easier to do nothing on borrowed money, and to drink, than to follow the château's example and grow prosperous. So the 1905 revolution found a shiftless, helpless, inert, benighted crowd, upon which it seemed to have small effect. It was too far from railroads or factory centers to have ever talked politics or built up political ideals. After the arrival of certain propagandists, who formed a village committee and urged the peasants on, they held meetings and listened with dull ears to promises, and to tirades about their misery, which was real enough, judging by the aspect of the town. There was no uprising, however at Bouromka, in 1905, and our three villages lived through the troublous epoch with only some few hot-headed, discontented men to show for it.

Cossacks who, having come to police the property, settled down with happy Slav illogic among our villagers as friends, chose Bouromka women for wives and remained for good, and that was about all we knew of the first revolution. But elsewhere disturbances, which were much greater, had shaken the government into various new measures, making for advance and reform, and our district profited by these. Since the emancipation in 1861 all land of the peasantry had belonged to their communes or "Mir." Now it was divided up among individuals, in terribly small plots, of course, but still each was owned outright, and could be bought and sold, or cultivated by the man to whom it belonged.

Our people realized the advantage of this personal possession immediately, and some who wished to enlarge their fields worked and saved and bought out others, who, not loving the country, but caring for other things, went with their acquired capital to the large cities, to work in the shops and factories.[1] Sometimes they even emigrated to far-away Siberia, to acquire there new interests and a broader atmosphere. Their going made agricultural workmen rarer and put up wages for those remaining at home. This was all to the peasant's advantage, of course, for we proprietors felt inclined to hold our people as best we could, especially such of them as showed intelligence, trained or untrained, and we gladly paid the new prices. We could use to advantage on our estates men with modern ideas and capacity, so we encouraged the new development by every means in our power.

Thus it came about that one leader in the villagers' "revolutionary" group became our head machinist and was paid city wages and given a cottage in our courtyard. From being called "Thou" he became "Mr. Tiltzoff," and he took tea on occasions with the superintendent (who before had looked down upon him), since in the new order of things he was one of the mainstays upon whom our administration leaned. There was another man, handsome and of a high-bred type of face, Axientieff [Aksent'ev], who, with flaming eyes and old Greek features, had the grace one meets with often in Little Russia, while he doffed his cap as if he were at court. He could make his men and cattle do anything. A natural [l]eader he was, though he drank on occasions, and could neither read nor write. He had the reputation of being "very red," but he had shown up splendidly once at a fire, when organizing the arrangements for life-saving, and again, when there had been a marsh to deepen and turn into a lake in the park grounds, he had forced men and horses to do work supposedly impossible, by the sheer strength of his will-power. We had admired him, though we were told of his defects. Considering his qualities to be greater than his faults, my husband used his influence to try the young man in a serious post of responsibility, and to gradually promote him to the position of head of the farm stock and second in command for the agricultural work on the estates. Proud of his place and of the implied confidence, Axientieff had thereafter proved himself admirable at his work.

Ten years later, when the war came, when no vodka and fair pay had made the village rich, the place and our people were good to look upon as never before. Though many of the best men were mobilized as soldiers, they returned on leave occasionally and brought back news which educated the multitude. This little corner learned something of the outside world, through tales of East Prussia, Poland, and Galicia, where the soldiers fought and saw many sights of interest, and where they grew to

---

[1] One goal of the government reform was to accomplish this: to induce a movement to the cities to provide cheap labor for industrialization.

know a civilization more advanced than was that of their home. Meantime, also, the women of the village were learning much, and could do a man's work on our lands or theirs. They handled their family incomes, decided the daily questions of their own and their children's lives, they guided their households and learned to spend money at will—for food or ribbons, for furniture and clothes.

The Austrian prisoners who worked among us had been educational elements in many ways, while the greatest influence of all was that of Batioushka, the new village priest. He had come with his wife to Bouromka just before the war, had not yet grown tired with age nor inert with discouragement, and he worked and lived among his people, teaching them not only to pray and confess their sins, but also to build up their fortunes and their health and spirits. He trained them even to amuse themselves, which they had never done before, and he put a new intelligence into their heads and a new zest into their bodies. Houses grew better, food more varied and healthier, and village life was busier and gayer. But even with all this there was still a long distance to travel before our semi-Oriental country could catch up with the western parts of Europe.

Then came the winter of 1916–17, when vague rumors reached us from the North of factory hands who were striking in the cities, of lack of food there, and even of misery at the front, where the soldiers were not being well fed as heretofore, and where discontent was rife over the hard life, while ammunition was still woefully lacking because of bad transportation. And who was to blame? asked the people, and the answer was: The government. Had not the strong German party, with the Empress and her proteges in charge, done many wrong things? They had sent the Czar to the staff, one heard, and had driven the Grand Duke away; he who loved the people and knew about making war... It was said by Peter or by Ivan, who returned on leave, that a man had visited their regiment and had told how he knew all of what occurred in Petrograd. It was quite true, some ministers were trying to sell us to the enemy, while the soldiers fought and died, and some others at court were writing to the enemy's government, and provisions were deliberately kept from the firing-line. There was each day less bread and meat in Petrograd, said this wise stranger. Almost no food or fuel reached the poor in the capital, though those who stole from the people lived in the greatest luxury.

One could see how things were going, since even here in the village tea and such small luxuries were becoming scarce. Later on came "travelers" to the village, who were "wise," and who knew what was occurring in the world, they said, and they remained on a few days, fraternizing with the people, reading "red" newspapers to them, and saying many curious things, among others that the Germans were not really bad, but much like us, that soldiers might fight battles and yet between times be friends with the enemy, and even exchange provisions occasionally across the trenches, receiving coffee and other excellent things for loaves of the black bread which wearied our men. What was bad was the German Government, and the

Kaiser, but had we not troubles with our own government and the protected few at its head? It was impossible that one's Czar should know what happened everywhere, or how many there were who cheated. He could not possibly see everything.

Now the government was selling bonds for a new loan, and one of the "strangers" said he knew there was no more gold to pay for these, so the paper would be good for nothing and the peasantry had better not buy it. Of course, he added, officers, police officials, and the bureaucrats would say one must do so, but such men were all in league, and had always been ready to exploit those who were beneath them. They did not even want our masses to know reading, nor have any comforts, and now they were down on the Duma, which would soon be closed by proclamation from above. The people were strong, however, at last, and were learning to understand, so the tyrants must beware.

Thus through the months villages, even far away in the provinces, were prepared by agitators for what was to come, and when at last one day in early March 1917, they heard of the revolution they were far from surprised. In Bouromka the people took it very quietly, and felt at first no difference, only they hoped to see a mending of their troubles. Isolated as our peasantry had been, living in one of the richest provinces of Russia's black-earth district, they felt the general misery perhaps less than did the rest of Russia. Their individual ownership of property had made for conservatism, and well-being was also fostered by the instruction we had helped to give them during several years previously. Every effort had been made to put the best possible advantages allowed by the government within their reach, even to the extent of a new school and a small public library, which under the protection of the village church, helped the younger element vastly.

It was difficult to do much in this line though, as the ministry of education allowed no books put into the hands of the peasantry, except such as were approved by their own censors. The regular schools were either under the same authorities or supervised by the church, and were all that was primitive in their programs, but the people improved greatly in spite of these difficulties, and both Bouromka's schools overflowed with children, who were clean and better dressed than ever before. On the whole, the inhabitants of our villages were sensible of their progress, and were contented and quite unambitious politically, and also they were suspicious of new doctrines. They seemed entirely uninterested as to the Emperor's abdication, much to our surprise, and equally so as to the rest of the revolution, save only the right they now felt given them to govern themselves by a committee. They proceeded at once to elect one, showing great common sense in their choice of members. It really represented the best elements of their group.

What delighted the people most was to hear that they "were free," whatever that conveyed to them, and that they were to have all the lands. From where, they asked, was this to come? Should they take over to themselves the estate of Bouromka totally, with its riches in cattle, and stud, and farms? Should they divide it among themselves?

They had some hesitation about this, since they wished the proprietors no harm, they said, and had always lived well with the latter. Besides, how would it be divided? Ivan, who is a ne'er-do-well, must not have as good ground as Dimitry, who is thrifty, and then, which would take the meadows, which the forests, and which the agricultural steppe-lands, with their black earth? If the house and park were to be divided, too, who could live in such a palace, for the whole village could not find room within its walls? And a rumor came which was very disturbing, saying that they alone would not be given Bouromka, but that, from the North and East, where the earth was poor, would come people to our rich provinces of Ukraine, and that we must subdivide equally with all of these.

Dimitry, who had saved and had bought as much as fifteen acres only last year, and those fifty men or more of the village who owned anywhere now from twenty to one hundred acres each, must throw in their fields too for the general subdivision. In short, all the country would be parceled out, till every one in Russia received his small legal share of ground to cultivate.... No, this was a mistake, and quite impossible, said our group of well-to-do peasants; how could men not "ours" think of appearing here in Little Russia and swamping us, and take away our hard-earned profits? By what right, when we had striven and saved, and each created his small fortune? "If it was so, then let things stand as they are, and let our Princes keep their land, and we each ours: and we will go on with our work." The committee said workmen must be better paid, so higher wages were demanded and conceded, and for the moment land remained undivided, at least in this corner of Russia.

As far as the rest of the country went I cannot say, but the administration of the Bouromka committee was most reasonable, and was advantageous for every one, as it decided all questions with great fairness and common sense, and the members showed themselves very conservative. Michael-Petrovich, the head intendant of the estate, was adroit and blessed with great capacity for handling men, and by his diplomacy through six or eight long months he managed to live with his own people in peace and perfect understanding, to sow and reap and sell our harvest, and to put things in order for the winter. Faithfully he served in this his employers, as he had always done before.

The autumn of the year 1917 brought great changes. Just as Michael-Petrovich thought all was well the Bolsheviks took over the government in Petrograd, and the Ukrainians took over Kiev. To Bouromka came, one day soon afterward, a new committee from outside, preaching fiery red doctrines. It was composed of a delegate or two from the factory workmen's Soviet at Poltava, together with student and Jewish propagandists, and they settled down for some time in the village. They preached to the peasants the oppressions which all the world had practiced till now on the poorer classes, and the millennium which at last was dawning for Russia. Our people were coming into their own, but they must rise up and punish the masters, who so far had kept every good thing to themselves. They would conquer here and then send ambassadors out, to carry the new gospel into other countries, and give to those the same liberty as would exist at home. To prove their good faith, the agents had brought with them vodka in large supplies, as a gift. Before, this had been the people's solace, they said, and it had been suppressed by the upper classes only to deprive the poor.

Also they brought gold. Strange gold, not with our home double-headed eagle and the usual stamp of the Russian Emperor's face, but with curious Gothic words and signs we had not known before. The people wondered as they listened to the strangers' tale, for it seemed this gold was sent to them by their brother republicans, across the frontier. At first they took it with suspicion and showed it to the elders of the village; these in turn heard from Rabinovich, the village Jew, that whatever the stamp, it was certainly good gold, and worth more than even the old-regime paper money, not to mention the small, miserable "kérenki" scraps of provisional-government money.

The vodka the strangers brought was also found excellent. One felt warmed up, stronger and braver for drinking it. Some of the women protested, and Batioushka forbade, but the men said the women knew nothing, and Batioushka wore skirts also and did not count. What could he judge—he who had never cared for it? They, who had returned after three years at the front, knew well that vodka was a pleasant thing, and they had tasted little of it in the hard life on the fighting line.[2] It was, indeed, fine to be free again of the discipline in trench and field. True, their officers and they had been together for three years, fighting Germans and Austrians, hating them, striving, and dying, often with empty stomachs, almost constantly with empty guns... It was very strange and difficult to understand the great changes... When their call had first come, they went under fire at once, and what a fire—with terrible sufferings from gas, and cold, and heat, and lack of care!

Food, munitions, clothes, letters from home, and everything else had been lacking, or came always late. Yet they had believed in the Grand Duke and his greatness, and he was at the staff. He wished them to hold on still, and to fight the enemy for their country's sake and that of their own hearths, as well as for the Little Father, their White Czar, and many times the things they patiently expected did arrive somehow finally, and with these were sometimes little gifts from home, even things the wives had cooked, or knit, or sewn. Rolled bundles were sent, too, containing a fresh change of linen, with tobacco or sugar, and now and then a knife or book, or a bit of gay soap or a colored handkerchief. These were from the officers' wives, while the officers themselves clubbed together occasionally to give their men warm woollen things, or better food, when in some town near by provisions could be bought.

---

[2] The references here are to the village priest (Batioushka) and the prohibition on alcoholic beverages in Russia that was declared suddenly at the beginning of the war. Few countries have entered a major war and at the same time cancelled a major source of revenue, the state vodka monopoly. By 1917, however, control over the vodka warehouses had loosened and made vodka a weapon in the revolution.

If ammunition was lacking, the officers were as sad as their men, and they had talked to the latter as to their own children, encouraging them to hold on with what they had against the enemy: sticks or stones or bricks, but generally guns remained unloaded. Officers and men had stood together, were wounded or killed, and fell like flies during the slow retreats. During these times refugees fled inward toward the center of the country, while our troops had held the lines in spite of all disadvantages to give opportunity for this. Then slowly the armies had ceded, mile upon mile, of a land which was being set on fire as they quitted it. Fields with vast grain crops, châteaux, forests, parks, towns, and villages were one vast sheet of flame, sacrificed to prevent the enemy profiting too much. The whole world seemed a burning hell to march through, in the summer of 1915. A shrieking horde of misery drew back before the foe.[3]

The Grand Duke had been furious at the necessity of this suffering, and he had demanded the severest punishment for those who caused it, but nothing had happened, except that the Grand Duke himself had been sent away. This went to show, the soldiers said, it was no good to complain since, whether great or small, one could only be beaten for it. Things went from bad to worse forever after, and, as the months passed, officers couldn't help their men as much, perhaps because, as they said, they were too poor themselves. All life at home had grown expensive, and those who came out to the front in the last mobilizations had been much older men, or else young boy recruits. These brought reports of wickedness and cheating in certain high circles, of troubles ever greater among the lower classes, and of the revolution which was promised soon...

Then it came, and they heard the Emperor had quietly left his crown and throne and given over his power to the people. In the army officers were now to command only with the consent of their soldiers. The soldiers were to have committees and to decide everything, even as to their obedience to military plans. They had the right now to debate upon these and to discus, until they understood them. Many agents at once had circulated among the troops, pointing out how the officers would hate all this, would dislike to have their power taken from them, and would not willingly accept the soldiers as their "comrades."[4] In many battles, one must admit, the officers had shown immense bravery. They had thrown themselves forward in recent charges, often quite alone, hoping their men would be carried along by old habit, and they had been assassinated thus in quantities at Tarnopol, or so Nikita had related to

---

[3] This depiction of "scorched earth" policy of Russia is more associated with the invasion of Napoleon Bonaparte in 1812 and with the German invasion of 1941 than with World War I.

[4] This is an accurate description of the result of the action of the Petrograd Soviet, which was endorsed by the Provisional Government in May 1917. It was in reaction to fear that the army units would stage a counter revolution and needed to be checked by soldiers committees, especially at the regimental level. Though not universally deployed, it was especially effected in the most radicalized forces in the north, in Petrograd and in the Baltic fleet.

the village when he returned from there. In his regiment, he said, out of thirty-seven officers, thirty had been killed, and in Dimitry's regiment, in the same battle, twenty-seven out of thirty had been left upon the field, while not a soldier had died, save perhaps a very few from stray bullets.[5]

The ranks had stood still or had fled, and some of those new fellows, who called themselves high priests of the revolutionary ideals, had even laughed or jeered when the older veterans wished to follow and to help their lieutenants and their captains, who were being shot down like helpless dogs. Possibly it is just for each new government to make some group or class into martyrs? But it was hard for our lieutenant, said Dimitry. He was but eighteen, and had always been kind and ready to help his men, and he had thought of them always before stopping to think of himself. Still the Bolsheviks' agents seemed very wise ...and they could read! They said it was surely so: that now was come the time when the soldier was free. There were many of our men at the front to fight Germans, the agents proclaimed, and the enemy was ready for peace anyway. He could never reach our provinces before the end of the war.

It would be much better, therefore, if those troops who came from Bouromka, or from farther East, went home and helped "protect the revolution" there, and organized free government, with committees such as they had seen in the army. Besides, all the land was to be divided very soon among the peasants, and, who knows? The village elders might arrange that the best bits go to themselves in others' absence? Surely, therefore, there was no time to lose in leaving the war, and even if the officers thought differently they could not audibly object, nor could they punish desertion, since one of the new laws said most clearly that soldiers were now free to obey or not, according to their own judgement. Truly it was now a good time to be alive!

So, with illusions freshly poured into them, the village men had returned to quiet Bouromka, riding on the tops of cars part way, and for the rest in first-class carriages, there sleeping in the corridors and on the platforms. One night, some said, they had taken possession even of a reserved compartment, smashing its windows to get in, and there some women and two children slept, who had been at first greatly frightened. But the soldiers explained to them there was no place elsewhere on the train, and that they would not disturb, only they wished to travel and had found no other means. One had sat on the floor, and two more on the upper berth, from which they had brought home as gifts to their wives the pillows, blankets, covers, and the sheets![6]

---

[5] This is probably an exaggerated description of the "Kerensky offensive" of June 1917 on the Southwestern Front, which resulted in initial success but was thrown back with major losses. It was the last offensive of the Russian army in World War I, considered by some historians a badly planned mistake. See Louise Erwin Heenan, *Russian Democracy's Fatal Blunder: the Summer Offensive of 1917* (New York: Praeger, 1987).

[6] The author describes such scenes personally from her extensive travels during the war and revolution in *Revolutionary Days*.

During the trip they very much enjoyed talking with the women travelers and telling them of their life under fire, and they played with the children and received apples and biscuits from these, because they had brought water for tea, or had helped amuse the young boy, a nice child, they said, like many in the village. Finally they arrived at Palmyra station, and came from there on foot for over fifty versts (approximately 20 miles), sleeping in the fields under the stars. It was good to feel one wouldn't be awakened by a bomb, said the deserters, and to know that very soon these fine acres would be all theirs. They had found the village quiet, somewhat discontented to be doing without tea, sugar, and other luxuries, but otherwise of old. Only a committee of elders existed, and were governing since the spring.

With Batioushka and the Prince's head intendant, they were managing everything, about like in olden days. This must be changed quickly and surely, and also, it would need much time and trouble to bring back into their proper places the village women. All of them, Matrona and Warka, Louba and Sonia, and even mild Evdoxia were not to be recognized! Dressed in fine clothes, ordering about the Austrian prisoners, smiling and powerful, capable and wasteful, talking much of their new right to vote! It was so amazing that the recently arrived lords and masters for a time quite lost their capacity of action. Then each one got his breath again, and did as he saw fit within his own house.

Vania had knuckled down and worked under Louba's orders, while the Austrian had remained in the house, and become his friend. Dimitry had soon put out the intruder, and had Sonia well in hand, while the others had made arrangements between these two extremes, according to their mental and their physical capacities for handling so delicate a situation.... They all told of their experiences at the front, and of what the wise men had said, and the elders understood that this much be all quite true, since the information the agents had given them was all "printed on paper"!

These "rules," the men said, had been read out to the soldiers from the papers, but privately, of course, because the officers must not yet know of the great promises for the future. Sometimes one did feel sorry for one's officers, and for the proprietors, who, also, were like those of Bouromka, yet it was only justice, and the wise agents explained that some good people must suffer, since so many of their group had done harm, and after all even the best had joined with the worst to deprive peasants and soldiers of their rights and hold them down.

It was very shortly after the soldiers returned from war that the outside committee settled in Bouromka. Ready-made by the chief soviets at Poltava, with vodka, gold coins; also printed papers, prepared to read at meetings, which latter were held daily. Speeches were made. The peasants were told, till they clearly understood, how they had been wronged, and then suddenly one day the student, who had possessed a silver tongue, cried to his audience:

"Come, if at last you are convinced, come with me and we will go to the distillery now; attack and capture it, and drink the vodka of which you have been deprived too long. It is a cold night, and our supply here is finished. What is there, will be warming when you have drunk as much as you wish, and afterward you may bring back a cow or two for the children of the village, who shall thus have better milk, and you shall take the château's oxen also, to plough your fields. These oxen are no longer, even in name, the Prince's, but are strictly yours now by legal right, to take and keep."

The men hesitated, but vodka was again passed about and soon infused daring. It was a fine moonlit night, so the walk to the farm courtyard was tempting and easy. A hundred or more of the bravest spirits were moving in that direction shortly, singing a wild chorus, led by the enthusiastic, wise strangers. Axientieff heard the rumors and the noise, and he rushed to meet the crowd of rowdies at his locked courtyard gate. He called on the workman or two who were up on night guard duty, and he sent a hurried message to our intendant-in-chief, who lived at the other courtyard, a mile off.

Before the latter could arrive with help there appeared a disorderly throng of peasants, shouting, crying, swaying as they marched, and though Axientieff made an attempt to harangue them, and his white face and blazing eyes did make the front ones hesitate, he had been swept aside very quickly by the paid leaders, while the rollickers pushed on and broke in the distillery door in spite of its locks and of the government seal upon it. Then the village men, frantic with the alcohol's odor, as it fermented in the vats, precipitated themselves to quench their thirst, first from the small hogsheads, and then even from the vats themselves. They drank deeply, until they fell down, completely unconscious and incapacitated.[7]

It was then the leaders acted. They rolled quickly a number of barrels into the courtyard and out into the road, where a wagon was waiting to cart this precious fluid (their best ally) away to their village headquarters. They looked about, and one said to the others: "Much breakage, no respect for seals, the second intendant injured, the vodka stolen, and the men who have succumbed are our creatures hereafter."

And another answered: "Yes, the owners may retaliate; that would be advantageous, for when the feeling is as good as here our work is much too slow and expensive."

---

[7] The edict on prohibition issued by Nicholas II at the beginning of the war came as a surprise to the population, with the producers of alcoholic beverages especially unprepared. Consequently, sizable quantities were left in storage in warehouses at a number of distilleries. Hence they became a target in the waning of controls and discipline during the revolution.

The background causes were the growth of the Russian temperance movement in the years before the war and a belief, perhaps mistaken, that Russian soldiers would fight better sober. The removal of the celebratory use of strong liquor, especially vodka, was deeply resented by the lower classes, especially since those who could afford it were still allowed to drink wine and brandy. For a thorough discussion, see Patricia Herlihy, *The Alcoholic Empire: Vodka and Politics in Late Imperial Russia* (Oxford: Oxford University Press, 2002).

The most famous incident of this kind occurred in the seizure of the Winter Palace in Petrograd in the climax of the Bolshevik Revolution, when many of the participants ended up in the wine cellars.

"True," said a third. "I had hoped we could attack the other courtyard and perhaps even the house tonight, but now we must wait, for these swine are so slow and stupid, and besides they are dead drunk and cannot even move."

Just then they all started as if frightened. Had some one overheard their remarks, which were spoken low and in German? But it was not so; it was a man lying on the edge of the vat, who had lost his balance and had fallen into the fermenting spirits. There, all unconsciously, he was drowning, yet none of the leaders stretched out a hand to save him. They merely looked, shrugged their shoulders, yawned, and turned away to walk back to their quarters at the village.

Within a week another raid occurred, on the remains of the distillery, and, strong in the artificial courage the vodka gave the crowd, it had then interviewed Michael-Petrovich at the intendant-in-chief's own house. They had confiscated, in spite of his protests, all the cattle, the horses, the machine-shops, and the stables, with their supplies of implements and harness, wagons and fine carriages. These were the people's too, and would be given over to them very soon by the government law, so they were merely anticipating, said the wise men who led the wreckers. In the machine-shops Tiltzoff and his few helpers had resisted, while at the stables and the stud, the old coachman and a few faithful servants had done likewise, but with the same results as when Axientieff had been swept aside at the farmyard a week earlier.

Our protectors were only about twenty in all, and there were many more than that of the village hotheads, some of whom were growing into first-class revolutionary leaders. The three or four strangers were clever inspirers of action, and were spokesmen ready with quick replies for every protest of the intendants. So all gave way before the rule of the strongest, and there was a sudden wish expressed to visit the château. This was done immediately. The ancient collections of arms, as well as the cupboards containing our modern guns used in the shooting season, were handed over to the "committee" by the head house-steward. They were carted away for safe-keeping in the village! The various cupboards and the wine-cellars of the château were all sealed, and clothes with books and everything else necessary to the family's life were thus left locked up in comparative safety, but were, of course, no longer attainable by their ancient owners—ourselves.

The intendant, his wife, and their fourteen children were left tranquil in their home, while the housekeeper, the majordomo, and various other ancient servants were allowed to remain in their rooms in one wing of the château, till it should be decided to what use the immense place could be put: whether that of a house of public amusement or a school. During two or three months this question was daily brought up for discussion at the village meetings. The leaders recommended complete destruction, and said that it would be great trouble and work to keep such a vast building heated. The village elders, with their peasant's common sense, advocated leaving the house as it was:

"One must leave something to the Princes, and the house is nothing to us, since we have the land already and all that goes to make it rich. Besides, their clothes and dishes are their own in all justice, for the new law speaks only about the land. And then who knows? These wise men talk well, but perhaps they make mistakes, and some day we may hear of different rules again. The Princes may return and ask what has been done with their palace, and clothes, and other things. If all is lost, we may well be punished for stealing. Yes, truly, better we leave the château alone."

There were some timid spirits, who already trembled as to the results of their present bravery. "We know," they said, "now it is all take and enjoy, and soon after it will be restitution and payment called for: and we shall be beaten then!"

"Who can beat you now? For this is a republic," cried the leaders.

"Naturally, naturally, we have heard that. First come people and say to us: be for autocracy, it is strength, and the sovereign shall love and care for his people, and all will be well, and we sing the anthem and cry hurrah, and are for an autocracy. And next comes some one who says: be for a republic, and it will be well, for the land shall belong to the peasants, and they will grow rich and great, and he teaches us a song which is of liberty, and tells us every one is singing it on the streets in Petrograd, so we learn that new song, and cry hurrah and seize the land. Yet who knows? Perhaps we may still be unhappy, for even now our grain is taken forcibly from us, whenever it is found, and we are paid in dirty paper slips without value. We have less food and comfort than before... Later maybe some man will come and tell us there is a republic with a Czar in Petrograd, and then we shall again cry hurrah, and learn the song of that King, and we will both own the land then, and also be taken care of by our Princes, and that would be the best of all!"

Even with the vodka's help and the foreign leaders' best persuasions, it took some time to accomplish their errand of complete political and economic debauchery, where previous good relations between proprietor and peasant were against them; and especially where all the heads of departments on estates came from the latter class, and so understood their own people well. After five or six months' residence in Bouromka, the strangers won their way, however, to the weak spots of their audience's simple understandings, and they paid for this popularity by encouraging every vice and abuse which was latent in our village.

One evening finally, in the spring of 1918, as darkness descended, the ancient majordomo and old "Grandmother Anna-Vladimirovna," the housekeeper, were having tea together in the latter's comfortable sitting-room, when across the distance of the park a noise reached them—something between songs and buzzing and the tramp of many feet far off. "A meeting," said Moses-Kouzmich.

"Louder than usual; they have been drinking again," answered our tranquil housekeeper, and they discussed for the five-hundredth time the revolution from their own view-point:

"All these fools know nothing of what they talk about," said the old man. "What need have they of more than the good God and the Czar have given them? And when they shall have done away with all the high-born people, who will they serve, I would like to know? And steal from comfortably? And who will care for them? Speransky and all of our seigneurs here have helped each one of us who was intelligent or capable of moving forward, and I for one (who am eighty-three, and wiser than the false prophets these madcaps run after), I tell you Anna, who are young and but sixty-five, that I will not serve in the house of peasants become rich, who cannot read or write! I know little of the Czar and the government, but we are well off here, and when I was in St. Petersburg, fifty years ago, with our Princess Marie-Alexandrovna, I saw many others were as content as we are. When one has lived in our aristocratic palaces, one knows the difference well between them and such a house as even rich Dimitry of the village would keep."

"Moses-Kouzmich, I who was head nurse to all their small Highnesses, know well you tell the truth, and each of us who have been dressed, and warmed, and fed, and who have pretty cottages in the village to retire to, and a sure pension to live upon, feel as you do: but the new generation has gone quite mad and realizes nothing! Why, even the nieces and nephews whom I feed always from the château pantry, and send provisions to of the best in my storerooms, are that ungrateful they would pull this roof down over our heads if they could... Strange, that noise; is it not approaching? Listen!"

And going to the window, she drew the curtain open and looked over the valley, which held the park with its great trees and its crystal lake now reflecting the full moon. A vast noise filled the little room as she opened its window and leaned out: and as she turned again it was with rapid movement not usual to her fat body. "Heaven help us, Moses-Kouzmich; run and shut and bar our door, while I telephone Michael-Pètrovich. It is a great crowd coming up the Speransky-Allee, and the procession is illuminated by torches, and they are singing, but not good songs. It is as if they were all crazy! Thank heaven, the valuables are sent to Kiev since long, and all that silver, too, but my pearl brooch and gold earrings and watch, what shall I do to hide them? In my mattress, perhaps? Or only in my pocket with my keys? Who ever would have thought that I would live to see and hear such things? But, of course, Michael-Petrovich will quiet these people and put them in their place."

And she disappeared, frowning, down the corridor toward the telephone. Old Moses-Kouzmich, somewhat hard of hearing and dull of mind, went off nodding and muttering to the door, but he reached it only in time to meet the intendant, who had long ago realized the storm was brewing, and who came running, followed by Tiltzoff, Axientieff, and his other lieutenants. Even Kalaschnikoff, head of the huntsmen and kennels, came with his long whip, and Bibikov the veterinary, and the old coachman Dimenti, with a certain number of other men true to their responsibilities, arrived, ready to measure their wits and strength against the strange committee's power. In a few minutes the crowd was on them, with shouts and threats and snatches of song, nearly all swinging torches.

"Come to burn the bourgeois house!" they cried. Some already tottered from vodka, while others were as yet only red of face and thick of voice, shouting first: "Tyrants!" and "This is all ours." They finally joined in the cry of: "Give us the cellar keys, or you shall be burned with the palace which you have served!" Long parley; the leaders egging on the muddled-headed mob; the intendant with his men and the village priest and elders trying to keep their people within bounds. With great presence of mind "Grandmother Anna-Vladimirovna" announced calmly that she had lost her keys last week, and in proof she turned her pockets inside out, so all could see that they were quite empty. Then the crowd was told by Michael-Petrovich that the cellars had been sealed by the the village's own revolutionary committee long ago, and even were the keys here, it would not be the law for him to open the iron door.

But his wish for peace and his tact were of no avail that night against the inflaming words and the alcohol his rivals distributed, and soon the great iron doors were broken in, and a wild orgy was under way in the cellar and in the courtyard, while a chosen few, less helpless from drink than the others, found occupation in systematically destroying first its furnishings, then the house, throwing the former into the courts and gardens, where paintings, china, bronzes, and wood carvings lay is dismal heaps, and embroidered silken rags or fine carpets served to light bonfires. Before the morning a greater flame than these went up, and the ancient picturesque pile, which had been the proud château of the old regime, had died![8]

The sun came up and shone on a sad mass of blackened walls, gray ashes, and broken treasures watered everywhere by rivulets of rare vintage were strewn about. In the midst of all this lay many wounded, while numerous others were lying merely sleeping off the effects of their party of the night before. Axientieff had a bleeding arm and hand, Tiltzoff a swollen face where a heavy blow had fallen, and the intendant was all black from smoke, as he spoke with them in a low, hoarse voice: "I have been able to save so little in the confusion," he said. "Only some papers and a few small things. What will the Princes think?"

And the other two replied: "You have fought bravely, Michael-Petrovich, and you will be condemned by these hooligans to sure death for defending all this, and

---

[8] Though the workers and peasants were inspired by the anti-capitalist and anti-aristocratic ideology of Marxism, other factors were also important, such as the breakdown of law and order in the countryside. Another was the rise of Ukrainian nationalism and the independence movement, which had created a crucial issue for the Provisional Government. This came to fruition in the wake of the Bolshevik Revolution of October 1917 and the declaration of the independence of Ukraine in January 1918. The violence described here may have been partly the result of popular reaction against the largely non-Ukrainian landholders in the region, and the Cantacuzène family was not even Slavic. For a background outline on the situation at the time, see Michael Palij, *The Ukrainian-Polish Defensive Alliance, 1919–1921: An Aspect of the Ukrainian Revolution* (Edmonton, Canadian Institute of Ukrainian Studies Press, 1995), 1–11.

have done your best. Go you, therefore, with your wife and children to the district town nearby, and remain there at Zoltonosh. We are old revolutionaries of 1905, and we will remain in our places here, since, alas, these fools are our own families and friends. We will do all we can to save what is left of the property; faithfully we promise it. You shall report to the Princes, and then send us their orders, and we will do everything to carry them out."

And so it was. Even until now these men have stayed at Bouromka in the two courtyards, representing the old owners' interests, as against their people, and trying to carry out what the intendant ordered. Of late they have obtained some restitution of goods which were stolen. Anna-Vladimirovna luckily was spirited away from the fire of the evening's attack, and has lived since in her own cottage, which is all that remains to her of past grandeur. She continues to scold her nieces and nephews for having no more provisions from the château by their fault, and she repeats constantly the tale of her last tea with Moses-Kouzmich, and of the poor old fellow's death on that same night. A heart stroke carried off the ancient, snobbish, but devoted old serf, who could not adapt himself to the idea of all his world becoming insane!

As for the German Bolshevik leaders who had brought about the ruin, they stood awhile looking on that night, till toward morning one of them gathered the others in a group. "At last our work is done here," he said, "and we had better go, for who can predict what these dullards may think of our success tomorrow, when they finally come to? We start on our road at once, then, and shall be far away before another day. We can demand double pay for the months spent here, I think, for our task was truly one of the most difficult in all this land of idealists and fools, and we have done it well at last."

And so, when they came to, late next day, the people had lost their foreign leaders, and were at great pains to remember what had occurred, and just why the château lay now in ashes. In their own group many were ready, however, to take on the role of the men who had just sneaked off, for they felt now a gulf existed between the ancient proprietors of the land and themselves, too wide a gulf ever to be bridged again. Some were troubled greatly at finding how things stood. It was worse for the people than ever before, in certain ways, since they must live on through the summer and the harvest-time, and they were not prepared to do so without guidance. They had no organization, and the peasants who would gladly work for money under earlier arrangements, would not work for love of labor now any more land than was actually of use for their own needs.

Yet at hand, confiscated by the village, were many of the fine implements and horses of the ex-proprietors, and the earth was there—though on it no fields of winter wheat had been prepared. None were even ploughed, and six precious months were lost, with neither food, nor grain, nor ready money to show. The Austrian prisoners had long since fled, and our own men, returned from the war, refused to work at all.

Every one was master now, free to rest, and sleep, and drink whenever he pleased, and every one felt more inclined to govern than be governed.

Meantime the days passed, and it was late spring. Delegates from the city Bolsheviks and from Kiev's new Ukrainian government came through the village, ordering peremptorily the peasantry to give grain from their slender stores to feed the starving towns.[9] The people hid what they could, and sold only what they were obliged to, for the worthless money; then they worked in the fields haphazard, being forced to it only by a fear of famine. The fine implements were mostly spoiled already, since protecting sheds and repairing shops had been burned, and their new owners had not seen to protecting them from the late winter snow, or springtime thaw or rain. The men and women and their animals were equally exposed to wind and weather, and they went untreated now when ill. Many were ailing or run down physically, as they were mentally, morally, and materially.

All the riches of the country had been theirs in those first days of revolution, but sloth and dirt and drink, and lack of knowledge as well as lack of organization, were laying the health and fortune of a whole race in the dust, taking all savor from its triumph, all confidence and hope from much discouraged hearts. Vodka, their first enemy, was their false friend again now, dragging our people lower with each day, while the enemy's agents were always passing through the village, ready and able to lead the simple peasant on to his destruction.

Suddenly one day it was learned the Germans were settled in Kiev as official masters, and then it came about that squads began to scour the country for grain and other provisions with which to feed themselves first, and even for enough to send back into Germany. What they could the peasants still kept back secretly; the rest was confiscated.

Open resistance was impossible, for the victims were both threatened and often whipped, and they knew that other villages round about that had dared fight the German tyranny had been burned, while the inhabitants were butchered wholesale, or even gassed! Tortured with such inconceivable cruelty, necessarily one bowed down to the fresh despotism, hideous as it was. During the months of Teuton occupation a vast retrograde movement was inaugurated in the provinces of Ukraine. The "national" Hetman, General Skoropadsky, who was, alas, a Russian, joined Von Eichhorn's government, and helped the latter to carry out his policy, making only one condition—that the rights of the landed proprietors in the Ukraine should be enforced against their own peasantry and against the Bolsheviks.[10]

---

[9] This was the result of the Food Decree of May 1918, which declared that all production belonged to the state, and the peasants could retain only some for their own needs. It resulted in much slaughter of farm animals, reduced seeding of fields, and a major famine.

[10] Pavel (Pavlo) Skoropadsky (1873–1945) was a Russian army officer of Ukrainian (not Russian) descent who won distinction in the Russo-Japanese War and World War I, rising to the rank of major general. After the declaration of Ukrainian independence in January 1918

So it turned out that for the safety of their personal fortunes, some few of the nobility in Kiev, through Skoropadsky's bargain, were tempted into aiding the Huns. These latter, who elsewhere in Russia were paying Bolsheviks to destroy the upper class and create anarchy, were in Kiev and its environs punishing the peasantry and helping the top strata. Our enemies' calculation was simple enough. From the Ukraine they needed grain which the peasants had, and as it was a country near their own frontier, they also preferred to keep law and order and our class organization as it had been; also they had found the Ukrainian Hetman with a military force ready to join them. In the rest of Russia they perfectly realized that every one with understanding or education was against them, so they had turned to the worst groups to carry out their designs, and had cynically counted on being always strong enough to make order later, when it should suit their convenience to do so.

Our peasants did not follow out the arguments, but they found it natural, traditionally logical and just to be beaten into semi-slavery after they had taken by force what did not belong to them. This had always been their fate so far in history. So now, under German tutelage, they ploughed and sowed obediently, and harvested the grain-crops, driven into it by whip and insult. The grain went partly for the German dictators' benefit and partly for that of the old proprietors. This last share was paid into one or another of the banks of Kiev, and the ex-owners of the land were officially notified of their credit.

As to the peasantry who had worked this year as never before since the Dark Ages, they were given a mere pittance. Oppressed and miserable, hopeless and inert, save under the lash, besodden when free from punishment, the villages lost again their fair coquettish beauty. The inhabitants' clothes were torn, their boots and harness worn out or requisitioned (for the victors needed all the leather in the country), and the cattle and horses became as thin as the people themselves. All were fair prey to illnesses. Old scourges which had been almost eradicated with care, had reappeared; tuberculosis in various forms, and many other maladies, claimed numerous victims. Yet, at the end of the autumn, the enemy had succeeded in making our peasantry pay heavy taxes and also levies in money and grain had been made by their agents.

Into the bank at Kiev, by order of the new conquerors, went eighty per cent of the value of livestock and implements which had been wantonly destroyed. Also the peasants had officially returned the lands to the old proprietors, and had paid rent down, for two years ahead, on such fields as they wished to keep farming. This was done to prove, the peasants fully admitted, that they had stolen lands and cattle, and that they

---

and the establishment of a republic, the subsequent German occupation resulted in a coup d'etat in late April and the installation of Skoropadsky as hetman (leader).

During the summer of 1918 Germany was desperate for food supplies for its starving army and home population and saw Ukraine as providing relief. This helped very little because of the conditions described here. In fact, the German effort in Ukraine drew vital resources away from the Western Front.

had no rights and no longer any pretensions to these riches. When, in our case, the proprietor's family was absent, due official notification of what had been done by the German-Ukrainian administration of Kiev was sent to them.

We were notified, for instance, that we could obtain this money from the bank at any time convenient to us, and that the valuation of our stock and implements for the refund had been made by our own intendants. So it was the Germans hoped to make themselves acceptable in the conquered province, at least to the aristocratic element, and, alas, in some cases they were only too successful in this. In the late summer Von Eichorn was assassinated by a young Russian, and within a few weeks the same fate supposedly overtook Skoropadsky. Both were dead, in spite of the pomp and military protection with which in Kiev they had surrounded themselves. Rapidly the artificial organization disintegrated, till within a few weeks chaos reigned everywhere, worse than ever before in the villages and small towns.[11]

It was a reaction against the enforced German discipline of the previous months, and certainly in all this misery our people roused one's pity by their helplessness, though much of the trouble was of their own creation. From being overdisciplined and undereducated they had been plunged without preparation into a riot of riches and vodka, backed by a fiery propaganda. No wonder that all boundaries were at once broken down—and they destroyed themselves and us. After this short orgy the prophetic vision of the peasant who asked "When shall we be beaten?" had verified itself fully, with the German armed dictatorship. And now that is also past, and the peasants sleep away their winter days, waiting what calamity will strike them next, and wondering how they can defend themselves.

Already the Bolsheviks have begun an invasion of the Ukraine from the north and east, since in their other strongholds food is exhausted. From the southeast, Cossacks announce that they will overrun the country and establish order according to their ideas. The peasants have a little grain and firewood left, but no clothes save rags, which were once so gay, and they are barely living, barely holding out as yet, with small hope of help! They are fighting cold and vodka, disease and underfeeding, lack of medicines and of the doctors whom they themselves have driven away. They are paying the heavy contributions levied by each new conqueror in turn, and mentally they are brutalized to silence, but are frantic as driven beasts in their fear of what each day may bring. So far the poor mujiks [Russian term for peasants; colloquially, good or strong man] have not given or received the least promise of better things.

It was little news one heard through the winter months from Bouromka, even at the best of times, as our post never came more than four days a week, and was brought by horses from a railroad station fifty miles away, but we know the people, semi-armed, are rising in our village as in those about, trying to resist the anarchistic tyrants who are now exploiting them. For the rest, their ferocity of destruction has

---

[11] The report of Skoropadsky's death was a false rumor.

long since worn itself out. Feeling crushed, the peasants sought revenge, first on those whom the false prophets told them were to blame, then on the latter themselves, when their prophecies proved wrong, and finally on the tyrants who abused them in the terrible German reaction. Undoubtedly, they had thought the Germans and ex-landowners were in league to force restitution from them.

While there was certainly some justice in their paying for what they spoiled or stole, and in their being made to admit that what they did was wrong, at the bottom of their minds, I think the feeling must exist they have not altogether deserved the punishment given them, for not they alone are responsible for the troubles. Undoubtedly, they are tormented occasionally trying to find a way out of the difficulty, and I can imagine Batioushka [the local priest] and the elders meeting at the priest's tiny cottage near the church, and their discussions of the dismal past, and of all the ground that has been lost to the poor village which lies spread out in placid sunlight at their feet.

The elders have probably lost hold of the situation, and one can hear them sigh heavily as they utter their complaints:[12]

"Batioushka, we have been truly in the dark, but it has not been our fault. Who could foretell and who could sufficiently prepare us for the great feast of our liberty? Of our people so few were educated, and our patriotism was for the 'hata' and the township, and perhaps even for this province, but it went no farther, since we know nothing of the rest of Russia, save that our religion was for the White Czar. If we had more learning, we would have made better arrangements for the new government. Surely the latter will still come to us when this black night of the terror is finished? It will be a long time till then, and full of pain, perhaps, but at last one might hope the rich and the poor, the great and the small, would join with one another and create a new country on the foundations of our present disappointments."

Batioushka answers:

"In spite of all the trouble, I am for the revolution, glad the old regime's ailments and sins have been destroyed, though that ancient government encouraged us and made us higher as a class than we priests shall ever be in the future. But religion itself will not suffer, and who knows? The old and the new, the Orthodox, Catholic, Protestant, Mohammedan, and even the Jew, shall perhaps be equal one to the other before the law, some day, and the church will preach joy and healthy living instead of gloom and punishment.

"We must plan a new education for our young priests to arrive at this, and for our doctors and all the teachers of the people. Russia must clean its house, and it is possible these tragic years are eradicating the bad as well as the good in us, and teaching us much which we never would have learned save by our present experiences. The new regime will be born a child, young and weak, and can only slowly grow up; the future is bound to the past by instincts and ideals, loves and hatreds, which are

---

[12] The author follows by putting her own reflections on the situation in Ukraine in late 1918 in the voices of local people, mainly the village priest.

inherited. But some of the traits of our nature, in fact most of them, were always very beautiful. We shall be great yet, I think. Listen, you who are the elders here, and then teach your children to believe that we are down now to our lowest depths, for we have been in German hands.

"For centuries we have been ill-used by this same enemy, given only their crumbs of civilization, and obliged to bow down to them, and now their agents have been here among us, imparting to us all sorts of lies, both as to our allies' wickedness and as to our revolution's power, and all this was told to a people wearied and worn by war. Why our allies did not tell us their side of such questions, I do not know, for we were far away from them, alone to fight all the battles on this side of the firing-lines, and we suffered and lost much more than they. More than three million of our men were killed, and two more millions have died of starvation or disease. When upon all this came the revolution, with the Germans ever ready to teach us the full meaning of it, we naturally fell prostrate in their hands.

"But see, already there are those preparing to rise again, and fighting as their ancestors of the steppes did in the Dark Ages against the Asiatic hordes who came to oppress them. The enemy's squads were ill-received in summer, and now it is even worse for the Bolsheviks' representatives who come to tyrannize. Maybe with time and thought our men shall again turn their minds to honest work, and will grow up to understand that liberty to do and responsibility for what is done must go together; also, that national funds must not be squandered, since they are nothing else than the money we ourselves pay into our state coffers. Perhaps, also, it will come to us that the villages and cities need one another, as do the rich and the poor also, and when this knowledge is accepted, all will be well. It is even near now, since you are all beginning to miss the city's luxuries and the château's care, and the money which your honest labor brought you: and you have found out that all of these, vodka and sleep alone cannot replace."

The elders slowly nod assent and reply:

"True, Batioushka, and if you believe this yourself, that all which is so bad now can at last be overcome, then we shall believe also, and there are others who are tired of the disorder, and who will join in trying to help. Perhaps there are neighbor villages which will act likewise? We finally understand now that no injustice of the past can be righted by stealing. Though certainly we have much need of land. The Princes should and must give us some of theirs, or all, but let us try to find a way out of this and other difficulties quietly."

Batioushka, full of pity for his flock, is ready to help them in every way he can and believes that the rapidity with which the peasant (with his woman and his child) blossomed in the few years which immediately preceded the revolution, shows of what progress the Russians are capable if rightly led and rightly understood. One was tempted to dream dreams then, and I also am still quite prepared to believe that a race which has thrown off, or absorbed, Tatars and Poles, Norsemen and Mongolians, together with refugees and colonists from all over the world, can still rise up and shake off German foe or Bolshevik traitor. Certainly though it is a difficult task to rid a country of such a heavy load of misery as the present one weighing on the Slav people, and then to build our national life anew!

How it shall be done only the future can show. At present the old people and the children are dying, and the villages need clothes and coverings, provisions and machinery, and every other sort of material help from the big centers, and they cannot obtain these since the cities refuse co-operation. So the peasantry holds back its own small stocks of hidden grain, while the townspeople riot for lack of bread, and the whole seething mass, which once was placid Russia, has this fight between urban and suburban groups to add to the other troubles of the frightful revolution. Russia offers to the world the most dismal tragedy which history ever presented!

In Bouromka, always far from the beaten tracks of civilization, the priest, though his own rosy plans are in the dust, still labors on and prays among his little group, and the brave few who have withstood the present time's temptations try to think and plan with him for all the rest, and so to minimize the great harm done. They, like many Russians everywhere, still feel the frenzy of our reign of terror must end in time for the whole nation—Prince, Bourgeois, and Peasant—to join hands and to rebuild our country on a new foundation. They know Russia has not yet had its day, historically, and that the disease from which we suffer is not degeneracy, but one caused by wild young forces too long suppressed, and then unleashed suddenly and overfed.

With at least one hundred and fifty million out of our one hundred and eighty million people still so undeveloped that they cannot sign their names, it is easy enough to lead them far astray. Every one helped to do it, friend and ally, through misunderstanding, no less than our foe through clever calculation. Till now all the civilization given us was by ordering the adoption of certain superficial forms, taken in total from the Orient, or again from France, Italy, or Germany, at the command of some enthusiastic Emperor or statesman.[13] The significance of these forms was never explained to the people, nor were the measures ever modified to suit the Slavs' own nature.

Underneath this veneer our people remained with their ancient ideals and primitive desires, a folk of patriarchal times. Finally, when the revolution came, the Slav giant stood up, and dropping his artificial garment, he stretched and shook himself until the whole earth trembled! All the world stood aghast at the result of its own labors, and foreigners are puzzling their brains as to what shall be done to quench the fire, stop the noise, and bring these wild demons back to law and order again. And while they talk, the delirium gains ground and many things are being burned. All the world risks perishing, and they who would like to preserve in a recognized form their civilization must act soon, or it will be too late.

---

[13] The author is subscribing to the Slavophile view that the reforms introduced by Peter the Great and others were detrimental to the true Slavic civilization and destiny.

As history counts, the time may not be long till our dramatic chapter will be finished, and until the Slav, untamed by the outsiders, may at last tame himself, rise up purified and strong to surprise the world by his own powers for civilization of a new type. Somehow every Russian, whether of high station or low, with whom I have talked, seems to have a prophetic feeling of this coming development. An old prophecy upholds the theory, if one is superstitious. Made long before the war by Count Leo Tolstoy, of whom the Czar, in 1910, had asked one, it announced the coming cataclysm, and it very much upset the ruler then! The paper was kept for years in his Majesty's secret archives, I heard. In a trance, the old writer, then almost in his dotage, saw all Europe in flames, and predicted such a war as the universe had never known before.

After this he said:

"The end of that great calamity will mark a new political era for the world. There will be left no empires nor kingdoms, but there will be born a federation of United States, and there will exist four great giant races: the Anglo-Saxons, the Latins, the Slavs, and the Mongolians, and I see a change in religious sentiment, and the church as known now will fall. The ethical idea will nearly vanish, and humanity will be almost without morality, and then a great reformer will arise about the year 1925. He will lay the corner-stone of a new religion, God, soul, and spirit, with immortality, all will be molten in the new furnace, to form a new power of spirituality, and I see the peaceful dawn of a new day at last. And the man determined on for this mission is a Mongolian-Slav already walking the earth. He will be a man of active affairs, and does not realize now the position in history assigned to him by his superior powers."

Some Slav to lead the world, and from the north or east he is to come? Only on the great silent steppe-lands and in the forests of Russia are there any Slavs with a strain of Mongolian blood. Even at this hour of supreme agony there are many of my compatriots, earnest in their spirit of devotion and self-sacrifice, who with the instinctive patience of their blood, wait for an occasion when action will be possible, trying to find help and save their race, never losing courage, never losing faith in the cause of a new Russia.[14]

---

[14] This prophecy, unfortunately, proved to be wrong, and Ukraine would suffer even more devastation during the civil war that followed.

III
The Reign of Terror

The first time we heard of Bolshevism by name was at the beginning of May—or to be exact, April 20, old style—1917, when an uprising of this ultra-radical group in Petrograd threatened to overthrow the first provisional government and to establish anarchy in the Russian capital. The Bolshevks paraded the streets at that time with black banners on which threatening mottoes were printed large, for all to read, and there was much shouting and street-fighting and salvo-firing. It was after several days that the atmosphere again became quiet and normal, and then the peace was obtained only by the sacrifice of Miliukov's position in the Cabinet and the acceptance by Kerensky of the soldiers' and workmen's committee as part of the machinery of government.[1]

Such was the official birth of the "Bolshevik" or "Maximalist" party, whose name came from the word "bolshoi"—big—because this group demanded the biggest or maximum of concessions from the revolutionary administration's weakness.[2] Since its first appearance Lenin was the declared organizer and chief of the party. He had come from Switzerland, direct through Germany, at the opening of the rev-

---

[1] Paul Miliukov (1859–1943) was a professor of history at the University of St. Petersburg and leader of the Constitutional Democratic Party (Kadets after its Russian initials, K.D.), became the first foreign minister of the Provisional Government and the effective head of the government. He accepted the war aim of the previous imperial government to claim the right of annexation of Constantinople and its Straits territory. A reaction from the left parties proclaiming "peace without annexation" created an outcry in early May 1917, resulting in his resignation. This was a blow to the moderate forces behind the February Revolution and precipitated the rise of Alexander Kerensky (1881–1970) from his initial position as minister of justice to minister of war and then minister-president, the effective head of the government from July to November, when it was overthrown by the Bolsheviks.

[2] The author is misleading as to the origin of the term. The name Bolshevik originated at a congress of the Russian Social Democratic Workers' Party in 1903 in London at which that faction won the majority in regarding rules of membership and control of the press. The name stuck, and the party was henceforth divided into two factions: Bolsheviks (majority), led by Vladimir Lenin, and Mensheviks (minority), led by Iulii Martov, usually indicated by a small "b" or "m" after the party name. Some, such as Trotsky at the time, refused to join either group.

olution, and had established his headquarters for propaganda in the charming little palace requisitioned by his staff from the frightened ballerina Kshesinskaia.[3]

An irony of chance placed this cradle of the new doctrine exactly opposite the ancient fortress of Peter and Paul, where in a secluded cathedral lie the bodies of all the Romanoff Emperors, from the great Peter, builder of the church, down to Alexander III.[4] I fancy these autocrats must have turned in their graves at the idea of their neighbors' theories and actions.

The germ of Bolshevism, like much else which has hurt the world of late, came straight from Germany to us, and by following facts this seems absolutely proved. When in July Lenin's headquarters were raided, German gold was found there in large sums; also during various uprisings of anarchistic tendency German gold was found both in the hands and pockets of those who were creating these disorders. In numerous places where specially violent demonstrations took place, German official spies were recognized and caught, disguised as Russian, and all the organization of the Bolsheviks has been so thorough and their movements so carefully carried out as to preclude these being the result of an effort of our benighted, uneducated, and inexperienced Russians of the extreme lower class. They might perhaps have been capable of some one crime, but were much too helpless to conceive and execute a long, complicated, and systematic program such as this party has carried out during the past two years.[5]

Petrograd was not alone in possessing German agents for this special work. All over the country such groups were at work. At Kiev my husband was fighting them, and himself had in hand Austrian and German papers and gold, while he

---

[3] The mansion of ballerina Matylda Kshesinskaia, former mistress of Nicholas II, had been looted during the February 1917 revolution and thus became available as the Bolshevik headquarters. Lenin did not enter Russia until the middle of April, six weeks after the revolution began, with a dramatic arrival at the Finland Station, where he issued his radical April theses.

[4] In recent years the remains of Nicholas II, victim of the murder of the imperial family in Ekaterinburg in July 1918, were also interned there.

[5] Here and following the author succumbs to the "German blame" theory that was widely circulated and believed at the time. Hatred of Germany was constant, so it was natural to blame that country for any ills befalling Russia. Many of the so-called German agents were most likely German-speaking Russian-American Jewish supporters of the revolution, such as Leon Trotsky. Ironically, the return of many of these exiles to Russia was funded by the Russian Provisional Government.

The supply of German gold to the revolution has generally been discounted by modern scholarship. Germany did not have gold to spare in the last year of the war, little evidence of such transfers of aid to the Bolsheviks exist. Probably more American money went to the Bolsheviks than German due to misdirected loans by the United States to the Provisional Government, such as special funds to pay the sailors of the Baltic Fleet in Finland with hard currency, which went indirectly to radical parties. See Norman Saul, *Sailors in Revolt: The Russian Baltic Fleet in 1917* (Lawrence: Regents Press of Kansas, 1979).

arrested several of the enemy's spies, who in the Ukraine posed as local nationalists. At the great staff headquarters of Moghilev, when came the last mutiny before the Provisional Government's final breaking up, the commander-in-chief, General [Nikolai] Dukhonin, was killed by an Austrian officer disguised in Russian-sailor uniform, whom the general recognized and called by name before he fell. In many a village such as our own Bouromka, months after the March revolution—when we were still living quietly and on good terms with our village peasant committee—a new group of five or six men appeared from outside, bred discontent and trouble, bribed the people with gold—and not Russian gold—excited them with speeches, and finally fed and inflamed their brains with vodka till they could successfully lead the crowd to excesses which were quite beyond belief. Then the foreign committee members diplomatically disappeared, leaving our peasants to face consequences very hard for them to bear.

An instance of the unnecessary destruction which was the work of such agents is that of Bouromka. When our main village was abandoned by the group of outsiders, one of the richest estates in Little Russia—consisting of thirty thousand or more acres of intensely cultivated farm land, in the black-earth section, with meadows and woods, herds of oxen, studs of both work-horses and thoroughbreds, dairy-farm and forges, shops, buildings, a mill and a distillery, not to mention the value of the château and park, with the rare furniture, plants, hothouses, and collections—had been by degree completely destroyed, together with all the farming implements and machinery. This result was accomplished during a few weeks, while the outside committee men resided at Bouromka.

After they had finally gone, the frantic, desperate peasants came to their senses sufficiently to realize not only that they had inflicted great wrong on us, but also that they had harmed themselves, by making it impossible to cultivate this land they had annexed in total by the committee's advice, since the wherewithal to work the place had been ruined beyond repair. Later the peasantry's "elders" helped our own intendants to make out the lists and estimates of our losses, and the latter reached the sum of eight million roubles, of which one and a half millions' worth—in live stock and implements largely—were found and returned, or paid for, by some of the less heedless peasants. The rest was clear loss.

And Bouromka estate is but one of many hundreds which in Russia have suffered from conditions created and kept going by German organization! It suited the enemy's policy perfectly, almost to abolish us and our peasantry together, and then to step into the richest part of Russia and re-establish law and order. Thus they tried to put the nobility under obligations, and to crush and exploit the humbler classes, drawing on them for both grain and men to replenish their own fatherland's losses in food and labor. This system has succeeded in many parts of Russia, where German overlords, in command of everything, are still using our resources either quite openly by requisition, or through their secret agents, the Bolshevik red guardsmen, or even by the cunning of politicians exploiting us. When a province or a city is crushed and trampled to complete exhaustion, the conqueror's agents at once retire and leave the place to recover itself as best it can, or to die out entirely.[6]

Long before the opening of the Great War, there were hundreds of thousands of Germans in Russia as elsewhere. Some few had intermarried with Russians, and their children, born and brought up in our country, belonged to the Orthodox Church and were good subjects of the Czar, but the vast majority—merchants, professionals, colonists—had remained loyal to their ancient fatherland, spoke German, lived as they had in the old country, and became very prosperous at the expense of their surroundings. Technically, they took out naturalization papers in our empire, and they were, of course, allowed to move about, making observations freely. They were of the greatest service to the enemy, both before and all through the war.[7]

Afterward, at the revolution, they also did everything to further the plans of their head men in Berlin. They were those who largely prepared the ground for the revolution, and who both in the laboring classes and in our army made much propaganda. Before the first movement of the revolution (in early March 1917), these agents in the barracks of Petrograd sowed disloyalty and indiscipline among recruits and reserves that made up the garrison of our capital.[8] When the crash came, during the first wild days it was found by officers attached to the Duma's committee that the Catherine Hall delegates of the workmen and soldiers had produced spontaneously and without thought (in the terrible period of general amazement and panic at the turn of events) both the famous "Order Number One to the Army," introducing committees into the military units, and thereby destroying discipline completely on the firing line, and also the proclamation to the garrison of Petrograd which permitted its members

---

[6] The author is obviously swayed by anti-German sentiment. If the reference here is to Baltic Germans who owned estates in the Baltic provinces, they were among the most loyal to the Russian state.

[7] It is difficult to ascertain what group of Germans the author is referring to. The largest number were Volga Germans, who emigrated to Russia in the 18th century and settled along the Volga River near Saratov before there was a Germany and were loyal to the Russian Empire and solidly Roman Catholic or Lutheran in religion, and the Baltic Germans, their homeland annexed into Russia also in the 18th century. All served well in the Russian armies of World War I. True, there were some Germans serving in manufacturing and business in Russia, but little evidence of disloyalty there either. Suspicion of their loyalty by ordinary Russians, however, was genuine at the time.

[8] It is interesting that such an important American observer of the scene should be so misled as to the "German menace." Many of the initial victims of the revolution were naval officers with German or Swedo-Finnish names.

to remain permanently stationary within the city, without ever being sent forward to the front.⁹

These two measures were brought to the provisional cabinet for signing, almost in the first hour of the revolution, and our minister, either troubled by the many dangers they and the whole country must face, and therefore anxious to placate so powerful a group as were the workmen and soldiers of the empire, or else merely dazed with surprise, affixed their names without serious resistance. Where these two papers came from, and how that seething mass of half-crazy humanity in the Catherine Hall could produce two such clear, logical orders at such a time, was an inexplicable mystery, except perhaps by inference, since both these papers were immensely useful to the German enemy's cause.

As a positive act I know that one officer—a personal friend of ours who chanced to be in the capital on sick leave from the front, and who had rushed with others to the parliament to offer his services in the cause of law and order—reported to his chief at once, and later testified to the fact that the only typographical plants working in the town during those early revolutionary days were run by German workmen, who had taken possession of them under German-speaking master printers. He, our friend, was unable to obtain sufficient service to type papers, which [Mikhail] Rodzianko had wished printed quickly for immediate distribution, because they were so busy preparing the Number One Order. Captain K—— heard and saw all of this himself. He said that as fast as the thousands of sheets were ready, they were taken off directly by special messengers, to be delivered to our soldiers at the front, without the knowledge of officers. These messengers were Germans also, or men in the German pay. This whole move was attended with rapid and extraordinary efficiency, at a time when Russians of the working class had gone mad with excitement over their new liberty, and could not have been brought to labor at anything, least of all to go off to deliver papers along the firing-line, leaving amusements of the Petrograd streets.¹⁰

Police were suppressed at the frontiers as elsewhere during the first week of the revolution, and for six days, barriers being down, thousands of German agents poured into our country, spreading out to points where duty had been assigned to them—spying and reporting, organizing propaganda, uprisings, and committees. Within the month, though things looked quiet on the surface, one often felt the fermentation

---

⁹ Cantacuzene is correct in her analysis of the order of the Petrograd Soviet that applied only to garrisons in the city but was extended, unfortunately, by the Provisional Government to the whole country. Many military units, however, especially on the Southwestern Front, ignored the order. The measure, however, would lead to the "July Crisis," when the Provisional Government attempted to send units from Petrograd to the front over the objections of unit committees.

¹⁰ Much of this is an exaggeration based on rumors and naturally antipathy to Germans. Germany, as well as other powers, was unprepared for the overthrow of the tsar and had few agents prepared to enter Russia. Lenin, finally with German help, entered Russia only in April.

underneath, and the cabinet members sat insecurely in their places governing a very fluid state.

The revolutionary preparation by Germany was never sufficiently noticed nor pursued then, and the work of the enemy with the Catherine Hall party and as printers and messengers speaks in its results. Afterward, with the arrival of new reserves from Germany, the work was at once begun of forming an official group. Lenin was its head, the Kshesinskaia house its quarters [not until June], and while the leader and his satellites preached their red doctrines to Petrograd's public as the gospel of the lowly people, their unofficial agents circulated about over the whole country, breaking ground, as it were, bringing in new recruits for initiation and creating discontent; thus they drew together the committees, both of soldiers and of workmen, with the Leninites. Saying a sympathetic word at the right moment, they were distributing everywhere leaflets of Karl Marx, translated and changed to fit the ambitions of the Russian poor, and they succeeded in inspiring pretensions which had never before occurred to their converts.

By July 1917, the Bolshevik party had gathered to itself all the discontented elements in the great cities and all the army's rebellious spirits, and there was strength behind it enough to frighten Kerensky and force him to give way.[11] "Land and Liberty" was this group's early cry, which meant little or much, according to its interpretation by conservatives or anarchists.

Count P———, who about this time was obliged to give up a large Red Cross unit at the front which, through three years of war, had done wonders to help our wounded soldiers, told me his reasons for abandoning this work. He said:

"I tried to argue out the situation with my men, both those who formed my unit as well as those whom we were having treated. The new liberty to them had been made to represent that the stretcher-bearers and the hospital's floor-scrubbers ought to run our whole administration, while the patients were to obey or not our doctor's orders, as they saw fit. Several of the patients had died from eating what was forbidden them, in absolute defiance of directions given, and then the other wounded had proclaimed noisily all this was the doctor's fault, as his medicines were bad.

"Once I went into the hospital garden and began to talk with a sanitary who was resting there in his off hour. I still hoped good might come of an explanation if I made it simple enough, so I told him: 'See, Ivan, if I sit on this bench and you come and sit by me instead of standing there—that to my mind is the new liberty they speak of, where neither you nor I inconvenience one another, and both are comfortable equally, but if you were to tell me that I must get up and you would like to sit on this same place where I am now as well as your own—that would scarcely be fair, since you would be taking away my seat, when you cannot possibly sit in two of them at once.'

---

[11] True, Bolshevik propaganda eroded Kerensky's popularity, but opposition to the war was the central cause, as well as his poor leadership in general.

"'Yes, Excellency,' answered Ivan, 'I have always thought this too, till now, and felt content, but the new people say that idea belongs to old times, and the new liberty is for me to keep my place and all I have, and add to it what is yours also, and certainly we find that will be an agreeable arrangement, since there are many things which belong to others and which we want.'

"So Ivan and I, having worked together over our wounded for three long years, were now separated completely by the new theories which had been poured into his brain, and there was nothing more for me to do but to pack up my things and leave our unit to the care of new masters. Soon the service would not obey their own elected soldier chiefs, and as funds gave out the whole hospital first ran wild and then fell to pieces; yet the men forming it had been devoted and loyal, and full of fervor and energy to help their struggling, suffering brothers at the front before the poison reached them.

"It seemed as if those who had led them astray by such impossible doctrines ought to be punished. The best men became violent Bolsheviks, bent on their own destruction and on ours, and whatever comes to them, they never will be satisfied, since their elusive ideal will always be some steps beyond attainment."

At least a dozen men and women whom I knew had about the same experience with their Red Cross workers, and these groups disintegrated, as did the army and every other organization in Russia, while little by little during the same period the Bolsheviks gained power steadily.

Leon Trotsky—alias Bronstein—arrived in July, and added his strength to the movement. He came from the East Side of New York City, where he had till then been doing useful work among Americans for his German masters and their cause.[12] He admitted being an anarchist, and also that his original name had been Leo Bronstein until he moved to our unfortunate land, when he had taken a Russian name. He probably outshone Lenin in magnetism and eloquence, and was better trained in German methods and more experienced. Certainly whether from that, or because his original home country backed him more suitably, he seems to have injected much greater energy into the agitations which he led and to have organized them better. He was infinitely violent and tyrannical as compared to other leaders. He promised more, and has shown himself unashamed of using any instrument which offered itself to his hand, and he had already by early November 1917, gathered enough power to overthrow the tottering provisional government, lock up its ministers—save only Kerensky, who ran away!—while he, Trotsky, personally assumed all power as tyrant and autocrat.[13]

---

[12] Leon Trotsky (1879–1940) edited a Jewish newspaper on the Lower East Side of New York before his departure for Russia in 1917. He and his family were delayed by being held up by British inspectors at Halifax, which delayed his arrival in Russia. There is no evidence that he was a German agent.

[13] This may have been the perspective of some as Trotsky headed the Red Army, but in fact he was subservient to Lenin and the Politburo of the Communist Party.

THE REIGN OF TERROR

This new Robespierre inaugurated at once a reign of terror, or tried to do so, for even with the seizure once accomplished most of his Russian followers still hung back, and with innate idealism expected the millennium immediately to fulfill all promises made, without undue effort or ferocity on their own part.

Of course nothing came of this hope, since it had never been in the plans of the originators that their followers should reap any good from their projects. The riches of the country they meant to draw for themselves out of the tempest they were stirring up, and only complete slavery was to be the part of the mujik, whether he hailed from town or village. But he, the victim, must be kept, of course, ignorant of such plans till he should be prostrate beyond recovery, and to gain that end it was necessary to tempt him onward, over the road he seemed almost loath to follow. Also, the various classes in Russia must all be put irretrievably one against the other, and misunderstandings, when they did not exist, must be created which would carry the groups beyond possibility of reconciliation.

Zealously the agents set about this special work. Step by step they carried out a fixed program. Our people of the lower strata, who were so ignorant they could neither read nor write, naturally wanted all those things which were dangled before their blinking eyes, so immediately they fell an easy prey to Bolshevik machinations. They, who had gone through the terrific years of war, who were very needy—in the north, especially—of both fuel and food, believed at once any false prophets, who appeared from they knew not where, and offered them shining gold and provisions, and above all vodka, of which they had not tasted for three long years. And then, beyond all this, the newcomers promised there should be a paradise on earth—no more work and no more fighting! All the riches of the world should be had for the mere taking, and it was not stealing and murder they were asked to practice, it was explained, for everything in the new government was to be "nationalized," and belonged to the humble masses, who were both great and good and long-suffering!

They were told all that was given to them thus by proclamations was already legally their property, and they had only two duties to perform: to carry out the law by appropriating what was at hand and to "defend the revolution"—which meant fighting counter-revolutionary plots and parties. This seemed easy enough; it only required occasional arrests, requisitions, and now and then the shooting of a suspected bourgeois, with raiding of houses, shops, and cellars, both public and private. All this was delightful through the excitement and booty it furnished!

By degrees, as heads became heated, the whole of the poorer elements became one drunken horde. Even the German directors could no longer manage the mobs except by giving them what they asked for and by promising more and always more. Each day brought new necessities, and to keep their places the demagogues must be forever ready to humor the wildest caprices and to invent new license and new orgies, so thought would be stifled on the part of those whom they wished to hold well in hand.

This became especially difficult, because so many of the prophecies did not come true, or when they did they proved unsatisfactory. Men who were led to burn château and farms, stock and implements, and to whom the land was given, were not content finally, because after they had the land they could not labor at so much of it merely with their hands, and all the tools and organization for bringing forth its fruits had been done for by the heirs to it themselves. How were they to draw money from the bare earth alone, be it ever so rich? They couldn't suffice at the work and, besides, they didn't really want to do it, since part of the new paradise promised had been that no one need labor unless he chose.

In the factories it was the same; there were at first wonderful days and nights, when the men had stood up to the owners, had talked of their new rights, and taken their freedom when and how they pleased, meaning naturally a complete holiday at full wages. The managers had protested, then for a time had paid, and had finally gone bankrupt and closed their shops, or simply left them to the management of the strikers. Some owners had fled and saved their lives, others had stayed and been murdered, while the buildings and machinery generally had gone up in flames. The factory-hands who wanted to stand by their employers were either driven off or, when they proclaimed too loudly that the conduct of their comrades was outrageous, they were put to death as renegades to their own class. After all this was accomplished and there was time to realize what had been done, naturally no pay was forthcoming, and from cold lodgings the workmen sallied out into the streets, ready for any adventure which might be suggested. Riots and noise, drinking, stealing and knifing, the inspiration was ever present in the thought of all that was to be, but had not yet come true, and in the gnawing hunger at their vitals.

Of such men the "Red Guard" was formed, and a more dangerous crowd could scarcely be. Trotsky saw to it they should be kept amused and satisfied, and he paid these men first, and well, with the money which came regularly from the Berlin banks when he could find none nearer to home.[14] Disorderly, undisciplined, rackety, untrustworthy, no reliance could be placed on them for any regular service, not even to back up the government's orders, or for maintaining any kind of organized life. Lawlessness was the special occupation of every Bolshevik, who applied his party's doctrines to himself and to the acquisition of his own personal desire of the moment. Any one who disagreed with the new scheme must either flee the country or give way, unless he cared to be shot if noticed. Remaining alive meant making oneself as small as possible on all occasions or paying with one's life for attracting undue attention.

As an indication of what the Bolsheviks were capable of in breaking all rules of hospitality and showing treachery even toward foreigners who were in their hands, I need cite but one instance: the experiences of the diplomatic missions, which departed from Petrograd at the moment when, after the peace treaty of Brest-Litovsk, German

---

[14] More important than money, though probably not German, was allotments of food, obtained by his "Food Brigades."

conquerors were to occupy our capital. The actions of the Trotsky-Lenin government were then quite on the Hun pattern. The Japanese and Chinese missions accompanied the American Ambassador's as far as Vologda, half across European Russia on the Trans-Siberian Railroad, while the British, French, Italian, and Serbian missions refused to take this route—quite around the world— to reach their homes, and they started, with the Bolshevik government's permission, for the Swedish frontier, by way of Finland, a trip which should have lasted about thirty hours. They were harassed and held up on the road, in their special trains, for between six and seven weeks, the British being the only mission which finally succeeded in getting to the frontier at all! The others were turned back after this long trial of their patience, and were forced to go to Vologda, where they remained with the Americans until July 1918!

During four or five months constant discussion continued between the little group of stranded diplomats at Vologda and the Bolshevik government at Moscow. The latter had offered Petrograd to the German masters, and had retired themselves to the more southern capital, accompanied by Hun Ambassadors, who were really dictators. Now they invited—and kept insisting on acceptance—the members of the foreign missions to join them at their new headquarters. At first they tried to tempt these by offering villas to the missions if they would but come to Moscow, thus recognizing the red government.

This invitation was steadily refused, because the Allies felt themselves already as near to the Soviet's people as they cared to be, and because if they went farther south they felt at any moment—when the occasion rose which might make such action advantageous—they might be seized and held as hostages. Evidently the object of Trotsky's government was to play off the Allies against the Germans, who were accredited to the Kremlin. The confidence the Teuton Powers felt in Trotsky's word can be judged by the fact that Austria and Germany each insisted on sending to Moscow two or three regiments of their own troops to defend their embassies... In spite of which Count Mirbach was murdered within six months![15]

Radek, a member of the Bolshevik Soviet, had come with the invitation to the diplomatic corps all the way to Vologda, and after he returned to Moscow with their refusal the stranded party received an alarming telegram in the night of July 23, from the Muscovite capital, saying it was unsafe for diplomats to remain at Vologda, and that another day might mean escape would no longer be possible![16] Thereupon

---

[15] After participating in the negotiations for the Treaty of Brest-Litovsk, Count Wilhelm von Mirbach was appointed German ambassador to Soviet Russia in April 1918. On July 6 of that year he was assassinated in Moscow by a Left Socialist Revolutionary. This led to a campaign of terror waged by the Bolsheviks against that party, which had also badly wounded Lenin.

[16] Karl Radek (1885–1939) was a Polish Jew from Austrian Galicia who had never resided in the Russian Empire but came to Petrograd in 1917 to join the revolution. He played a major role in the negotiations with Germany at Brest-Litovsk and later in negotiating the Treaty of Rapallo in 1921. He added a sane approach and fluency in German to these agreements.

Mr. Francis and his companions decided to use immediately the special train which they had kept ready on the track for five months past and to beat a hasty retreat to Archangel.[17] They consequently asked for a locomotive, which it had been arranged they were to obtain from the station-master on demand, but the Soviet government heard of this action and made inquiries as to the proposed departure and the destination of the train. The information demanded was sent by the Vologda officials, where upon Chicherin, Minister of Foreign Affairs at Moscow,[18] sent word to the American Ambassador: "Archangel is an unfit place for diplomats to life, and going there means leaving Russia definitely."

The little group left, all the same, for the northern port. They reached it only to find the Soviet representatives warned of their coming and waiting there with orders from Moscow, which renewed complications for some time longer. During this period the diplomats lived through many dangerous hours, and were treated in turn as both hostages and prisoners. At times, however, they themselves were in command, especially after an Allied fleet landed a goodly number of marines. They even made a forced trip to Kandalaksha and returned in time to assist at the overthrow of the Bolsheviks, after which they attended to much of the settling of the Archangel government's policy, upholding the new and struggling provisional officials who lately had been established there.

It shows the influence of the Germans, if not their absolute control of Trotsky, that they twice demanded the American Ambassador be banished from Archangel, in support of which demand they made various accusations. Trotsky, cringing to his masters, gave the necessary orders, but these were not carried out, because the Bolsheviks were no longer in charge at Archangel when these papers came, and the American Ambassador remained in possession of the field until November 1918. Then he left Russian shores by his own decision and because of impaired health.

One might feel surprise no opposition was attempted in the great centers where Bolshevism flourished, but when one remembers how this party came into existence it seems natural enough nothing could be organized against it. The enlightened members of society were not only in the minority, but the many requisitions since the first movement in March 1917, had deprived them of arms and ammunition of every description, while the red rabble owned firearms which had been in factories or arsenals, and

---

[17] The American ambassador, David R. Francis (1850–1927), a Missouri politician and newspaper publisher, was appointed to the Russian post in 1916 with no diplomatic experience. He received much criticism, notably from George F. Kennan, for his tenure, but on the whole managed a difficult situation as described in Ralph Barnes's *Standing on a Volcano: The Life and Times of David Rowland Francis* (St. Louis: Missouri Historical Society, 2001).

[18] Georgy Chicherin (1872–1936) assumed the position of Commissar of Foreign Relations in 1918 to relieve Leon Trotsky to concentrate on building the Red Army. He served in that post though increasingly crippled by illness until 1930, when his assistant, Maxim Litvinov (1876–1951), took his place.

even all those used in the army, except such as had been surrendered to the German conqueror, destroyed or thrown away during their wild routs of the past summer.

The Teutons, until now, have kept these so-called troops of the Red Guard well supplied with ammunition. I find myself hoping sometimes, that in a gesture of revenge all this ragged and disappointed misery will turn on the German leaders, and serve them with the treatment they so justly merit by the vast swindle they have practiced on our criminally childish groups. To rouse them the enemy's loathsome game was dressed in fine ideals. Made of Utopian hopes never to be gratified was the sheep's clothing these wolves wore. Little by little they proceeded to debauch their converts till these became mere tools the enemy used shamelessly for the destruction and dismemberment of Great Russia, Germany's most powerful foe. This once accomplished, the Huns were quite ready to turn away, and indifferent as to their victim's fate.

Even after all these months of the loathsome system, the monsters who invented it have drawn little good from their infamy; firstly, because the same propaganda they created has rolled back in a great wave upon themselves; secondly, because as yet Germany has been too busy on her western front, and at home, to turn soldiers and officials into Russia in numbers sufficient to take complete possession of us, as she would like to do, also, the Boche [Germans] has been unable to gather in the quantity of food and labor from our provinces on which he counted, but he still trusts he will manage to remedy these points as soon as peace with the Allies is really signed. Then he will have a free hand in Russia, he foresees, in exchange for concessions made to the Allies elsewhere.

All parties in Germany will be willing to give up everything else, if only Russia remains to them, for none know better than they the real value of our resources and the qualities of our race. They see our unformed, groping millions as docile material in the hands of their own strong disciplinarians, turning present defeat into an eventual glittering victory of their fatherland. Therefore, while ambassadors discuss general peace and politicians are settling burning home questions, the enemy can afford to let the pot in Russia simmer down, hoping their agents will keep enough propaganda going and that the disorder they have ordained will continue till they are ready to go into Russia and take complete charge. Whether the Huns have miscalculated in all this or not, only time can show.

By degrees their schooling is giving results which bear the "Made in Germany" stamp; as, for instance, by the recent delightfully frank declaration of Zinoviev, the Bolshevik tyrant at Petrograd, in a speech to his confederates of the Russian capital.[19] Doubtless these men were at a loss to understand why, after having made the peace of Brest-Litovsk with the Huns and become their creatures—even fighting the Allies in

---

[19] Grigory Zinoviev (1883–1936) was a leading Bolshevik and member of the original five of the Politburo. He devoted much of his efforts to the founding and mission of the Comintern (Communist International), and the promotion of world revolution. Eased out by Joseph Stalin, he was arrested and, after a celebrated show trial in 1936, was executed.

desultory fashion through a long year of weary misery—suddenly the policies of the Peoples' Commissars are changed to the point of accepting an invitation sent from Paris to meet and confer with representatives of the winners of the war. These simple citizens of Petrograd cannot comprehend why, while his army is still battling with Bolshevik troops in the northern snows round Archangel, the American President should wish to send them peace messengers and to invite them to a meeting on an island in the southern seas.[20]

But Zinoviev is cleverer, and he explains at once the statesmanlike point of view! And his discourse is published in a Bolshevik paper at Petrograd for all the world to read. He said: "We have accepted this invitation, which has come to us Bolsheviks unsolicited, because we are poor and need help and provisions of all kinds, which these new allies—now tired of fighting us—will offer in exchange for certain promises on our part. The promises we shall keep only as long as we are pleased to do so, and then we shall act as we see fit, and treat this agreement as we would any other scrap of paper. There is no obligation to hold to such an arrangement, once it is no longer convenient for us to do so; and meantime we stand to gain those things which we desire, and will demand of the Americans."[21]

Small wonder that the various other Russian parties showed disinclination to accept the tryst offered, and refused to try healing all Russia's ills by discussing them with Bolsheviks. It would take courage indeed to go as representatives of the Allies to the Prince's Islands after Zinoviev's frank avowal of the Soviet government's intentions.

In the hands of plotters such as Trotsky, the professed ideals of the Bolshevik party had been so thoroughly debased that now, I fancy, the crowd about him is only held by fear, or by a constant appeal to its worst instincts. Religion—deep-seated of old in our Orthodox peasant and soldier, and only slightly less so in the city factory-hand of Russia—is slowly being killed off. The churches, which held crowds of poorly clad bodies with exalted faces in the first months of the revolution, are empty now, their facades are disfigured, and their jewelled icons and candlesticks, crosses, and missals are stolen, or destroyed in the melting-pot; the priests have mostly fled, or they hide themselves in misery, and all that was once holy is desecrated. This by what was once the most beautifully devout group of humble Christian worshipers. Before

---

[20] The reference here is to the "Prinkipo Proposal," an attempt by the Big Four of the Paris peace conference in January 1919, to initiate a discussion of the Russian situation among all the various factions claiming authority in Russia. Inspired by an appeal from Maxim Litvinov, assistant commissar of foreign affairs from Stockholm in early January, it was then promoted by Woodrow Wilson, to take place in a neutral setting far from Paris on Prinkipo, the largest island of the Turkish Prince's Islands in the Sea of Marmora near Istanbul. The Bolsheviks accepted the invitation to participate, but other factions refused to have any thing to do with a meeting that included the Bolsheviks, so the conference never took place.

[21] The invitation was accepted formally by a radiogram of February 4, 1919, by Georgy Chicherin, commissar of foreign affairs.

THE REIGN OF TERROR

this newest regime appeared, they had brought all their troubles and their joys to the foot of the cross, with a splendid faith, in which they lived, fearing God and loving one another.

But religion, though forced to burn low, is not quite dead in Russia. In Moscow the old Patriarch, head of our Church, has dared to remain at his post and to live on, helping his flock as best he can. This ancient hero has even boldly bearded the lion in its den, calling it to shame. Escaping murder by some miracle, the venerable man has published a message to the "Council of Commissioners of the People" which is characteristically courageous. He says in part:

> You who regulate the fate of the people, to you I address these words, as you are preparing to celebrate the anniversary of your revolution of October, which gave you the power. But the blood you have spilt in a year cries out for celestial justice and constrains me to address you in bitter words. At the moment when you took possession, promising them peace without annexation or contribution, you sold out the people!
>
> You gave Russia a peace so humiliating that you lacked the courage to publish all its articles! Our country is debased and divided, and as a gauge of the contributions imposed on it, you are secretly paying Germany money accumulated by others that yourselves. You have debauched our national army, and in doing so you have robbed it of its soul—the soul which inspired it to so many heroic deeds. You have incited soldiers, till now brave and indomitable, to give up defending their land. You have extinguished in their hearts the flaming conviction that none can show more love than he who gives his life up for his people. You have substituted for patriotism an inanimate internationalism, and you know well at the same time that the proletarian sons of other nations answered with devotion the first call to defend their nations' frontiers.
>
> You have refused to defend our country against the exterior enemy, yet you do nothing but mobilize armies; and against whom are you leading them? You have divided all our people among themselves and inspired them to fratricidal war; you substitute hate for Christian love; and in making peace you rouse only envy and jealousy!
>
> This civil war you have lighted, you know well can have no end, for you are trying to establish the triumph of a specter of universal revolution and are sacrificing to it the workmen and the peasants of our land. It was only you leaders who needed this humiliating peace with an outside enemy, so you would be able to carry out your intention of destroying forever interior peace. No one's life is now secure. Innocents are constantly suffering and being killed, without any form of judgment, accusation, or defense. Those whom you keep as hostages and whom you execute in this manner are merely victims of your hideous thirst for revenge for crimes committed by others

whom these did not even know, and who were often your own collaborators. All classes of martyrs—from army, church, or civilian groups—have been accused vaguely of propaganda against your revolution; but no proof of this is in your hands.

What insane cruelty on the part of men who pretend to the title of benefactors to humanity at large! Torrents of blood have not quenched it. You have pushed the people to pillage and to the destruction of all that was not theirs. First the rich, under the pretense of fighting the 'bourgeoisie,' then the well-to-do peasants you have sacrificed. You have multiplied the number of mendicants, even while you realized that in deteriorating all these citizens you are bringing the whole country to ruin. Yet you incite continuously all the rough elements of the population to facile and unpunished acquisition of anything which for the moment pleases them; and however you hide your acts under fine names, murder, and pillage, and violence, will always be infamous crimes; and will call down the contempt of the world at large, and heaven's vengeance.

And you promised liberty—which is a boon when it guarantees safety and happiness, when it is equal and does not turn to arrogance; but this is not liberty which you have given the people, for you have favored the development of the vilest passions in the lowest element of our population, and you have left unnoticed crimes which are unutterable—murder, theft, and rape. And you oppress all civic freedom and the dignity of man. When no one dares buy provisions, or rent a room to live in, or travel, without your personal permission, it is not liberty; and when whole families or the occupants of an entire house are thrown into the streets without reason, again it is not liberty.

Is it, then, liberty to have our people divided into artificial groups, of which more than the half are preyed upon; and when no one can declare his convictions—political or religious—sincerely without fear of persecution; is this liberty or tyranny! Where is the liberty of word, and act, and press, and faith you promised? You forbid even the entrance of the Kremlin to the Russian people, whose sacred property it is, and whom even crowned autocrats had allowed to enter always! You have destroyed the parish, and the schools, and all charitable institutions which have cared and helped the nation's misery in years gone by...

I do not even dwell on the breaking up of Russia, yesterday so great and powerful; nor on the disappearance of our transportation, the lack of food and fuel, which threaten our cities and even many villages with complete annihilation. The tragedy is but too evident, and the horrible epoch of your regime will remain for long reflected in the souls of our compatriots, where you have replaced the image of God by that of the beast...

It is not for me to judge terrestrial power, and all forms of government will have my benediction, if only they serve God in protecting good and exterminating evil... To celebrate the anniversary of your seizure of power, end completely the persecution of your neighbors, and of other innocents, stop the flow of blood and the violence and the ruins which are now about us, protect loyalty, establish law and order, and give back to our people the peace for which they pray! If this is not done, you who have raised the sword, shall perish by the sword!

(Signed) Tikhon
Patriarch of Moscow and of all Russia

His manifesto was published in Moscow on October 26, 1918. But in spite of this old champion of the good cause, every crime in the calendar is not only still permitted but encouraged, while lawlessness remains the order of the day. In Petrograd and Moscow misery for all, with famine, typhus, cholera, and foul air caused by dirt and decay inconceivable, reigns. Water, light, street conveyances, telephones, and other public services have completely collapsed, the brilliant, beautiful capitals stand rotting and helpless through the months. Their show buildings are mostly in ruins, either from bombardments or from sacking by the mobs; food, when obtainable, has reached prices impossible to pay, for I read recently that butter was one hundred and forty-five dollars a pound, and dog-meat ten dollars, while pork at forty-five dollars a pound was snatched at![22]

From time to time from Smolny [Bolshevik/Soviet headquarters] or some other confiscated palace, where either Trotsky, Lenin, Chicherin, or Zinoviev resides in slovenly state, an order is issued, given out in form of proclamation to the multitude. Occasionally the latter pay no attention; sometimes they listen and disapprove, then the new law dies at its birth. Once in a while some proclamation captures popular fancy, and then these children of the gutter rush off to play the new game proposed, whatever it may be.

In spite of starvation, theaters, operas, and ballets are continuously open, with free seats for all. No man does any work. Yet one can't sleep always through twenty-four hours during months and months. The banks and shops and palaces afforded interesting occupation at first, but these are done for completely now; the bigger restaurants and hotels are also closed down, after their cellars were looted and their furniture and windows had been smashed. Possible fun, consequently, had been greatly reduced; no one could think of work, of course, under any circumstances.

---

[22] This may seem an exaggeration of conditions but is not. 1918 was a year of economic and social collapse extending throughout the winter of 1918–19, one reason for the Bolshevik acceptance of the Prinkipo invitation. The situation was also a major factor in the harsh decrees issued by the Soviet government to address it, especially the Food Decree of May 1918 that declared all agricultural production, except for enough to support a peasant family, state property without compensation. This only made the situation worse, with wholesale slaughter of livestock and fields left fallow, the period known as "War Communism."

Labor which must be done is attended to by a small portion of the inhabitants, whose fate makes one's heart ache, for they are the real martyrs of the revolution—I mean the ex-officers of our great army. In the capital small squads of them have joined together, and are allowed to earn the pittance on which they manage to keep alive, with the wives and children who are generally dependent on them. One such little band is hewing wood in a courtyard, another is cleaning snow from the main streets, where once they paraded, commanding a marvelous army of heroes; others sweep, or serve cabbies and their friends in the small eating-houses which these frequent.

An acquaintance of mine, who had fragile health, and was the gay young ex-colonel of a crack bodyguard regiment, is so lucky now as to have found a place as salesman in a tiny booth at one of the bazaars. There he measures tape and lace for the old market-women and scrubs the shop for its owner. The latter felt enough pity to take him in and give him protection till death should claim him. In his hours of fever, as he tosses on his pallet, perhaps he imagines his strange surroundings are but a nightmare, which will cease with the morning's dawn, and that he will wake to find himself still leading daring scouts in enemies' countries and winning a St. George's Cross—which he did during the war—or leading a mazurka at a great court ball, as was his wont in still earlier days. Or perhaps he dreams that he is helping one of his soldier's families, since he had always spent his income in this manner. His theory was that as he had no estates with peasants to look after, the men of his command were his nearest responsibility. Instead, it is to scrub floors, shivering and coughing, that he rises again, and patiently, in half-dazed wonder, he asks himself when it will all end.

The officers who were free to do so fled to one of the several units in Denikin's or Krasnov's volunteer armies.[23] Earlier still they mostly went into the "shock battalions" on the firing-line, and were, if possible, killed. But where a woman and small mouths depended on one, and there were no money and no trains for flight, a man had to stay in some big center and face the crisis out. Immediately when the Bolsheviks took power the officers were disarmed, their epaulets were dragged off, and their rank and pay were both suppressed, even to the small pensions of such officers as had been wounded, or who had won a St. George's Cross for signal gallantry on the field of battle.

With every means of living gone, one must tramp the streets to find work, and take whatever offered, and though the new rulers did not want to labor themselves, they objected to seeing others do so, thus putting them to shame. So here, there, and everywhere the officer was told no room for him existed in the new scheme of things,

---

[23] General Petr Krasnov (1867–1947) was a Don Cossack leader (elected hetman in May 1918) and general in the imperial army during World War I. He became an early "White army" commander at the beginning of the Russian civil war. Emigrating to Germany he was a leader of the right-wing exile community and wrote novels about the Civil War experience. In World War II, he joined the German war effort and commanded occupation units in Yugoslavia. Repatriated to the Soviet Union, he was executed.

and he was reviled and baited, repulsed and humiliated from every side. Many fell, faint with hunger and discouragement, on the streets or door-steps, where some pitying soul perhaps would take them in, warm, and wash, and feed them from small secret reserves not yet requisitioned, or they would lie unconscious till some adept pupil of the German conquerors passed by and kicked the fallen body into a gutter, putting the officer out of his misery forever with a blow upon the head.

Avowed and intentional degradation of our people, after the German model, has been thoroughly practiced, so that aside from crushing our religious beliefs the Bolsheviks had quite openly encouraged immorality, anyhow and everywhere. In at least two cities—Saratov and Vladimir—proclamations issued by the Soviets announced officially the "nationalization of women" and the adoption of all children by the state.[24] Consequently the complete abolition of homes and families, with all the strength, responsibility, and happiness which these may mean to a community, is deliberately aimed at. As no results of this measure's success are yet announced, I feel privileged to doubt whether these newest laws have actually been enforced.[25] I venture to believe they never will be, since in the general chaos existing people are apt to do what they please, and Russians of every station whom I saw during nearly twenty years loved their hearths and homes, their mothers, wives, or children with more intense devotion than I have met with elsewhere. Therefore, I think to defend these many a man even in such mad surroundings would risk drastic punishment.

An ex-member of the ancient national Duma, just escaped to the Crimea from Petrograd, made the following deposition on August 19, 1918:

> It was decreed that all persons who were suspected of having communication with the Allies, or any sympathy for their cause, were to be immediately shot, without trial, on the decision of the inquiry committee of the Bolshevik government. After this, arrests and executions in the capital rose to a frightful total. Every night the red guardsmen gathered up crowds of former officers and conservative civilians, and took them to Kronstadt, where part were always immediately killed and part imprisoned. One officer I knew escaped from there by some miracle, while out of a herd of three hundred and sixty persons who were arrested with him, two hundred were executed before his eyes. Some months ago President Uritsky, of the Inquisitional Court, was assassinated, and the Bolsheviks at once took five hundred of the best known

---

[24] In the chaos of the times, it was easy to proclaim ultra-radical measures with the understanding that there could be no enforcement. It satisfied the whims of some of the radical inclinations.

[25] Author's note: Since my article was published I have read that these laws were so unpopular that they had to be repealed.

citizens of Petrograd and held them as hostages.[26] I was personally among these, and was kept two days by the Committee of Inquiry; then I was thrown into the state prison.

The conditions were dreadful; we were one hundred and forty people in one room, where because of lack of space one could not lie down at all; and we were obliged to live in such filth that we were all covered with vermin. Both cholera and typhus broke out, and as the prison had no hospital ward, those who were ill continued among us. By way of medical aid we had the visit of an assistant surgeon, who came through the prison from time to tome. A real doctor's services were refused us. We had no medicines, and for food we received a salted-herring porridge twice a day, which was often decayed; each man also received an eighth of a pound of bread and a small bit of sugar per day. The most remarkable fact is that though I was locked up for two months in such dramatic conditions, I underwent no inquiry, and no accusation was ever presented against me. It was as if I had been merely forgotten.

No newspapers are allowed [to be] published in the Bolshevik domains, save only those approved by the Soviet, which constantly show their German training and inspiration. From the *Bulletin of the Soviets* of December 3, 1918, the following extract is eloquent of the feeling toward the Allied Powers. Freely translated the article says:

> Lloyd George, Clemenceau, and Wilson! These three men are directing their armies to oppose Bolshevik Russia, which is rightly esteemed by them to be the most dangerous and resisting power in the world to their theories. An Allied navy is now sailing from Constantinople to Sevastopol, probably intending to land troops, and the Allies also think they can attack us from the southeast, through Rumania. The British navy is only waiting to clear out mines from the Baltic in order to throw itself at our red Petrograd. We know quite well a struggle is imminent, and we exhort the Bolsheviks to surround all the north of Russia with an iron ring of discipline…that same discipline which our government abolished some months ago voluntarily in the cause of liberty. A council of defense of workmen and peasants has been instituted, and the task has been allotted to it of organizing the defense of Russia in its struggle with the Allies. Not only the army and navy, but also all matters of commissariat and transportation, as well as of military industry, must be put into the hands of a military regime—that is, a regime of violent labor and discipline.
>
> This is being done in accordance with the situation of the country, and is necessitated by the imperialistic bandits' action—that of Lloyd George,

---

[26] A follower of Trotsky, Moisei Uritsky (1873–1918) joined the Bolsheviks in July 1917 and lent his organizational expertise to the revolution until his assassination by a Left Socialist Revolutionary in August 1918 as part of a "reign of terror" waged against the Bolsheviks.

Clemenceau, and Wilson! We are compelled by them to make our country a military camp, as every day the cynicism and the falseness of these conquerors' policy become more openly declared. Wilson, who yesterday was an eloquent protector of the liberty of nations and the rights of democracy, today fits out formidable forces to bring order into our Revolutionary Russia! Wilson is the leader of the fight against Russia, while Lenin is the man whose strong arm holds the torch of our civilization aloft, to enlighten the whole world!

In a Kiev Bolshevik newspaper put into my hands I find another equally eloquent but entirely contradictory official communication:

On November 19, 1918, was held in Moscow an extra session of the Council of the Peoples' Commissars—the Bolshevik government—and it was debated how Russia would meet the advance of the Allied troops which is shortly expected. The chief of the Bolshevik armies, Leon Trotsky, rose to announce that the army of the Soviets would probably not be able to withstand the enemies' offensive. "Being so numerous the Bolshevik forces are deprived of the concentrated strength of organization, whereas the fall of Germany has had the effect of augmenting recently the arrogance of the Anglo-French coalition in a proportion difficult of evaluation. At this time it suffices that our front should learn some rumor of the approach of an Allied detachment for the news to produce immediately colossal disorders in the ranks of our red army, making it almost impossible to persuade our men to battle!

I cannot vouch for the truthfulness of all these statements, but only for the fact that the newspapers containing them are really in my hands, sent me by a friend escaped within a month from our sad home country. I am inclined to believe that Trotsky and Lenin must really have much anxiety as to their powers of defense in case of an attack by a proper force, well led, for I personally saw the Bolsheviks on several occasions fighting, and while they always created havoc, and infinite tragedy lay in their wake, they never carried out their plans, but were easily distracted by some side issue, and showed themselves ready to stop for food or drink, or to throw away their arms and carry off, instead, some booty which captivated their fancies, and which in turn they soon dropped to follow a new scent, or merely because the burden of it wearied them. Never had they organization above, nor obedience below, in their ranks except when they were led by Germans, who frightened them.

Our people, always childish, have been especially so through their shame and misery. They have shown ferocity only under strong incentive and capable mastery, whereas left to themselves they have been chaotic, noisy, wasteful, wanton, careless, dirty, gluttonous, and many other things which have brought them to their present straits. But never are they by temperament bloodthirsty, nor systematically cruel, as were the French peasantry and citizens of 1792. Victims who have barely escaped with their lives—and they are numerous—have been all helped to freedom by some good-natured, unlearned giant, who had been set to guard them, and though Russia has seen torture and death accompanied by every sort of crime, these have been desultory cases, or else were exacted by foreign tyrants and inspired by foreign theories. Many, many of our people were drawn to those first Bolshevik leaders or have since followed the bloody banner because the propagandists held out promises of good things—of peace, and happiness, and prosperity, and the true millennium, and land and liberty for all.

The converts saw much in the new doctrines at first to satisfy their craving for ideals, which is never quite eradicated from the mentality of the Russian, of whatever class he may be. They were told all men would be brothers, content and rich, and they saw gold and were treated to food and drink when they were starving. Small wonder they were impressed with this apparent generosity and believed in the mirage of good to come, and when the Rubicon was passed, they found themselves outside the pale and were obliged, they thought, to stay there, or else it was explained the expected results were just beyond the next bend in the road, which seemed so difficult to tread. So they were tempted on.

Afterward the culprits were either frightened or their sense of morality was blunted, and wrong still dressed as right was dangled before their eyes. Then finally the worst elements came to the surface, both in individual characters and in the crowds, and all were dragged, led, and cajoled into the trap of their present misery.

Many a self-styled Bolshevik among peasants or working people, or among the soldiers I personally have known, has confided to me that he joined the party because "it was either be a Bolshevik or be shot", and it was promised him he should have all things, after a short period of disorder and trouble. I feel certain many of these men are sorely disappointed now in results, and want a change but they dare not say it, even in a whisper. In the crowds of Bolsheviks I have seen there were, of course, some heavy criminal faces full of brutality, but the vast majority bore the signs of a dull, hopeless misery and of surprise and fear. Mostly there are mere cowed and broken wrecks in the populace which drifts by one on a Russian street; all look beaten and torn by the storms to which they are subjected.

I have not been alone in noticing these markedly distressing types, for nearly every traveler who had recently come out of North Russia testifies, consciously or unconsciously, to the sorrow and deep agony he has recognized. After all, these men and women to whom so much was promised are still hungry, cold, and without homes, even more wretched than before the revolution, for they have lost ideals and hopes and the softness which was the natural atmosphere of life in the old Russia. The beauty of their cities is gone, and their churches all closed, so that they are shut off even from the outside frame which brought a ray of warmth and sun into their tragic lives. I am told there is much desire for improvement, but no one dares be caught by the present authorities expressing a wish for it.

One can only hope and pray a change may come, from within or without, before Russia shall have reached the point of exhaustion when rebirth is impossible. In various corners of the great empire parties seem to be forming to throw off the yoke and crush the tyrants and the anarchy, which proves our people have still a vital force and a warm, beating heart. These small groups are, alas, not strong numerically in proportion to their courage, though they are growing, nor are they furnished with the material wherewith to fight. They must get to their feet somehow and be supplied, before they can aspire to crush the dragon who is at large in the fair home domain.

Will the spirit of St. George and that inherited from Joan of Arc come to the rescue? And shall Russia see Columbia's sons also coming to bring her law and order? Or must the Slavs go through the purgatory of German ownership and renew their terrible experiences of past centuries and of Tatar mastery? Even in this last case I know the Teutons, as the Tatars, would finally be laid low by our younger, more primitive and stronger, race, for our Russia is still in its childhood, and has fallen through ignorance into the hands of thieves.

One wonders where the remedy will be found to cure the deathly ailment. Mostly in the strength of the many worthy men who rose up and from the first moment joined in heroic bands, and who have never ceased their struggle against the terrible odds. Such is Denikin's army. Perhaps aid may come also from outside, since there are many voices among our ancient allies crying out in favor of offering us a helping hand. These would give of their present strength to the prostrate sister, who did her part so grandly in the first years of the war, while they themselves were weak and unprepared, and who has since paid dearly for her sacrifices in the general cause. Such voices are very powerful ones, and come from men of varying creeds and parties, and as I read their speeches I am filled with hope that succor may be tendered, and that it may be soon!

In Paris the great Lloyd George spoke for Russia to his colleagues, and then his plea was upheld by Sir George Buchanan, who had lived in our country for many years as ambassador from his Majesty the King. They know our value well, and here in America there are also men who speak with equal conviction and enthusiasm on the same subject, and who say that our great empire must be saved from further depredation at the hands of the Germans, or of the latter's inspired agents; that such riches as ours must not be left to the exploitation of the world's enemy indefinitely. Each man who knows the truth adds his word of warning as to the danger to the whole edifice of Christian civilization from the spread of Bolshevism, and each one most solemnly asserts that if the world is to be protected from the dread disease, then Russia must be quickly helped and saved!

IV
The Crimea's Effort—Denikin's Army

Many months had passed, during which the population of the Crimean coast suffered and gazed wistfully out to sea, when one day, about the middle of December 1918, an allied fleet sailed into the harbor of Sevastopol. As soon as the flagship dropped anchor the commanding officer, British Vice-Admiral Calthorpe,[1] was waited upon by a messenger, who put the following official document into his hands:

The Minister of Foreign Affairs of the Provisional Crimean Government, to the High Commander of the Allied Fleet in Sevastopol Harbor.

In consequence of our recent negotiations of December 9, I have the honor to inform the high commander of the Allied fleet of the following particulars concerning accommodations which can be afforded Allied troops landing in the Crimea, and concerning provisions which will be supplied to them. By the 16th of December the government can install at our capital, Simferopol, 400 men in barracks, and in town-billets 600 more; at Dzhankoi, 300 men; at Evpatoria, 500; at Feodosia, 500; at Karasu-Bazar, 300; at Toganash, 100, and at Perekop, 100. Toganash and Perekop which are thirty and sixty kilometres from Dzhankoi, will necessitate transportation, and this the government can also furnish for the number of men designated. All these groups total together 2,800 men, and equal number can be quartered in Sevastopol itself.

The Crimean provisional government will pay for the troops' installation, and will furnish the Allies with firewood and coal. Also the provisional government considers itself in duty bound to supply the following provisions to Allied troops: One pound of bread to each man daily; two pounds of sugar monthly; 80,000 bottles of red and white Crimean wine in casks; 4,000 pounds of dried fruits; 120 litres of rum.

(Signed) Vinaver,[2] Minister of Foreign Affairs

---

[1] Vice-Admiral Somerset Arthur Gough-Calthorpe (1864–1937) was commander of the British Mediterranean Station since 1917. He had served earlier (1902–05) as British naval attache in St. Petersburg.

[2] Maksim Vinaver (1863–1926) was a founder of the Constitutional Democratic Party and a former member of the State Duma. He was a supporter of Paul Miliukov and in 1918 served as

So it would seem the Allied fleet, on reaching Crimean shores, found an organized government alive in the midst of the general chaos which Russia nowadays represents to the imagination of the outside world. This government was a new-born thing, for when the central provisional government fell at Petrograd, in November 1917, and the Bolsheviks took over the power in the north, a period of general unrest was inaugurated all over Russia. The whole country was immediately victimized by uprisings of various Bolshevik groups, or of "nationalists," such as the Ukrainians, Letts, Estonians, Finns, and numerous Caucasian tribes.

Stretching into the Black Sea, the Crimean Peninsula had remained calmer than the rest of our immense country. With almost enough resources to be independent, with small, well-to-do cities, a population of comfortable Tatar or Little Russian peasant proprietors, with a large group of rich and aristocratic refugees scattered in villas along the coast, able and ready to pay well for safety and comfort—it had a better chance of being overlooked by the new propagandists, and as it was on the road to nowhere, it was used neither as a battle-ground nor as a passageway for the various conflicting forces. The Crimea's main fear was of financial misery, an effect of Bolshevik ill usage of northern banks. Also, the province suffered from attacks of armed soldiers and sailors, or other criminals disguised in uniforms, who made up occasional parties to steal and kill, and who motored over the country doing what harm they could.

At first the towns had been very tranquil, and the only signs of the times were the arrests of members of the imperial family, who lived along the cliffs from Livadia to Tchaire [summer palace of Grand Duke Nikolai Nikolaevich]. These unfortunates were threatened, not by the quiet Tatars who lived round them, but by the same hooligan elements—vague, torn-off shreds of the rabble in the north, and because money did not come through, the financial establishments in Simferopol, Yalta, Kerch, and elsewhere, necessarily limited their clients to the smallest payments. With provision prices immensely high, it was a problem how the victims could get on. Thus in dread of daily suffering and in great danger they lived, hoarding their small resources and provisions, worried by rumors and terrified by occasional demonstrations, when villas round about were sacked, inhabitants driven from home, ill treated, and frequently wounded; sometimes even murdered on the spot.

Soon the treaty of Brest-Litovsk and the equal treachery of the German Government and its agents—who were Trotsky's and Lenin's representatives—brought our country into the enemies' net completely, ended the war, and opened wide the doors of Russia to the Huns. This was in the winter, spring, and summer of 1918. Moscow had a German Ambassador then, Count Mirbach, who dictated his

---

foreign minister of the Crimean provisional government. In exile in 1919 he edited the emigre Jewish journal *Zveno* (Link).

country's policy to the docile Trotsky, while Skoropadsky, Hetman of Ukraine, joined forces with Von Eichhorn, Hun dictator at Kiev, and did the latter's bidding.[3]

In the south our Caucasian peoples, always wild and proud, broke away from this new Russia. They had been held to us before only by the brilliancy of our court, which appealed equally to all of the antagonistic mountain tribes, through their love of splendor and of visible power.[4] Other considerable districts of Russia, also secretly encouraged by the enemy, fell off now, believing they were to be really independent and free from tyranny, but they all found themselves immediately absorbed by the diabolical German octopus, which stretched cunning, supple arms and gathered in the whole country's riches, whether in grain or in men, repaying these only with empty words and with Utopian promises.

Never was there such misery in any nation as in ours through that time, when, unable to gather herself up and reorganize, frantic with fear and suffering, torn with the violence of contending parties and ideas, helpless and prostrate, Russia was all but dying. The various provinces called "independent countries" were treated as mere colonies by the invaders. Lithuania, White Russia, the Baltic States, Georgia, and the Crimean peninsula were all proclaimed "free," but the latter was the only one which called itself "Russian," and it alone had not been either mentioned or represented at the conference of Brest-Litovsk. Germany was sending her troops over all the northern country, and also through Rumania into Bessarabia and the Ukraine, while Turkey invaded the Caucasus. Suddenly, without explanation or excuse, the Teuton soldiers appeared in the Tauride Government (including Crimea), and installed themselves at the capital, Simferopol. They told the people of the Tatar race to rise up and create a national free state. "Were they not Orientals, and were they not living since long under the rule of Russian conquerors? Now at last these were laid low, and it was time for the poor, downtrodden Tatar tribes to form their own government and elect a khan of their own race, putting themselves then under German protection, or else joining the kindly Turks, who were their coreligionists."[5]

---

[3] Field Marshall Hermann von Eichhorn (1848–1918) was in command of the German army in Ukraine since April 1918. He was assassinated by a member of the Left Socialist Revolutionary Party in Kiev on July 30 that year just two weeks after Mirbach, the German ambassador in Moscow, met that same fate.

[4] Some of the Caucasian people, notably the Chechens, successfully resisted Russian occupation and rule for many years in the first half of the nineteenth century and remained resentful of their loss of independence after their conquest, especially in the late twentieth century.

[5] At the time, the population of Crimea was approximately 50 percent Russian, 30 percent Tatar, and 10 percent Ukrainian, though the Tatars were the only indigenous people, centered around the legendary Bakhchisarai in the interior of the peninsula. The Russians were concentrated along the resort coast and at the naval base of Sevastopol, the largest city in Crimea. The Russian numbers grew in 1918–20 because of the flood of refugees from the north.

Everything was done by the Germans to awaken chauvinism among the Oriental portion of the Crimea's inhabitants, while the imperial group of refugees was ostentatiously well treated. Their guard of Bolshevik sailors was changed at once for one of ex-officers of the old-régime army, who were now given as their unique occupation the duty of keeping safely the Empress-Mother, and the various Grand Dukes.

Somehow or other, however, this German propaganda met with small success. Our officers were glad enough to protect the lives of a group of helpless refugees, who until now had been in danger, and the latter were equally well pleased to be rid of their previous guardians, but both imperials and officers were against the Teuton enemy they had fought valiantly through three long years, and whom in that time they had learned to know so well. They continued to dislike the Germans even now, in spite of the sudden change of front the latter affected. It seemed somewhat naive in the Huns to act as they did, and it showed the measure of their own principles for them to think the Dowager-Empress and the Grand Duke Nicholas (and others of that party) could be their allies under any circumstances.

A khan was named Prime Minister—Sulkévich, a Mohammedan Tatar—and the natives of Oriental origin about him were constantly caressed and courted, but whether from real wisdom or from indifference, or because they had been content with their previous life as it was, the Crimean Tatars in these new conditions were as inert as the imperialists, and gave small attention to German flattery or advances. Anyhow, they formed only one-third of the population, and they had lived on excellent terms with the Russian majority until now. Sulkévich and his German protectors became odious after a short time. There was one great advantage in the Teuton occupation, however. It was that railroad communications with the north were opened and banking operations were possible again, so provisions and money could be arranged for and brought into the Tauride province, while even some few men with interests in the north or Ukraine could make an occasional trip on business, or for political reasons. This was the only benefit of our enemy's short reign.

From January to May 1918, was a painful and dangerous period. There were uprisings forced by the Germans in many cities, while villas all the way along the coast were destroyed, the well-to-do population slept with loaded firearms within their reach, and every refugee hid or buried the few treasures he had brought south to save. All faces became worn and gray with anxiety; those who could do so, left isolated suburbs and villages and went to the larger towns, where crowded, and in intense discomfort, they lived on from day to day. Nerves suffered terribly from the strain, and men watched anxiously over their women and children, trying to keep up courage, to protect the old and delicate from shock, and to educate and bring up young people in circumstances far too abnormal to be healthy.

Yet the living forces in our Russian race did not die completely out, for as early as last October a meeting of representatives of the municipalities and of the country districts was held, and it was then and there decided to make an effort toward the reconstruction of Russia, beginning in a small way with Crimea. During the next month—until the last of November—this movement struggled against the government of the Khan Sulkévich, who was still upheld and protected by German troops. When the armistice was signed between the latter and our old Allies in November, the enemy found himself no longer strong enough, nor willing, to support his protégé, and Sulkévich was persuaded to resign from his post in favor of a new local ministry, provisionally formed, which still rules the Crimea, and which hopes for Allied co-operation.

This ministry declared it took and held the power only provisionally, until such time as Russia should be one state, with a chosen, fixed, and popular form of government. Wherefore this governing group was composed not of Crimean elements alone, but of all the material which could be used for the promotion of law and order in the land, without any reference to the previous places of residence, or the political opinions of its various elements. A strange conglomeration these men made, if regarded from the point of view of party politics, either in ancient days or in those of the revolution. All were sincere, energetic, and capable men, of great ideas, and all were practical patriots, their one present aim being to keep this corner organized and safe for life and property. It was their ambition to create a feeling of love of country, with a small well-oiled administrative machine, to be ready and at hand on the day when, God willing, Bolshevism and German influence should be overthrown together. Then one might hope to see our Russia breathe again, reborn to a new life under their care.

The ministry as formed provisionally was headed by a Prime Minister, Krym, who represented Crimea in the first Duma, and later also in the Council of the Empire. Vinaver, Minister of Foreign Affairs, and [Konstantin] Nabokov, Minister of Justice, were both St. Petersburg men, also ex-members of the Duma, and they had been elected to represent their districts in the great revolutionary constituent assembly which never came off.[6] Incidentally, toward the end of the old régime, they had both been appointed members of the Russian Senate, and they had been much in the Crimea in previous years and knew that country well. In the young government Bogdanov held the portfolio of the Interior, and he also had held a seat in the Duma for a long time, while since the revolution he had been named Commissioner of Crimea.

These men were of the "Liberal Cadet party" [Constitutional Democratic] in old days, and are all democratic in opinion, though not Socialists, but the latter group also had voices in the new organization, for there was a "Revolutionary-Socialist" Minister of Public Education, Doctor Nikonov, elected also to the unborn constituent assembly by his radical party, and since that miscarried, he has been acting provost of Sevastopol. Bobrovsky, Minister of Public Works, was a Social-Democrat, and

---

[6] The Constituent Assembly was elected before the Bolshevik Revolution to decide on the constitutional make-up of a new democratic Russia when it met in January 1918, but, since it was not controlled by Bolsheviks, was disbanded by force after a brief meeting. Konstantin Nabokov was the uncle of the writer Vladimir Nabokov.

Stewen, Minister for Trade and Commissariat, was well known to all the Crimea. Admiral Kanin, in revolutionary times elected commander of the Black Sea fleet, dismissed by Bolshevism, also had a brilliant reputation and career, and took the portfolio of Marine. Consequently there was no retrograde element, and no Bolshevik, in the Cabinet formed at Simferopol—in the autumn of 1918.

Bark, Ex-Finance Minister, with a group of followers, had wished early to re-establish some sort of security in the economic world, and he had formed an independent financial committee for Crimean interests.[7] He was elected its president, and was then asked to hold out a hand through his association to the new effort of government. Gladly this was done, for now, as in old days, Bark is both liberal and patriotic, always quite ready to offer the strength of his own personal power and his association's resources in the country's service. [Sergei] Sazonov, equally brave, enthusiastic, and broad in his views, consented to go to Paris and represent to the Allies Russia's needs and miseries; he would plead for their help, so sorely needed to keep this new effort alive.[8]

At its birth the young government called upon the inhabitants of the province to uphold it, by a proclamation which, freely translated, read:

> According to the resolution of the country, state, and municipal councils, the Crimean Government comes into office at a critical moment. The war is nearing its end, but our immense, united Russia no longer exists, though it had lived for more than a thousand years. Scattered over the present torn-up divisions of the land, bodies of evil-minded conspirators are bringing into existence sentiments of hatred, smallness, and selfishness. They are destroying what we had of culture and of law, of right and civilization.
>
> In these circumstances, we consider a firm decision to restore Russia to be the first patriotic duty of every citizen, and the first task of our whole nation. Some few states which have survived or have reformed, are now scattered over the surface of our country. They are separated by long distances, one from the other; but they will be ready to join such a union as we propose when it becomes possible, and inasmuch as Russia's peril is the consequence of anarchy and of wild passions, so its restoration cannot be accomplished without a reign of right, order, law, and liberty in each individual state. All efforts must be directed therefore to this main purpose.

---

[7] Petr Bark (1869–1937) was the Russian Minister of Finance during the war (1914–17), a difficult period. He emigrated from Crimea to Great Britain later in 1918.

[8] Sergei Sazonov (1861–1927) was the Russian Minister of Foreign Affairs at the beginning of the war and is sometimes assessed blame for his insistence on early mobilization; he was dismissed from that office in April 1916. In exile he wrote an interesting memoir, *Fateful Years, 1909–16*.

This provisional government, in speaking of united Russia, does not mean the old bureaucratic one—a centralized state built on the oppression or the injury of separate races, conquered and absorbed. It means a free, democratic country, in which the right to obtain culture shall be guaranteed to all classes and nationalities. At the same time this government feels convinced the wealth and welfare of the nations composing Russia can in no wise be founded on their opposition to unification. A tendency toward separation would make for weakness, and this policy has brought our country to its present pitiful state. It is of the utmost danger to normal life, which we all want restored in Crimea. Therefore the government appeals to the whole population, of every race and class, to help in its fight with our worst foe, and to support us in the most resolute measures should they become necessary, and we rely on an army which is ready to assist us in any way.

The government is formed of men well known to all the people, and who must be in permanent contact with the latter. We rely on the confidence of the inhabitants, and we beg to be trusted by them. Therefore until a Diet can be convened, the government has appointed the Congress of the Country and District Councils to remain in session, and we will be responsible to this body; which in turn will communicate to the government any necessary information as to conditions and opinions among our population. A law as to the suffrage, also one as to the Diet, will be presented to this Congress for confirmation immediately—on or about December 7—and the Congress will then fix the date of the diet's inauguration. We have been led to this action by discussions held on 18th of October and the 10th of November.

The government takes on itself the procuring of provisions, the guaranteeing of economic progress and security of interests for all branches of the population, and the fulfilment of just desires among the Tatar and every other nationality. The government acknowledges the difficulties of the task it has undertaken, and will use all its powers to solve our many problems. It appeals to the citizens everywhere for support and help! May pernicious catering to wild hatred pass unheeded, and may murder and other crimes cease; may anxiety, uncertainty, and danger disappear, and may all of us be united in one decision to push with our whole strength to a happy ending the undertaking of our salvation and the restoration of our country!

As for the army mentioned in this proclamation, General Denikin—whose record in the magnificent Russian army of early war days was excellent, and who in revolutionary times succeeded to [Aleksei] Brusilov and [Lavr] Kornilov as commander of the southeastern front—had gathered about himself long ago a large group of men, all volunteers.[9] Officers driven to desperation by the situation, both on our front and behind the lines, came to him asking only for the chance to fight and die. Soldiers who had gradually formed their own opinions of the Red Guard of the Bolsheviks came too.

Little by little these gathered, till Denikin counted 200,000 picked men or more. With very shabby and immensely varied uniforms, running from those of the Imperial Guardsmen to bright Cossack dress, the army was clothed, and they all had thin, drawn, haggard faces, though with determined mouths and eyes. They made up for their other defects of appearance by this grim look. None of them had yet lost their faith in Russia's future, and they turned to Denikin with perfect confidence that he could and would lead them somehow to success. His own personality—quiet, strong, and completely brave—was that of an ideal commander for such a force. At Ekaterinodar, where the country was friendly to him, and fed and housed his men and horses in exchange for the protection Denikin gave the inhabitants, he had settled his army, and it soon doubled.

Denikin's sympathy was at once with the Crimean effort, and he promised to the fragile government what help and support he could give. When the Allies came in December and were received by this organization with all the dignity of which it was capable, and while the populace of Sevastopol and Simferopol turned out in welcome, there were many discussions and consultations among the chiefs, much explanation as to recent developments, and also several proposals as to possible future action by the combined strength of the Crimeans and the Allies.

The latter were entertained with typical Russian hospitality, and though poor little Simferopol has less of brilliancy to offer than had the palaces and ministries of ancient days in Petrograd, the national heart behind these fêtes beat true, and the quaint semi-Oriental capital made a picturesque frame for simple receptions. English and French sailors and soldiers must have gathered interesting impressions from their experiences, and they were doubtless pleased to have nothing to do with the Bolsheviks, and no one to fight against upon their landing, as had been necessary elsewhere on Russian coasts.

Soon the government decided on a mobilization in the Crimea, to include ex-officers up to the age of forty, if they were able-bodied, and all other men of military age as soldiers. These were ordered to join Denikin's forces, which so far had depended entirely on volunteers. He had largely gathered men of aristocratic traditions from the old crack-guard regiments, and they had gone into his unit as simple

---

[9] General Anton Denikin (1872–1947) was a distinguished infantry officer in the Russo-Japanese War and World War I. He replaced Kornilov after his death in July 1918, as head of the Russian armies in the south (Ukraine) and led a valiant effort during the early Civil War to overthrow the Bolsheviks. This effort collapsed in July 1919 causing a large flow of refugees from Ukraine to the West. Denikin found refuge in Paris, where he published several volumes of memoirs.

soldiers, willingly doing any work in the ranks for what they considered to be the good cause.

The new Crimean administration also made a calculation of monetary and material losses, at the hands of both German and Bolshevik criminals, in the province of the Tauride, for future reference. Another surprise to the Allies when they came was the organization of General Krasnov at Novocherkassk, who, like Denikin, had drawn a large following of volunteers about himself, and who was proving his talent as a leader and administrator of immense energy and power, holding his followers, winning his surroundings, maintaining discipline and creating another oasis of strength and patriotic organization in the great desert of misery which surrounded him.

Both these generals have moved about in various directions. They have inflicted already several defeats on the Bolsheviks and on the Germans, but the armies of both are wretchedly poor. Ammunition, uniforms, underclothes, food, supplies of every sort, money to pay troops, transportation for them—all of these are lacking, and the units have only their heroism and what the small provincial population back of them can offer for support.

When the allied representatives went recently from their ships to confer with Denikin, at Ekaterinodar, they were received by the general with the utmost simplicity. There was neither space nor money for official receptions at his headquarters, and he showed nothing to impress the deputation save the evident burning spirit of his soldiers and that of the commander at their head. He spoke to the strangers and said:

> During the last four years of war, an echo on the Vistula and the Bug Rivers answered to the sound of each battle on the Somme or on the Marne; the triumph of victory, like the keen sorrow of defeat, was equally felt by all the Allied armies. Though ours were divided from yours by a thousand kilometers, we were rightly linked to you by fraternity in arms. The Russian army was destroyed a year ago, not by a military or moral, or even technical superiority of its adversary, but only by the Germans' plotting and a blow from behind, which came through the propaganda of anarchists who were the enemies' agents at home here among us.
>
> The volunteer army which I command has risen from the ruins of all this, and during the various political revolutions, surrounded by enemies and treacheries, it has continued to fight hard for the sake of Russia. These are conditions heretofore unheard of in military history. This army remains faithful to treaties concluded with the Allies, and in spite of its vast losses and many temptations it has repulsed the hand of the enemy, which it recognized was stretched out maliciously.
>
> The Germans have taken much bread from Russia, and they have paid for it with ammunition left in Bolshevik hands. These are the cartridges which the red armies have used against us in civil war of late, and our fight has

torn off the mask which Germany had worn till recently, though the Teuton policy has been hard on us Russians since long before the war. Our people have much warmth of heart, and they can well appreciate nobility when it exists, even in enemies, and so it was that after the battles of Borodino and of Sevastopol in the past, we became friends with you, the French and the English, and that now we sincerely rejoice in your victory.[10]

We believe that present events in Russia are but a tragic episode in our history. After this period of commotion, which has been violent and painful, will follow one of calm and of great reconstruction; but our wound will remind us of the past for a long time. As Russia renovates herself, and gathers strength and might, even to complete restoration, she will never forget those who may give her help today, and who stretch out their arms to her in her great trouble.

Such was Denikin's spirit at the end of December [1918]. Is it surprising that by the middle of February his volunteer army had pushed back the Red Guards, sweeping the country northward and eastward to Kharkov and Poltava, and almost to the Caspian Sea, taking 30,000 prisoners? So far all this has been done without help from outside. On the southern coast of the Crimean peninsula the nobility also has raised its head again. In spite of the nervous strain of two whole years past, the Empress-Mother,[11] unsurpassed in bravery, again refused the Allies' invitation to leave Russian soil, and decided she would remain until she felt absolute certainty as to the fate of her two sons, reported assassinated at Tobolsk and at Perm. It seemed Her Majesty did not believe in these deaths, and that she inspired all those who surrounded her with faith and courage in spite of many hardships. Crowded into the tiny villa of Ai-todor, living in the most difficult situation financially, the old Empress remained the same dignified personage as in the days of her glory and riches.

Many years ago, when I first went, a stranger, to Russia, I was told by some one who had observed her through her reign: "The Empress-Mother is a success always, and were she not a sovereign she would still be a charming and much loved woman." And in the humiliations of the revolution and in the months since then, I have often thought how true that judgment was. In her young days a universal favorite, she led society, and every one then adored and followed her. Her least caprice was law, because of the charm and gentleness behind it, and in the court's brilliancy she managed to keep together a circle of warm friends, as she created also a beautiful

---

[10] References here are to the Borodino Battle of 1812 in resistance to the French invasion, and to the siege of Sevastopol during the Crimean War (1854–56).

[11] Maria Fedorovna (1847–1928) was the dowager empress: widow of Alexander III and mother of Nicholas II. Born a Danish princess, she was much admired in the West for her fortitude and beauty, celebrated by the popularity of "Dagmar" (her Danish name) dolls. From Crimea, she sought exile in Denmark and was featured in the film *Anastasia*, portrayed by Helen Hayes.

home life within the palace halls. Her widowhood later was full of quiet dignity and charitable work, and though she still kept up friendly and family relations which were altogether delightful, she retired almost completely from court and society life.

When the storm of revolution threatened and broke, she came from her retirement to warn and try to uphold, then to console, her son who, blinded and inert, arrested and dethroned, needed her greatly while he waited at his headquarters' staff for the decision as to his fate. All she could do was done, and immediately afterward she wound up her affairs and palace home in Kiev and took refuge with her two daughters at their Crimean villa of Ai-todor. There she lived on from month to month, crushed by the weight of her sorrows, yet refusing the chance of comfortable exile which was early offered her by the first Provisional Government. Russia was her home, she said, and the Russians were her people, and she would not leave them while there was any hope. Her Majesty's courage never failed her, though she was harassed with anxiety almost unbelievable for both her sons, and she herself had much to bear personally—discomfort and poverty, sometimes insult, and always threats, not to her alone, but also to those about her whom she loved.

Once an eruption of Bolshevik sailors at six in the morning occurred; they ventured to disturb the Empress-Mother in her bed. Rough men had walked without ceremony into the villa and into her room, ordered her to rise, and refused to retire or to wait till she could slip on even her dressing-gown. Perforce she must obey instantly in their presence, and then must watch them fumbling about among her clothes, papers, and all her small possessions, while she stood in night-dress and slippers, shivering. In spite of the disorder they created they had shortly to admit they could find nothing compromising in her baggage. Finally they laid a paper on her desk and ordered her to sign it, saying it stated she was found not to be mixed in any counter-revolutionary plot. She signed "Marie." "That is not your proper name. Sign 'Marie Romanov,'" came a stern rebuke, "or you will be made to pay dearly."

At the end of her patience finally, Her Majesty, quietly looking the tough spokesman in the eye, relied: "I know how to sign my name, and on that subject I take no instructions from you. For fifty years I have signed in this same way, and I do not mean to change. If you choose, you can kill me, of course, but you cannot alter the fact that I had my reign out and have not abdicated, so I am the Empress-Mother still, and that is my signature. Take it or leave it, as you please." The men grumbling took the paper and went out, leaving the Empress-Mother chilled with exposure in her unusually light costume, but quite undaunted and triumphant in the possession of her room.

Even in exile and poverty she drew round her devoted friends, who were ready to offer her their purses and their lives, and in captivity and trouble she still was a success. When the Germans came and replaced her Bolshevik guards by a régiment of officers, the Empress smiled gently and sadly on the latter, and won their hearts immediately, giving them new life and hope. From time to time, when allowed to do so by the revolutionary authorities, she received a few of the refugee aristocrats, who gladly came from the Ai-todor environs for an audience with their old Empress, and she talked with them and with their daughters, whom they brought to be presented to Her Majesty. Her days were spent as normally as possible, holding together a group of ancient associates, and she was apparently not further considered a danger to revolutionary ideals. Had she not fought the retrograde spirit in 1916? And had she not begged for the banishment of the occult forces?[12] And also she had implored her son, the Emperor, to join with the liberals in helping and loving his country. Even after all she has gone through, she still loyally clung to Russia, and lived on at the villa of Ai-todor.

There are others such as she among our imperial family, for her two daughters were remaining at her side, and farther up the rocky coast the Grand Duke Nicholas and his brother Peter were waiting patiently, hoping always to see their country make good after the storm.[13] Each of their homes had been raided, and the old splendid chief had acted as the Empress-Mother did, and with the same success.[14]

The Russian aristocrats, though of various types, have stood the test of the revolution surprisingly well, for they have been through much suffering from lack of money and the scarcity and high prices of necessities, also the impossibility of communication with their estates, or with the members of their large families, who are scattered over the country. In January 1918, an uprising in Yalta, as elsewhere, caused many of the nobility, and especially the officers, to be arrested, and some were shot. None of this group knows what has become of dear relatives who were last heard of at the front, or in the cities of the north, and who, one feels, are probably risking their lives daily, if they are not already dead.

Sympathy with the upper classes (accused of a counter-revolution), like being a member of these classes, was a serious crime in the eyes of the triumphant Bolsheviks, and at different times there have been regular persecutions, always accompanied by house-to-house visits, inspections, requisitions, and insults forever renewed. Living on through months of this has been very hard, and yet has been stood patiently. One

---

[12] The reference here is to Grigory Rasputin and his clique who influenced Nicholas II and his family by his ability to stop the bleeding of their son, Alexis, afflicted with hemophilia. He was opposed by Maria Fedorovna, who may have influenced those who murdered him in 1916.

[13] Maria Fedorovna had six children, only the two daughters outlived her: Xenia Alexandrovna (1875–1960) and Olga Alexandrovna (1882–1960). Their two cousins, mentioned here, were Nikolai Nikolaevich (1856–1929), commander in chief of the Russian army during the first year of World War I, and Petr Nikolaevich (1864–1931), grandsons of Tsar Nicholas I. Both found exile in France.

[14] For a description of the royal family and Russian nobility departing Crimea for exile abroad in April 1919, see Douglas Smith, *Former People: The Final Days of the Russian Aristocracy* (New York: Farrar, Straus and Giroux, 2012), 202–07. Smith's book mainly charts the fate of two of the most prominent aristocratic families—the Sheremetevs and Golitsyns—through the revolution.

day, about a year ago, ships of the Russian Black Sea fleet appeared on the horizon, steamed as near as possible to the shores in front of Yalta, and bombarded that city and the villas about it for three long days and nights. The inhabitants of the town took refuge in their cellars—men, women, and children living through the long hours without food and without fuel, with scarcely sufficient clothes, with no beds to sleep upon, and unable to guess when, if ever, these ships would sail away again, or if the bombardment would be followed by a descent and a general massacre. The most terrible thought was always that the enemy one dreads is of one's own race and people, a group gone mad with fear and poisoned by false doctrines, all of which were injected by Germans.

From outside came no news at all save now and then false, exciting rumors of hope and rescue by the Allies. These raised beliefs only to cast them down again, and make despair the blacker. Small wonder if nerves and health have suffered in a year and more, though the Crimea has been the most protected corner of all Russia. Pride and blood have told, and there have been both marvelous courage and great self-denial shown, and a Christian spirit rivaled by no other race, with patience always both of word and deed toward followers of inferior rank, who lived near the victimized highbred group to serve them. Nobles, officers, members of the former parliaments and the old government have saved some forms of organization about them still; some schooling for their children, and what resemblance they could create to a useful, healthy community. Always ready to meet destruction, they have smiled on with brave lips, and though going through so much, scarcely any of them have spoken or thought of vengeance. Each has believed in the future of the race; each one who could command.

Only the other day a letter came to me from a leading spirit in that little colony. After describing sundry measures being taken to help in the movement for self-government by the new provisional ministry, and after saying to me something of what had been suffered in the Crimea, the writer goes on to tell me:

> Recently I was in Yalta and I saw your people there, who are all well. Your brother-in-law had been north to your country estate, and had in person talked to the peasantry with most satisfactory results. I admired him greatly for this, as it is not eight months since your château and estates were sacked and burned... There are others here acting in the same way. I am impressed with the general faith shown by all, though I have to admit that most members of the society clan at Yalta seem a little nervous, which, considering what they have lived through during the past year or so, is hardly surprising! ... Now the Allies are really here, and I trust ready to help us in our effort at government and to back Denikin's army especially.
>
> One feels one may almost count on success in holding this province free of the poison already injected elsewhere, and perhaps—if we live—we may even hope to repulse the dangerous enemies from other districts little by little, thus

gaining more ground for law and order and a popular government. But necessarily a long period must elapse before the whole country, under whatever form of organization, can completely recover its tranquillity and prosperity after all of this lost time. Probably many of us will be killed before we are through with the work we are undertaking. But we are far from crushed yet, as vital forces go, and in every direction small attempts at resurrection and constructive work are apparent. You know my personal confidence is indomitable. We have always throughout history stood frightful blows and shown tremendous recuperative power, and we have vast primitive resources at our disposal, both to pay others for their help and to be developed for our own benefit.

Such letters show there is still life and hope for Russia, and that among those who have lost most no time is being wasted in laments. One evening long ago, early in the revolution, a small group gathered in my salon, and they talked of the future and of the new Russia to be built on quite different lines from the old one. To my surprise an officer suddenly said:

We could form again sometime the best of armies, and it will be well to have Denikin's force to use as a source of concentrated and creative strength for this purpose. If in time our peasantry becomes educated, so much the better; for then as soldiers the people will have gained in patriotism and love for the whole of Russia. We will not then have each man thinking only of his home village as his personal political unit and the one point he is called upon to defend. It has been so until now, and largely because the rank and file knew nothing of geography, could not read or understand. Our peasant soldiery thus stood unarmed against the wiles of any enemy propaganda. To them it was the village and the Emperor who counted, and when the latter fell away, nothing of common interest united the man from one part to the one who was a native of another part of Russia; so our army fell to pieces.

Politically in the provinces it was the same with our people, though agriculture usually makes for conservatism in politics. What could the peasant of your Bouromka village care for the trials and tribulations of his brother, who was living on the coast of the Baltic or the White Sea, or in faraway Siberia?

Places they were to him not even familiar in name, since he had never learned geography. So it was that he knew patriotism only in its most primitive form, and felt called upon to defend only his own "hata" from oncoming foes. Real love of country must be spread yet, with us, to include all of the race, and our people must become educated and well-governed, till by degrees every one of our peasants will be ready to enjoy his share of benefits, and also will do gladly his part in the general duty which must be performed.

While this is preparing, we officers, who know nothing of politics or of administrative organization, can only sit with crossed arms, looking on, or join Denikin and contribute what we can to the strength of the cause, thus carrying out our share of reconstruction.

The proprietors seem still to have confidence in their humble peasants, too, in spite of the disillusions which have been. Nearly every one speaks quite simply of going back to ruined homes and taking up life there, if not on the same old basis, then on new lines, and where one hears a sharp criticism or a threat of vengeance, it is generally because a foreign strain of blood runs through the veins of the speaker and puts him out of the understanding with his people.

With the officer, the ex-official, the Empress and the noble, joined also the bourgeois and the peasant of Crimea in this effort put on foot to reorganize. When the first movement took place in October last, and the present provisional government was formed, it was the lowly people of the country districts and those of the municipalities who worked in with heartiest sympathy. They had suffered least, of course, from the revolution here in this rich southern province—at least so far—and they were probably less disheartened and disillusioned than were the other classes, but they especially wanted to make the revolutionary movement a success and to establish its first ideals and principles on a lasting basis.

To preserve and keep the new-found liberty, which they had all but lost again under the German-Tatar rule, and to avoid the terrible mistakes they had seen made farther north, was a fine ambition. It was for this they acted through their representatives, elected at their early meetings, and who stood for the people's own democratic ideals. They, the poor people, promised to uphold and back this provisional Cabinet and Congress in its labor last October.

Again, in December, it was the people of the city streets and in the city parks and theaters who received the sailors of the Allied fleet and tried to prove their friendship as best they could, and this spontaneous, frank reception surely had as great a value as was represented by court ball or splendid banquet offered to one King from another in former years! When the announced mobilization took place the poor man and the rich both gladly gave all they could offer to their great cause, and certainly Denikin's army, with aristocrat and bourgeois, peasant and fisherman, Orthodoxy and Islam rubbing elbows, will stand to the most ardent republican for the perfection of democratic patriotism, well combined and organized.

So with the venture at proper self-government started on the Crimean peninsula before the Allies came, the experiment seemed full of promise from within. Since October much has been accomplished, and as if in answer to the prayer of every sincere Russian, the Allied fleet came to them two months later, apparently ready to uphold them morally and materially. After six weeks we read of the progress of Denikin's army with a glow of triumph. He and his volunteers pushed the hordes of the Red Guard back, and the reading of this news made exiles' hearts in foreign countries beat fast with new-born hope. It seemed to eliminate the danger of this little Crimean province being overrun by the barbarians paid to destroy it. Surely the brave leader with his unit is making good.

One wonders if the world will be touched to admiration by this splendid patriotism? These were men who have refused through all the reign of terror to admit defeat, and who after a year of torture were ready to recreate their country quite anew. They were brave and generous enough to give up without a sign of complaint the traditions they and their forefathers were used to through many hundreds of years, even to lose their fortunes without murmuring, and begin life on a new basis of democratic principles and of legal equality for all their race.

I, who have been a Russian for many years, though born in this calm American land, would ask every citizen to uphold my adopted people whenever and wherever it were possible. Denikin and his men are fighting for the cause of the world, and for its safety, and they need succor—mental, moral, and material—to beat down the powers of darkness. These seem to be threatening every country at the present moment with the poison of doctrines made in Germany to destroy the ideals and civic health of each and every self-respecting race.

Till help reaches her, the giant Russia must struggle onward toward her salvation as best she can, amazing mankind with her strange contrasts of defects and virtues. Always mysterious, at this moment our people stoop to the lowest depths in some parts of the country, while in others they soar far up above the clouds. "The Crimea—Denikin's army," seem words to conjure with, words which when written against the dark background of the terror's story will light the future student to comprehension and sympathy. Now already they mean to exiles a new strength of faith, a ray of hope, together with a better and tenderer charity.

V
The Ukrainian Movement

Very soon after the first revolutionary movement of March 1917, the factory hands in Kiev [Kyiv in Ukrainian] began to feel the general fermentation, which was in the air, and which over the rest of Russia was already causing serious uprisings and troubles. Wages rose; holidays, always numerous in the Greek-Orthodox calendar, increased, while work-hours became shorter. There were parades, where red banners with suggestive mottoes were carried, and in the small gardens and restaurants of the city a happy-go-lucky southern crowd fêted its new liberty. The dramas enacted in the north were lacking though, and at first the owners of manufacturing plants, or their representatives, remained in charge of their property as usual, and were unmolested. They felt, however, that things were going wrong, and that their men were becoming restless and unreliable, and might soon be out of hand.

When I returned to Kiev in mid-July 1917, after an absence of some months, I found anxious faces among industrials, and I heard the workmen were less contented, and that there was much agitation below the quiet surface which met a casual eye. Most of the great manufacturing plants were by then running in the hands of "committees," and were in a half-hearted way producing very little. Prices of sugar, flour, and all other supplies, in which Ukraine is ordinarily so rich, were rapidly rising. Only the soft climate and the sufficiency of provisions prevented riots, and as every one still believed in the constituent assembly promised for the early autumn, and considered the present disorganization to be only temporary, stories of such troubles as had occurred were passed about in a good-natured spirit of toleration. I heard many a factory owner tell of his difficulties and his discussions with his own particular group of "tovarishchi" [comrades], and generally the story was made an amusing one, and showed a keen sense of humor, even when the joke was on the teller. There was, as always heretofore, a warm, patriarchal, protective feeling for the men underneath, for whom (whatever their actual vagaries) the owners continued to care with paternal solicitude.

Once, as an after-dinner tale, which kept the salon full of our guests between tears and laughter, a friend told us the following very typical incident as to how his factory's management had been taken over by the "comrades' committee," and his superintendent sent away, and then recalled and reinstated by this same group of his workmen.

It was about a month ago, when our people first grew restless, he said. They came to Peter Ivanovich, my manager, one morning and surrounded the office of the factory; said they were not going to work any more under him, as it was now time for all factories to be nationalized; that they had been told this only the night before, at a meeting, by some great speakers. The latter had said it was cowardly not to take over the business and manage it themselves, dividing the work and then the profits equally among those to whom it properly belonged. Had not the peasantry been promised the lands? And factories and machinery were in equal measure the people's. This also the speaker had said, and they even were surprised these men had not thought of it by themselves...

Peter Ivanovich reminded them they had never felt any severity at his hands, that he was Russian, and of their own class, promoted and educated by the owners; that they had all of them received many kindnesses from the latter, such as hospitals with good care, free of all charges for those who were ill, Christmas trees and good garments, fuel and provisions in hard times, warm feeling always shown them, and of late raised wages and shortened hours, in accordance with the new revolutionary ideas.... All this the committee of workmen admitted, and their spokesman said they had not come to complain, but only to say that now they must be masters of the nationalized factory, and of all its implements, in order to move in the spirit of the times.

To give weight to his arguments, the spokesman again lengthily quoted from speeches of various revolutionary orators who has been at meetings attended by him. Peter Ivanovich then asked, by way of delaying his reply for a few moments in which to telephone me, and the crowd waited patiently in the yard, its leaders in our outside office, while he rang me up and informed me of the emergency, of the assembled multitude outside, who for the moment were quiet and still childishly confident that everything would be delivered to them at once, according to the prophecies of their leaders. He, however, warned me they would probably lose their heads and begin breaking things up at the least sign of resistance. I must decide on the course to follow, and he would execute my order to the best of his ability.

Knowing his resourcefulness and devotion, yet not willing to ask an exaggerated sacrifice of himself, I told him he might as well give way and let the men try running our factory, since it would probably save his life and be the best way of making them finally realize how much they and we needed one another. I thought it would be too simple, however, to give the property over to this crowd, just because it was demanded, when we had an excellent case and every right to our buildings and implementation; so I said I hoped he would at least protest, and tell them I would carry this before the government.

I asked if I should come out to him at once by auto, and uphold his authority, and did he need protection?

He half laughed and answered no, and that he would do his best and would try to save the situation. He added he would rather handle the matter alone, if I felt willing to leave it all to him. Naturally I gave him carte-blanche, and promised all my gratitude for his effort, however things turned out; I would keep the motor at my door, and would be sitting by the telephone in case he wanted to change his mind and call me to the works during the day. But there was no sign...

Time passed, and I learned that after much parley and some rough treatment, my Peter Ivanovich had been put into a wheelbarrow which was found standing in the yard, far from clean, and had been wheeled out of the factory limits and dumped on the highroad. His aids and foremen had been driven out in a herd behind him, and the workers had returned to their acquired estate in triumph and had taken complete possession. "Nothing is destroyed, though, Excellency," announced Peter Ivanovich when he appeared. "In a week we shall return to our offices, if I know my people." And though he had a black eye and a scratch or two, he looked more amused than dismal...

I had less confidence than he, and I began the preparation of a report to the authorities, asking to have my property returned to me... I hadn"t finished with this, however, when I was rung up one day toward noon. "Peter Ivanovich at the phone, and will your Excellency drive out to the factory? You will find me in the office at your service!" I was amazed, and lost no time in joining him. Respectfully, as in old times, the doorkeeper received me and helped me remove my dust-cloak, and as I glanced about I saw the chimneys smoking from our furnaces and heard the ordinary whirring of machines. I noticed no change from previous visits, save that a wheelbarrow, freshly painted and covered with red cloth, heavily fringed in gold, stood by the entrance.

Peter Ivanovich gave me his usual quiet smile. His eyes were bright and his color high. "We have just had a very pleasant procession this morning, Excellency, and my best hope is realized," he announced as he closed the door of his private office. "It was as I thought; our men when they took possession first examined the office books, which show what deficits your pocket has sustained in the past months, to keep things going here; they found the cash safe was quite empty. This office was, therefore, a disillusion, except as to the possibilities of establishing a comfortable club in it, for the elected heads to sit about in. And the machinery turned out, after trial, to be worse than the office, for it required labor, attention, superintending and expert knowledge to run it. The first two requisites our comrades didn"t wish to put into their business, and the last ones they did not possess for it, since all the upper expert strata has been driven away with me.

"To do them justice, they tried hard to live up to their new obligations, and they elected another committee, which has sat here for the past week, while clumsy hands and inexperienced brains blocked our machines with oil and dust, and more and more the whole place became confused. More and more also chaos invaded the little world, which was so used to be cared for out here. It seems the new leaders were very arrogant, trying to hold their subordinates by their pretensions, so the troubles grew, and when last Saturday night there was no money forthcoming to pay the workmen, and no fuel nor provisions were to be had from our storehouses, which were empty, the cry arose that our people had been better off before.

"'Let us go to Peter Ivanovich and ask his advice! He was much better with us than are these lazy louts, who sit here and do nothing for us. Perhaps he would be glad to return, when we tell him how troubled we are. He has sprung from among us and has always understood our needs.' So yesterday morning, as I was dressing, I heard a great clamoring, outside our house, and there stood a crowd of our workmen in the road, with a small group of spokesmen in front. Looking sheepish and sullen, and evidently humiliated, there were also the leaders in the recent difficulties, and these were being held and derided by their erstwhile followers. This seemed to me a good sign as I appeared on our small balcony. 'What do you all want?' I said. 'Peter Ivanovich,' answered one man, turning his hat and twisting it reflectively, 'we have tried for a week the way of the speechmaker's advice, and it was all wrong, though they seemed to know so much from book wisdom which we do not possess, and they had promised us such pleasant things; but we found their plans did not work out well with us. We are unpaid, unwarmed, and unfed by these rascals whom we had elected to command us, and now we have come to fetch you back Peter Ivanovich.'

"'But who dares to imagine for a moment that I could consent to return and risk my life among you brigands, when the next strolling propagandist at a street corner who tells you to throw me out again will be obeyed. No, you *would* have the factory. Go you back to it then, now, and leave me to my rest. I have deserved rest, God knows, after twenty years that I have managed you, and I don"t want to ever see you all again. I mean to go far away to other republics, where there is proper respect for law and discipline, and to work there; but never here again among a lot of knaves and fools.'

"With anxious faces the crowd listened, while the spokesman took up his argument again, told me the many small dramas of the past week, which had piled up into a mountain so heavy it had crushed them all, and how they wished to be governed again. Every one in the past week had wanted the first roles, and naturally each had a desire to be the committee, or at least to superintend some special group, while, of course, none of them had the experience for this. It had ended in a fight, and the pretentious tyrants had finally been overpowered and were brought to me now for inspection. 'See, Peter Ivanovich, how can we obey those who, for all their fine chatter, we found knew nothing more than we ourselves. They sat and smoked all day and played cards; but they did none of the things which you are always busy doing in your office, so we have come back to you. Please, come to us and direct us as of old.'

"Considering their helpless ignorance, I felt if these people were to be saved from future impostors and mistakes, I must still keep them for a time uncertain; so they would at least appreciate that I was giving way to their wish by returning. For two long hours I stood, therefore, on my balcony, they begging and offering me new attractions, promising me perfect obedience and devotion, and I holding off, refusing their invitations and showing myself completely indifferent to each added proposition.

"'Peter Ivanovich, only return and set the factory and us in order, and we shall fetch you from here in the best caleche to be hired in Kiev, and with a fast troika to pull it, so all the street will turn and admire as you fly by.' I really thought this very touching, but still held out firmly and answered: 'No, I need not bribes to make me return to my place or undertake my duties; but it is the day of liberty now you say, and I wish only for rest and to be left alone by such unreliable people as you are.' At last the crowd wept and implored. They could do nothing with the machines, they said, and were lost if the manager and his aids, whom they had driven away only in ignorance, would not return. Would I but state my terms, since nothing they had thought of to propose had moved me?

"Though in days gone by they have had the greatest kindness from us, and were naturally in the wrong, now I felt sorry for them, Excellency, for they are not like people of other lands, after all; these are but children in nature and in mind, and quite irresponsible for about half of what they do. Thinking they were sufficiently punished, I rose finally, stepped forward, and said to them: 'You are a mass of fools; firstly, not to recognize that we have been most liberal always, and have done and were doing our best to face these difficult times, and to carry you all and the factory through them, without closing down; secondly, to listen to those propagandists who naturally try to create trouble between us, because they are paid in proportion to the results they can show in the way of destruction and disorder in our land; thirdly, you have blindly insulted me with your offers of a luxurious equipage to drive me to my ancient work place, and by the suggestion of other bribes, as if you did not know me well enough to realize I would refuse.

"'Now, since you have at last learned your folly, and you merely ask me for my terms, I tell them to you, and you may accept or refuse at once, and definitely. If you accept, and then change again later, I shall say nothing to you, but shall quietly depart, leaving you to work out your problems alone. I consent to return to you only because I wish to serve faithfully the master of our factory, who has been a good employer to us all, and because I wish to save those of our machines which you have not yet ruined; even I would help such of you as will work well and are willing to begin anew.

"'My terms are these: You dragged me from my office and ill-treated me, and you drove out all my aides; you were all mobilized for that purpose, an untidy throng of humanity in your work clothes; you will go home, now, and collect all the men who took part in that demonstration of a week ago; you will all clean up and put on your Sunday clothes; then you will come here in orderly procession and will escort me and those of my party who consent to accompany me back with all due show of honor and respect. You tumbled me into a rough and dirty wheelbarrow when I refused to leave my place; now you will find again that same wheelbarrow, paint it freshly, and drape it with red cloth and gold fringe, and bring it here; I will sit in that in preference to the finest carriage, and you shall wheel me back to my office door. Prepare all of this for tomorrow morning.

"'Meantime, return today to the factory, and clean the machines, the floors and the courtyards as for a new start. I myself will engage to gather up what foremen I can find, and we will return to our work tomorrow with all memory of these painful days effaced, and will be ready as before to help you to the best of our ability, so we may all do our duty together.'" The heads of his audience went up, and with joy and gratitude the men thanked and blessed Peter Ivanovich for his generosity. Everything was done exactly as he had ordered. Early the following morning the same crowd of the previous day presented itself at his door in gay holiday dress, and with serious faces. The old wheelbarrow in its unexpected finery was solemnly brought forward, and my manager took his seat upon it, with a manner which made it a full-fledged triumphal car.

With his lieutenants about him, he sat tranquil, while slowly and quietly they all marched to the factory's office door. The place was clean as never since the buildings had been opened, and Peter Ivanovich on the entrance steps turned and thanked "his children" in exactly the old tone, whose kindly note had held their affections for many years… "Luckily, they had done no harm they could not easily undo. By their reparation and general cleaning up, and by their readiness to fall into line with their chief's ideas, they felt they had gone back the same road, to the turning which they had chosen wrong and had begun over again. They are good children, and see their folly, for which, after all, they are not really to blame so much as are those damnable German agents, who are always among us, spreading poisonous doctrines. I trust, Excellency," ended Peter Ivanovich, "you will not feel obliged to punish these men further; as while I did not promise, I think they hope for my complete forgiveness of the harm done me, and that they count on my protection to save them from further humiliation. After what they offered me by way of reparation, they believe I will not report their wickedness to you. They have lost two weeks' wages, anyhow, and I think we shall have no further troubles."

"I don't quite believe," added the storyteller, "in such Utopian results as my manager predicts, but of course I fell in with his schemes, and for the moment all is going well—till the next time some new prophet passes, I suppose."[1]

His anecdote sounded encouraging, as it was related, and the upper classes tried to be light-hearted, anyhow, and to hope that things would mend; but day by day the clouds piled higher on the political and economic horizon, the restless spirit grew, and principles and common sense were submerged, largely through the enemy's efforts and excellent organization.[2] Poor Peter Ivanovich did not live the year out, I heard afterward, but was killed in a riot, while the factory of my story went up in flames late that autumn.

In November 1917, after a week of terrible tension, and after long negotiations, much fighting, rioting and killing in our gay city of Kiev, and especially through false play on the part of the Austro-Ukrainians, the latter took complete possession of all power, and then established order according to their own theories. For a time the city was fairly quiet, and the pleasure-loving Little Russians led their loves unmolested, facing only difficulties of extremely reduced incomes, and extremely high prices on all necessities.

At once, in the beginning of their triumph, General Skoropadsky was elected "Hetman" of the Ukrainian Cossacks.[3] He occupied continuously the most promi-

---

[1] This long recounting of a conversation that an associate had with a third party is probably not word for word and more likely an exaggerated summation of several experiences of events occurring in the late summer of 1917. The dramatic shift in peasant demeanor would have been more likely in Ukraine than in Russia proper, but in any event would have changed again as the Civil War developed—as the author predicts.

[2] One of the problems by this time was the confusion about who the "enemy" actually was.

[3] Pavlo Skoropadsky (1873–1945) was born into a large Cossack landowning and army officer family of Poltava province in Ukraine that was also active in local provincial administration. His education, however, was oriented toward Russia. He graduated from the Page Corps in St. Petersburg in 1893 and married the daughter of Moscow governor Petr Durnovo. He had a distinguished service record in the Russo-Japanese War and in World War I, during which he probably knew Michael Cantacuzène. By July 1917 he commanded the 60,000-man 34th Army Corps, which was then transformed into the 1st Ukrainian Corps in an effort by the Provisional Government (Kerensky) to win Ukrainian support. At the end of April 1918 he supported a German-instigated coup d'etat and was installed as "hetman" (leader) of Ukraine. However, in November Skoropadsky was overthrown by a Ukrainian nationalist movement

nent place held by any Russian [sic] in Kiev, until his disappearance from the scene, which was after the departure of the Germans from Kiev. Just before his election, and before we left, he came to my husband, trying to persuade the latter to remain in the city and undertake with him the adventure which he planned. Of ancient Cossack lineage, though untitled, Pavel Mikhailovich Skoropadsky represented as blue blood and as fine traditions as any Slav in Little Russia. His own great fortune and his wife's, and their powerful relations, had placed them from early childhood in delightful situations.

He had graduated from the Imperial Page Corps, been immediately promoted into the first regiment of the empire (Her Majesty the Empress-Mother's Chevalier Guards). He had been made aide-de-camp to the Emperor, and having asked, during the Japanese War, for service in Siberia, he was sent there on a special mission and was awarded the "Golden Sword" on his return. After his Oriental campaign he was at once pushed forward by his court protections, and was given command, first of a regiment of the line, then of the "Emperor's Own Horse Guards," and following on these the command of the first brigade of the Imperial Cavalry of the Guard. Always an excellent officer, his attention to questions of service and his bravery kept him (with his name and fortune to help) conspicuously to the fore, and when the great war came, Skoropadsky's luck was proverbial.

In the first battles of the East Prussian campaign, the troops under him won the St. George's Cross for their commander by a brilliant feat of arms. Within a year he had received a division, and soon after temporarily was given a corps and promoted lieutenant-general. Fairly tall and well made, with (at the age of forty-three) a face of most guileless expression, extremely blue eyes and light skin and hair, he was always rather quiet in company and gave an impression of simplicity which was entirely false. Among his comrades of twenty years past, he had the reputation of such uncommon adroitness as to have been nicknamed "Foxy-Skoro," and those in his old regiment who knew him best were least fond of him, somehow, though with no definite reason to give for their feeling.

I remember at the beginning of the war, he passed a group of us one day, and an old comrade of his said: "Well, whatever else happens Skoro will come back a field-marshal."

"And if by chance, the Germans were to win?" asked a bystander.

"He will be at once placed in the highest court position William has to spare!"

"Then suppose we have a revolution by chance?"

"No; I don't mean to say he will do anything wrong for it, but somehow the thing will just come about."

---

led by Symon Petliura and fled to Germany, where he lived in exile the remainder of his life. For more details, see Serhii Plokhy, *The Gates of Europe: A History of Ukraine* (New York: Basic Books, 2015), 209–13.

"Oh, then he will be the modern Robespierre for awhile, the moment comes for him to play the Napoleonic dictator. Of course, he may get killed, for, to do him justice, he always plays his game with courage."

It was strange how truly his comrades understood the deep, still nature, and foretold the man's future. Though of the Emperor's suite, after the first Provisional Government was an established fact, Skoropadsky became its avowed admirer and friend, and he did much useful work for it at various points, around and before Kiev.

He was lucky, as usual, in avoiding the firing-line when the great routs occurred on the front. When the Ukrainian propaganda was at its height, he appeared in Kiev on leave, and Cossack dress, and his family traditions were naturally recalled to mind of many people, while the old Ukrainian name of Skoropadsky was constantly appearing in the public press. He himself met and cultivated various members of the "Rada," who were duly brought to realize that one of this man's ancestors had been "Hetman of the Ukrainian Cossacks" in early Russian history. Somehow, the suggestion was made that he was the ideal figurehead for the newly formed nationalist army.

Skoropadsky in the situation was naturally most anxious to accept the new title and post, yet he somewhat feared the opinion and criticism of his early associates, and of his own class generally. He at once called on a number of people to discover their point of view as to his intentions, and also, if possible, hoping to strengthen his position by persuading them to join in the move and uphold him. In a very few cases he succeeded, but it was a small minority who sympathized with his ideas and ambitions, and he was instead generally criticized.

To my husband, in a long conversation, he frankly admitted his views, saying he considered under the circumstances (and since the fall of the imperial and Provisional Governments) it was up to each man to save what he could for himself individually. His estates being in Little Russia, he had embraced the nationalist Ukrainian movement, and he meant to throw all his strength into it, if he could by so doing manage to hold the Cossack force, of which he had accepted the command, and protect his lands and those of his class from confiscation. He wanted my husband to join in this good work, throwing all Cantacuzène's influence and popularity into gathering recruits, etc. "But the Ukrainian party is Austrian, built up by enemy money and propaganda, and I have actually had the proofs of this in my hands during the six months I have been fighting it," was my husband's objection.

Skoropadsky immediately admitted this fact, and went on quite cynically to say that he felt such a detail to be of no particular importance as compared to the chance of keeping law and order, both in Kiev and in the provinces round about our city. He and others serving in military capacities, he continued, would have nothing to do with the political side of the Ukrainian movement and would merely be defending the country from the anarchy rampant to the north and east. "At any rate, Austrian or not, this is the most conservative effort on foot. I mean to work with it, and, if I can, keep our provinces quiet till I see what the future has in store."

"It will be the Germans' arrival very shortly," he was told. "They may delay a few weeks or months, because they know their allies, the Austrians, are in possession here, so they can afford, in complete security, to go on with their organization elsewhere, but soon they mean to come in here, and to feed on us later, and what will you do then?"

Skoropadsky laughed rather shortly and answered that he meant to work with these also, on certain conditions! If part of Russia, which was near enough their own doors to be dangerous in a chaotic condition or through its bad principles of government, they would be glad enough to make terms with any conservative elements who might be ready to negotiate. He, Skoropadsky, meant to hold on, therefore, even with the Germans, to a certain extent, and to bargain. He said he felt sure many of the nobility would support him and be glad to uphold his policy in exchange for the security he could offer them. He was perfectly cool and decided, and since that day when, for the last time, my husband and he spoke openly to one another and disagreed (as to the Russian aristocrat's duty in the movement), the Hetman Skoropadsky never for a single moment abandoned the course he had set for himself.

He gathered and drilled troops, who served under him the Ukrainian (Austrian-inspired) Rada. They were unable to do much in the way of real work, because all these men were undisciplined and refused to obey his orders about half the time. Often, when a small unit was sent to protect some factory, chateau, or other property, the soldiers out of hand joined with the mobs in sacking, stealing, and destroying. In Kiev itself, however, a fair appearance was kept up. The "National Army" paraded sometimes or occasionally did light duty as sentinels, but they did not prevent one or two uprisings which were more bloody than anything before their day had ever been.

The worst of these occurred in January 1918, when, for two weeks or so, the city was bombarded and suffered every misery imaginable. One family we knew sat in an underground cellar then for eleven days and nights, without comforts of any kind, with no possibility of bathing or redressing, and without food other than was brought to them by a devoted old man-servant, who risked twice daily to feed his masters. Grandmother, parents, and several small children, with all the household's domestics, lived through the siege in this way, but in many other cases a grenade, a bomb, or a shell came and found out hiding, miserable humanity. Casualties occurred also on the streets in great numbers among those whom hunger or other necessity forced out of doors on short trips about the town, and, as usual, the martyred officers made up a formidable company.

The young cadets who were known to have defended the provisional authority in the previous November against the Ukrainians and Bolsheviks were massacred without mercy. Every officer was, of course, suspected of sympathizing with the "Russian" cause, and hundreds of these were captured, tortured, and shot as "counter-revolutionists." One boy, whom we had known from infancy, barely eighteen and just promoted to his officer's epaulets within a year, was shot in broad daylight as he left his aunt's house for the street; a rough, who had been waiting, stepped suddenly in front of him in the doorway, and putting a revolver to his victim's eyes he fired instantly and without parley. There were many other such cases; about twenty of more of our personal friends were killed under practically these same conditions, merely for being in their uniforms and because of inferred antipathy to the "national" movement.

There were no judgments in any cases I heard of, and altogether about two thousand five hundred officers were executed in Kiev during that one uprising, with the Hetman Skoropadsky commanding the Ukrainian army there! Several women friends and acquaintances of ours were also wounded or killed in the streets "by accident." Naturally, all who could arrange to do so fled elsewhere. Enemy spies filled the town and ordered all things as they chose. There were many anxieties and dramas in the lives of the ordinary inhabitants as well as of the refugee nobility of Kiev. Small wonder some of them fell into line behind the Hetman, hoping to save whatever they could of their fast-diminishing fortunes and also the lives of those who were dear to them.

Help came from no other quarter, and the Ukrainian-Austrian-German authorities represented the only possible chance of safety. A lot of Russian aristocrats held out against the new regime, had the courage to live on in Kiev through these months, hoping against hope something would occur to succor them, yet dreading their surroundings and making themselves as small as possible. These paid heavily (in taxes, by bribes, and in all prices of necessities) merely to live unmolested, however poorly, in their homes. Their houses were used as billets for arrogant, uncouth members of the local army. They were subjected to constant requisitions; they were allowed no arms, nor defense of any kind, and their days and nights were made hideous in a thousand ways: but they stood firmly, nevertheless, by their ideals, bowed down to no foreign mastership, and had only such commerce with the enemy as was necessary with reference to payments, reclamations, passports, and such other business.

During this time Skoropadsky played well his chosen role, was seen moving in state about the city, looked imposing in his full uniform and fine motors, and did all he could to capture and hold the imagination of the populace, with whom he succeeded, at least in so far as to deter them from actual revolt.[4] He had a large number of troops and kept them generally at work, which they enjoyed, so that they were ready enough on occasion to prevent rioting by mobs, since they themselves were satisfied, fed, clothed, and kept out of danger. They "policed" the town, and it remained comparatively quiet. They were always glad to make foraging expeditions and to bring supplies back from the country districts for the citizens' use.

The city populace was a good-natured, gay lot, in general, too, and though of late it had felt certain discomforts of the times, it never knew the terrible sufferings of the

---

[4] Skoropadsky's rule in Ukraine was for only six months, from the end of April 1918 to November and the withdrawal of German forces, which allowed a Ukrainian nationalist, Symon Petliura, to take power. Skoropadsky fled to Berlin, where he maintained a semblance of a Ukrainian government in exile until his death in an allied bombing raid in April 1945.

northern metropolis. The people danced and sang on, therefore, and declared their perfect indifference as to the name or variety of any power which reigned over them. Glad of an excuse for noise and excitement, they now and then, of course, lost their heads in some demonstration and demolished a building or broke into a shop. So it was the Ukrainians received the Germans, and later the Bolsheviks, with a festival of bloodshed.

The factory districts were full of idlers and ne'er-do-wells who were producing little or nothing. Most of the machinery and buildings had been injured or destroyed, while the owners, managers, foremen, and experts had nearly all fled or had been killed. It seemed useless to resist the current, and the factory hands or their committees were completely in the saddle. The roughest elements turned burglars or pickpockets, and crimes on the street or in isolated houses were of continual occurrence. In the villages round about great animosity was felt against Kiev, the city which was requisitioning provisions, grain, and produce of every description. The peasantry were violent in their hatred of the new system, which they considered both unjust and unpleasant.

Occasionally one heard of a foraging party disappearing totally, murdered, it was supposed, and it was well known that peasants were still hoarding some part of their meager supplies, and were constantly ready to revolt if only they could feel themselves of sufficient strength to stand up for their rights. They needed supplies from the towns and factories, and they offered to make trades, but such arrangements were refused, and only an armed peace existed between the urban and country "comrades," a truce which frequently broke down.

During the time, Skoropadsky was the representative figurehead of the Ukrainian Government in all military matters and seemed to indicate to a certain extent the nobility's concurrence in the "national" movement; the civilian first role was being played by a man named Petliura. He was of the peasantry or of the lower ranks in the bureaucracy, had been one of the uniformed scribes in a government office at Kiev, and had been mobilized for duty during the war for a staff bureau there, because the mobilization officers had judged he would be of more use to his country with his pen than with a gun. So all the early years of the war he had sat making out despatches, or writing low-class copy...[5]

Certainly no one ever suspected him of having ideas! He was considered merely an arm with a pen. In the revolution he became excitable and less efficient, and

---

[5] Symon Petliura (1879–1926) before the war was a member of the Ukrainian Social Democratic Party and edited its newspaper and then the respected journal *Ukrainskaia Zhyzn* (Ukrainian Life). After 1914 he worked in the military drafting orders, requisitions, etc. and drifted in that direction, becoming director of the Ukrainian General Military Committee in 1917. Jailed briefly by Skoropadsky, upon release he became head of Ukrainian Directorate and commander of the army of the Ukrainian Democratic Republic in 1918 that succeeded Skoropadsky. He sided with Poland during the Soviet-Polish war in 1920 but lost his position by the Treaty of Riga in 1921 that gave the Soviet Union control of Ukraine. He was subsequently exiled to Paris, where he was assassinated in reprisal for his role in the mass murder of Jews in Kiev during the war.

attracted attention early through his extreme speeches and by the noise about him. Soon he was forming a group of personal partisans, then he showed cunning, considerable strength, and was mixed up in various agitations; finally he was imprisoned by order of the central Provisional Government during Kerensky's premiership, and was judged, acquitted, then liberated, while a large mob cheered themselves half mad outside the courts. This mob carried him away above their heads to his lodging, giving him a triumphal procession. He became an enthusiastic "Ukrainian," and was soon the head of the "nationalists" and their idol.

Perfectly unscrupulous, extremely adroit, well paid by the Austrians, having nothing to lose and all to gain, he developed tremendously, and ended by holding his own even with Skoropadsky and also against all other would-be leaders. He kept in the saddle and is still in power now with his own crowd, for I read quite recently in an American paper he was leading the Ukrainian armies against Lemberg. But in early 1918, Petliura and Skoropadsky, hand in hand, stood together awaiting the arrival and orders of their German masters. The latter came, and after the feeblest show of resistance, the conquerors were admitted to Kiev and were received officially by the "nationalists" with all ostensible honors.

To give the devil his due, Skoropadsky's army, of course, could not have resisted the triumphant troops of Von Eichhorn, as the Ukrainians were a vague and unarmed horde of uniformed picnickers. Petliura was not heard from during German occupation, whether because he was paid to subside into insignificance, or because he was frightened into a secondary place, but the Hetman of the Cossacks, General Skoropadsky, ex-aide-de-camp of the Czar, was a rare friend for the Huns, and he was petted and spoiled, and was made much of. He did make a good bargain both for himself and for his class. As he had foreseen, the German conquerors thought the opportunity excellent to win the aristocracy over to Teutonic "Kultur."

Skoropadsky drove about in Von Eichhorn's motor, held receptions and parades, gave his new chief valuable advice and information as to administrative measures he considered the dictator should take. He obtained (by German consent and enforcement) for all proprietors of landed estates official and legal admissions from the peasantry that the latter had lately stolen goods and land not theirs by law, which must be paid for, especially when there had been destruction. Of these sums paid by the peasantry much of the money went to the Germans, but thirty per cent really went to the old proprietors (or in their absence was paid into a Kiev bank in trust for them).

The peasants were whipped and made to work in field and factory again and to hand over what grain they possessed for the use of Kiev, but also and mainly for that of the German soldiers. Upon resistance several villages were gassed, and all the inhabitants left dead! The helpless country population now staggered on a weary road of abject slavery, privation, and punishment. In the towns it was the same; banks were kept open, business was done; the factories smoked again, and they turned out goods rapidly; the shops were encouraged to resume their ordinary aspect, and counters and windows were flooded with German goods, which, after the long lack of them, were bought up with avidity. Whatever scruples they had, it was reassuring to the upper classes to sleep quietly in their beds for a time again and to see their lives and property respected, to regain their lands and factories, and start working or selling.

They were living, in a word, under what seemed almost normal conditions, and, even if they owed it to their worst enemy and knew the day must come when the iron grip relaxed the whole edifice would tumble in a heap, they were glad of a breathing space of calm and prosperity. The poor man felt, however, at this time, he was arrayed against the landed proprietors and the capitalists of his own race, who were in league with the Huns and who were using the latter's force to crush him, the "moujik." It was a bad situation, and it promised worse ruins for the future.

Skoropadsky was invited to join the German Emperor at the latter's Grand Staff Headquarters, and accepted, and there his triumph continued. He was courted and praised, and a photograph was circulated about, showing him and William deep in conversation and smiling at one another. I fancy this one man was the only Russian perfectly understood and appreciated by the German mentality. Anyhow, his honors at the conqueror's hands lasted till the end, and though he saw Von Eichhorn assassinated, he lived on for some time before his own turn came (late in the autumn of 1918). It is told among Russians that Skoropadsky was not assassinated at all, but that seeing his game was up he spread the report of his own murder and decamped with the Germans when they retired officially from Kiev.

The fact that comparative quiet and prosperity reigned in the Ukrainian provinces aroused the envy of the rabid and starving Bolsheviks to the north and east. Their cities, like their country districts, were already squeezed dry of possible plunder by the Huns who occupied them, and their chances of recuperation were destroyed by the anarchy these tyrants had inspired and encouraged. Hordes of northern rabble were ready to overrun their own frontiers, driven by frantic misery and dread of the bloody terror they had lived in for months past. The climate and riches of the south seemed still sufficiently tempting, and after the Germans' official withdrawal from Ukraine, the strength of the local administration became insufficient to hold back an invasion. From time to time, therefore, waves of dilapidated humanity overflowed toward the south, and though the Teutons sent out such soldiers as were still left in the province to stiffen the Ukrainian national armies, these were not always able to hold back onslaughts.

Various cities on the frontiers of Little Russia were taken by the red guardsmen and were sacked. Many châteaux and villages disappeared completely, and in some of the latter the worn-out peasantry, glad to change one misfortune for another, if only by way of variety, joined the new conqueror's movement which attacked their own home-land. Twice the gates of Kiev were reached by the Bolsheviks: once the city was bombarded and the army of the reds repulsed; the other time they entered and held sway in the city by force of terrorism, till finally through ruse they were persuaded to leave. After Von Eichhorn's murder, and the reported murder of Skoropadsky, Petliura remained alone and took supreme command. In order to draw to his standard the most radical classes, whom he feared might join the Bolsheviks, he inclined his own policies more and more toward Bolshevism. By so doing Petliura's party principles became almost identical with the reds and the chaos in Kiev increased. The leader kept to the name of a separate government, however, and remained independent himself of Trotsky and Lenin.

With Von Eichhorn's murder the German power officially came to an end and many of the Hun troops were withdrawn from the Ukraine. This fact and Skoropadsky's disappearance meant for the few conservatives, who had backed this false authority for a time, the utter failure of their last hopes. Either they must fly now, or be killed eventually and meantime live in abject fear. Since months back this had been the fate of all the better classes, both in Moscow and Petrograd, while of course there came a great reaction after the repressions of the German dictatorship. Though anxiety and uncertainty were terrible trials, life was still possible in Kiev, until January 1919. At the very beginning of that month (the 20th of December 1918, Russian style), the "Council of the Country Districts and Municipalities" was formed in Kiev. The ultra-radical groups were therein represented by large majorities, and the council or congress passed the following resolution:

> The Congress of Country Districts and Municipalities finds the settlement of a ruling power for the Ukraine is most urgent, and that it should be decided immediately, because of the revolts taking place all over our land. Under the dictatorship there has been much commotion, with some movements which were truly democratic, as well as many which were only in favor of absolute anarchy, or were made with an intention of breaking away and forming small independent states. The Hetman's government, set up and supported by imperial Germany, has only deepened the rupture between Ukraine and Russia, and has allowed our people to be cruelly exploited by the foreign armies of occupation. Being rejected by all democratic elements, this government was maintained by the most reactionary and monarchical group, and it undertook violent repression of our peasants and workmen. In the interests of the Ukraine, this power must now be replaced by a purely democratic one. The civil war raging in our country is a great danger to all the south of Russia. It can but lead to the triumph of Bolshevism or to a reaction toward monarchy.
>
> This Congress supposes the continuation and reinforcement of civil war parties in the Ukraine can be prevented only by means of the establishment of a democratic government, which would be ready to enter into open agreement with all groups, classes, and nationalities in the social scale. Only such a government can put an end to the hard consequences of the Hetman's regime

and abolish civil war. It will also thoroughly guarantee the national interests of Ukraine, and the latter's union with Russia may possibly later be renewed.

As I read this, it seems vague enough as to its promises of present or future usefulness. The only thing it really has proved is the fact that by all parties at Kiev, the nationalists' movement, in spite of two Russian [sic] figureheads (Skoropadsky and Petliura), was acknowledged to be a German intrigue.[6] An article in a Bolshevist newspaper says at about the same date:

> The current of Bolshevism has now passed beyond the limits of the Soviets in Great Russia, and overflows into the territory of the Ukraine. The Provisional Government of the peasants and workmen, therefore, makes the following appeal:
> The members of the Central Executive Committee of the Ukrainian Soviets, in complete accord with the revolutionary workmen, peasants, and soldiers of the Bolsheviks, are now at the head of the communistic Bolshevik Provisional Government of the workmen and peasants of the Ukraine! All factories, materials, banks, trade-establishments, mines, and quarries are declared in the possession of the working people, and are forfeited by their present owners. All lands, with inventories of their contents in buildings and implementation, must also be taken from the proprietors, definitely and finally, and given gratis to the peasantry. In these measures the revolution advances with strong and formidable steps in its steady march onward!"

Shortly after this was published it was announced that the Ukrainian government, with Petliura at its head, was officially recognized by the United States administration, and I personally read an official telegram, published in the press here in America, in which the State Department at Washington made this announcement at the moment when Bolsheviks and Ukrainians were joining one another!

The chaos of the north seems to have reached out now through Ukraine into Galicia, Poland, and even Hungary, where civil war and anarchy are devouring the last signs of law and order. Communications have been cut off entirely from Kiev, and the last of the nobility who could escape have done so, abandoning their estates, which it seemed scarcely worth worrying over, as these were almost non-existing. Ours among others have, of course, been re-confiscated.

A last press sheet has come into my hands, sent by a kindly compatriot refugee in the Crimea. It contains a description of most recent occurrences in the Ukraine:

---

[6] Skoropadsky perhaps but not Petliura.

Events here are alarming and important in the highest degree. The south has been now entirely separated from the Ukraine, which has proclaimed its complete independence, and as a republic has set up a new government.

After the first revolution, March 1917, a Hetman was established by the vote of certain reactionary landowners, and was maintained by German troops in the face of all attacks. Now that the Germans are no longer mixed in the fight, renewed excesses have broken out, the revolt against the Hetman provoking a civil war between his troops and Petliura's. The latter has with great audacity established a Bolshevik republic. Petliura is admittedly a partisan (though insisting on independent authority) of the northern Bolsheviks, and this is why the latter are at present moving toward Kharkov. If the two armies should succeed in fusing at this point, we shall see a new disaster threatening all the south of Russia.

The railroad's administration furnishes us with the information that an invasion of the Ukraine by Moscow's red armies is inevitable, and that in a few days Kharkov will be in their hands. The few German troops left in the Ukraine will offer no resistance, of course, nor protection in this movement, neither would the remnants of the Hetman's nationalists be of the least support to any good elements among the local authorities, who might try to preserve law and order. Lacking sufficient resistance, the Bolshevist effort will probably be crowned with complete success.

Unless some succor comes from outside to aid the Dénikin army, one can count on the probability of the whole of southern Russia going up in flames, such as have already wrecked the north of the empire, and as are now destroying our Ukrainian provinces.[7] In this maelstrom the refugees in and about Iassy (Romania) will also necessarily be caught, after their long and patient wait for deliverance! They must feel, if they are still alive, that they have been abandoned and forgotten by all of civilization. At the end of December last [1918], when the Allied fleet dropped anchor in the harbor of Sevastopol, a message was delivered to them immediately from the members of the Iassy conference. It had been written on November 17 1918, and in part it said:

> The conference of Iassy, which includes representatives of every political party, with the exception of the extreme right and left (autocratic monarchists and Bolsheviks, before attacking questions of business have the honor of welcoming their allies!
>
> Our delegation is to communicate at once to the Allies the following facts of great importance: the south of Russia is traversing a very painful transition period, while the weakness of local authorities (which is the direct result of

---

[7] Author's note: Reports within the last week of April 1919, would seem to show that Petliura has changed his politics and is now fighting the Bolshevik invasion with some success.

the German policy and occupation) promises the inhabitants a bloody future, if the solution of its problems are deferred. Only the instantaneous military intervention of the Allies could now prevent the uprising of the extreme chauvinist groups, who would lead the country into anarchy and Bolshevism, and would finally abolish all possibility of the Allies attaining later even a necessary base of operations against the authority of the Soviets.

To encourage the only Russian army (Dénikin's) capable of organized resistance in these parts, the assurance of prompt support from the Allies is indispensable. While awaiting the moment when a considerable unit of troops could be sent us, a certain number of Allied ships appearing in the ports of the Black Sea, with a few detachments of soldiers in the large cities and at strategic points on the railroads, would suffice to keep up hope and to limit the action of anarchy. This preliminary demonstration should necessarily occur within a few days.

The French and British fleets arrived in Sevastopol about six weeks after this message had been written, and received it at the same time as the following one; the two being printed together in one (French) bulletin for their perusal:

Dated Iassy, November the 19th, 1918.

In supplement to the message sent three days ago, we add this further information, which we consider it indispensable to communicate to you, our Allies.

1. The chauvinist elements of the Ukraine have now organized, in the environs of Kiev, a revolt in which, besides the independents, a large number of anarchists and Bolsheviks are taking part.

2. This revolt is all the more dangerous, as the conservative Austro-German units of soldiery are breaking up, and are no longer offering any resistance to the invasion of Bolsheviks from the north.

3. Such an offensive means the immediate rupture of all lines of communication between the Ukraine and the Don River, and in this case the Donetz region, with its great coal mines (owned mainly by French capitalists), would fall into the hands of the Bolsheviks , giving them sufficient provisions of fuel to run industries and railroads for their own and German benefit.

It would seem, therefore, indispensable to take the following measures:

1. Hasten the descent of Allied troops, in whatever numbers possible, at Odessa, and occupy immediately Kharkov and Kiev.

2. Publish a clear and determined proclamation of the Allies' decision to uphold these elements of law and order.

3. Warn the German Government that the Allies will hold the enemy's army responsible for all riots in which it takes part, whether by distributing

arms and ammunition, or in forbidding to Russian officers' organizations (which, in the face of danger, show themselves still ready to defend law and order) access to the *depots of arms and ammunition which are still in the hands of the German troops!*

In case such dispositions are not taken immediately, and intervention by the Allies not carried out at present, it will probably require later a greater sized army and military operation of much longer duration to establish quiet.

Early in January these two messages reached the Allies' hands, and the reply has been surprising! It has consisted of the recognition of Petliura's republic by at least one of the Allied governments, and by the stoppage of any further effort to uphold the struggling groups in the right-minded south once the English fleet of a few ships was anchored at Sevastopol and after the French had entered the port of Odessa! In consequence of all this hesitation, during the past few days we have read of the evacuation of the latter city, and the probable surrender to the attacking Bolsheviks, together with all its riches in provisions; of the capture of Kharkov and other cities in those parts, by the combined Ukrainian and Red Guard armies; of the cutting off of Rumania, the attack of Petliura on western cities, the uprising in Hungary, and the general offering of the richest portion of eastern Europe to the powers of darkness![8]

---

[8] Author's note: Since this article was written it would seem that Petliura has defied the Bolshevists, and that the Allies have decided to recognize and uphold with supplies the Dénikin and Crimean movements.

VI
The New Russian View

Quite recently, in their patriotic desire and effort to save a great cause, the various Russian elements in Paris have joined hands and formed a small "Junta" on the outskirts of the Peace Conference. It consists of four committees. Men of all shades of opinion (from the Liberals of the old, autocratic regime to ex-members of Kerensky's last, and most Socialistic, cabinets) have gone into each of these committees whole-heartedly. There is no one who favors the re-establishment of an autocracy, however, and no single Bolshevik. All Russians, the members sitting side by side, are content to have reached among themselves an understanding, and feeling ready to make any concessions of their personal opinions for the general good of their country, they really amalgamate.

On the political committee's list figures many a great name of ancient Russia, with at least one which was of fiery prominence in a successful nihilist assassination plot about fifteen years ago. After pulling in different directions for so long, as long a time as the revolution has lasted, Russia had become a tower of Babel, incomprehensible to outsiders or to itself. An American, who met a number of my compatriots as they arrived in Paris to represent the north, south, east, and west of our home country, said to me that each deputation came with a special intention, apparently, of telling the Allies about its own plan for saving Russia, which must be followed exactly and to the exclusion of any other recommended by parties previously on the spot! No one of these delegations ever represented any official group which had accomplished anything, and each was accredited merely by themselves to uphold their own ideas.

Recently, quite suddenly, practical common sense and persuasive powers seemed to have grown up among the scattered elements, and rivalries have been reconciled. Still officially unrecognized by the Allies, these Russians have organized three other commissions besides their political committee, presided over by Prince [Georgy] Lvov, who was Prime Minister of the first revolutionary [provisional] government. A military commission is presided over by General Cherbachov, who commanded the Russian armies on the Romanian front in the early years of the war, when he distinguished himself both as a commander and administrator, and where he kept his soldiers well in hand, till long after all other fronts had disintegrated. Thirdly, there is a financial commission presided over by Monsieur [Arthur] Raffalovich, who for many years represented the Russian Ministry of Finance at Paris, and who had a most brilliant reputation in his domain. Finally, there is a commission for provisioning, etc., headed by Monsieur [Pavel] Tretiakov, one of Moscow's vastly wealthy merchants.

Since these groups are now divided up according to their special capacities, and not according to the individual or rival pretensions, with which they came to Paris, they have grown more comprehensible to outsiders and they promise to be useful. They seem prepared for practical team-work when opportunity shall offer, but when this time will be is still an open question. Certain persons, members of the group, in a private capacity have already attracted attention from the great Allies' ministers who are in Paris, and these men have been called upon to prepare the ground for mutual action on the part of Russia and her ex-friends elsewhere in Europe. It is to be hoped that before many months have passed ways and means may be discovered for settling the terrible problems of our salvage and development.

I asked the most practical and clear-minded Russian I have ever known what was his idea as to the form a successful effort to tranquilize our homeland should take, and I wrote down his reply, which seemed to me more promising than any of the numerous Utopian plans I had heard till then expressed. He was on his way to Paris at the time he spoke, and I found he had in no degree changed his opinion since a day in September 1917, when we had first talked of the probabilities ahead of us:

> I begin by saying that, in spite of the terrible experiences we are traversing, I still keep a deep faith in our future; but I think now that the enemy is, at least in part and officially, abandoning Russian territory, it is time party and personal and all other small questions should be laid aside and that we should all unite about one single banner, bearing as our motto merely that we would save and liberate our country from the anarchy and destruction caused by Bolshevism. It seems evident the Allies in their own interests would gladly help in this as much as they can, and would feel obliged to let us have the implements and other material help necessary for our fight. Perhaps even by occupying certain base positions they would liberate our available military units for active operations.
>
> At the same time, I consider essential a first move to re-establish immediately an exchange of produce and merchandise, to organize transportation and communication with the outside world, and to oblige our people to take up work again, after the complete pause which has lasted practically since the revolution began. I consider the fight for reconstruction must be Russian, and that through our own efforts we must reach our redemption. Whenever I say this, my friends fall upon me for not loving my country enough to wish for, and ask for the introduction of foreign forces and riches which would give immediate results; but I am against leaning too completely on outside strength, as long as there is living strength in our own race.

I'm convinced we still possess such vital forces, after observation of the efforts of Denikin and others, with the support of the Crimean government behind them, and there are other local movements of the same kind. It seems to me we must gain our knowledge through our sufferings, and our rebirth must come by our own labor and sincere patriotism. I feel satisfied we can and will work out our salvation in permanent form finally, though we must necessarily go slowly amid great difficulties and over very dangerous ground. Certainly we still risk being swamped by new waves of Bolshevism, unless our Allies are brought to see the absolute need of giving us, the liberal elements in Russia, some support, both moral and material!

"I have always perseveringly believed also in the immense good to be obtained from a better sympathy between Russia and your native country, Princess," the speaker added. "And during all my public life, I have, as you know, both advocated and carried out a policy in line with this idea, and have tried to establish closer relations with America in every department connected with my specialities. I still hope some day to realize such a situation. Your compatriots are practical idealists, and I think they will agree with me that it is in the interests of both countries if we can manage to stretch our hands to one another."

Of old, this thought seemed pleasant even when my adopted country was still an extreme autocracy and America represented all that was divergent in national aspirations. Now, it seems a plan possible to execute when at last the reign of terror shall be over, and when the new Russia will slowly, but necessarily, emerge from the furnace in another form, and will be doubtless very democratic. One begins to see, beyond all the present misery, the dawn of a new day, when, though much of the old charm of our brilliant traditions may be burned away and the fate of many martyrs must be still a saddening memory, we shall find strength to carry high our heads again and shall be faithful to new principles. Many millions strong, only remembering we are all of one great race in spite of past divisions and bitterness, we shall stand ready to work out our salvation, and that of our great land.

At present one lives in an agony of suspense as the slow and contradictory reports come, and the fever burns higher and higher. One hopes for the best as one hears or reads the Allied leaders' speeches, but one wonders... Will these dictators to the world *act now* at last? Will they uphold and strengthen their great Slav brother in his distress? He who so generously bled for them all through the first part of the war, and who saved Verdun and Paris then. In its agony Russia calls for help, and already there have been such vast losses and such awful sufferings which better, quicker action might have saved and healed. Even at this peace gathering in Paris many precious weeks have passed in vague discussion, with nothing done. Meantime the enemy is on the ground, working hard to further his own aims—attacking the last defenses of law and order. Will the outlaw win? Or will succor come at the eleventh hour?

Please God, great Russia shall survive, and after her trials she will know who her real friends have been, and will repay her debts to such as have proved true. Slavs can be marvelously grateful, I have often noticed, and our country has the riches of Aladdin to draw forth from forest, hill, and plain for gifts. Those who look on calmly must soon realize that upon the fate of Russia, in this crisis, will largely depend the future prosperity and peace of the whole world. So civilization cannot afford to turn away and pass by on the other side!

VII
Kolchak

As I am writing (June 1919) the Peace Conference draws to a close in Paris, and it is with quick-beating hearts that the Russian mission there work on for the world's and their own great cause. Russian refugees about them, or those scattered elsewhere over the whole earth, await the results of their representatives' labors and the verdict of the Allies, wondering what the latter's final attitude toward our home-land will be.

Six months has brought about so many changes. Last November, when the armistice was signed, Russia was quite prostrate, bruised and broken, and the red flame of Bolshevism, still fed richly with German gold, obeyed German instructions and continued the enemy's work against the Slavs. Denikin then was fighting hard, holding safe a small oasis toward the southeast of the great steppe lands. The Crimean peninsula was already recovering, but slowly, from a terrible short reign of Bolshevism, and these two units had joined their modest forces, exchanging protection on the one hand for provisions on the other. There were several more spots where law was still recognized. In the Caucasus a small space was protected by Krasnov and his Cossacks and volunteers;[1] in the north, about Archangel, there was a strong defense backed by the Allies, which had been organized largely through the efforts of the American Ambassador, to uphold Tchaikovsky, the peasant leader.[2] Elsewhere the red terror

---

[1] Petr Krasnov (1869–1947) was a Cossack officer in the Russian army, a descendant of Russian generals from the Don River region, and graduate of the Pavlovsk Military Academy. He commanded a Cossack regiment in World War I and was promoted in August 1917 to command as a lieutenant general the 3rd Cavalry Corps, a unit of which marched on Petrograd in an unsuccessful attempt to overthrow the Bolsheviks on behalf of Kerensky in November 1917. He then fled to the Don region and was elected hetman of the Don Cossacks and led a White army of 40,000 in opposition to the Red Army in that region in 1918. After his advance toward Moscow was turned back, however, he gave up his authority to General Denikin and fled to Western Europe. In Germany first and then France, he headed an emigre Cossack anti-Bolshevik center, and wrote several books and novels in behalf of that cause.

During World War II he sided with Nazi Germany and organized a force, mainly of captured Soviet soldiers, that served mostly as occupational units in Yugoslavia. Surrendering to the British army in late 1944, he was, in a controversial decision, turned over to the Soviets, who executed him in early 1947.

[2] Nikolai Chaikovsky (1850–1925) was a populist radical proponent of agrarian socialism and a leader of the Socialist Revolutionary Party that opposed the Bolsheviks. He spent a number

was being fought vaguely by nationalists: The Finns under General Mannerheim,³ and the Letts and Estonians in the Baltic provinces were doing this, while Petliura led Ukrainians forth on the same errand, so he said.

There was no communication possible between these groups, however, and they knew almost nothing of one another's actions or ambitions. They all had different ideas and plans to save at least the small locality in which each lived from Bolshevism. The Crimeans and Denikin alone kept in their program the idea of a final gathering together of all the states which once had made up Russia's domain. Perhaps it was because the men who chanced to be in these two groups were refugees from north and east and west themselves, and because they met by accident only in the southern province. As a matter of fact, however, every one's politics were as fluid as was the situation.

When the conference in Paris opened, delegations were sent out from all these small units, begging our Allies for succor to fight on against the scourge which was devouring Russia. Anxious as to conditions they had left behind them, uncertain of what news the morrow might bring, well-nigh worn out from strain, privation, danger, and the agony of spirit which their patriotism suffered—each set of representatives came to Paris with some proposal thought out in ignorance of conditions as a whole. Each insisted his idea was best for saving what was left of our country, and that his alone of all parties was bound to survive, since it had done so thus far.

Soon there were in Paris representatives of every political persuasion in Russia—upholders of the autocracy, who stood aside and were ignored, did not even ask for recognition; men, hoping still for a constitutional monarchy; liberals, who had been content in the service of the ancient government, but who frankly said they now were no longer for it; other liberals, who had been the frank opposition of our regime in olden days. There were also some of the first revolutionaries of 1917, and others who had opposed these as too conservative from the beginning. Every shade of revolutionist, socialist, and nihilist opinion was represented at the world's great center. When one reached the end of simple designations one began on the hyphenated party names—Social Democrats, Social-Revolutionaries, Radical-Revolutionaries, Independent-Democrats, and so on. All expected immediate recognition, each one as the best there was in Russia, and every delegation hoped to be taken at once into the Allies' con-

---

of years in the United States, where he founded a commune in Kansas, learned English, and won the support of a number progressive Americans. In 1918, he emerged as leader of the Archangel Soviet with American support. With the end of intervention and the loss of his base in the north, he emigrated to Paris.

³ Carl Gustaf Emil Mannerheim (1867–1951) was a Swedish aristocrat from Finland who established a distinguished military record in the Russian army and was close to Nicholas II. After the Bolshevik Revolution, he devoted his talents to the cause of Finnish independence and led the anti-Bolshevik forces there to victory. He emerged again as the architect of Finnish defense in the "Winter War" of 1939–40 and served as president of Finland, 1944–46.

fidence. They expected attention, and the gratitude which they felt was owing them for actual sufferings, and for all Russia's noble work during the first years of the war.

This mass of Slavs, attacking indiscriminately, was of course very puzzling and disturbing to the Allies. In the confusion of the first weeks at the congress, with so many serious questions concerning their own interests weighing on their minds, the various foreign statesmen felt they could not afford time or trouble to solve this problem of an unhappy group of violent partisans clamoring for hearings and for help.

"It is more than we can understand," they said indifferently, "when other questions are settled, if there are time and money and sympathy left over, you shall have some; meanwhile leave us to the great business of our own particular necessities. First, the League of Nations, secondly, the Germans, must be settled; that is what we came to Paris for. You are as chaotic as your land."

Our Russians thus tossed aside were for the moment dazed, hopeless, and silent. It took them some time to rise from such a blow, when they had come so far and with such complete faith. They only knew they had been fighting, at terrific disadvantage, the red peril which threatened all humanity, while the Allies did not seem to realize this in the safety and glory of a recent victory. So the Russians stood round on the outside, condemned to look on merely at the making of the peace.

Certain individuals were kind to them, through sheer pity for their sufferings, or remembering how they had carried the entire weight of the war in the beginning, while France was helpless to defend herself, and the Anglo-Saxons were not ready. Yet on the whole, now, when these old saviors of early days cried out for help, there was none to speak of at their disposal. In black despair Russians foresaw they must return home empty-handed, to watch the continued destruction both of national life and the last remnants of civilization. They had used in many cases their final funds to travel out to Paris, sure of the welcome they would receive, and there was nothing now left for them but slow ruin and death. No wonder deep tragedy reigned in the mentality of every compatriot in Paris!

Then there came a sudden change. One or two new men arrived: real statesmen, practical idealists, with a genius for comprehending things when they looked at them, also a genius for organizing. They brought power, fire, and courage into the group, and these sentiments remained fresh and new always afterward, drawing inspiration from such depths of faith and patriotism, drawing persuasive eloquence from such real talent and capacity, they really could not fail. Theirs were long years of experience, too, and theirs a deep confidence in the good common cause. The Allies must and should be made to see their own advantage in standing by a prostrate sister. If the latter were allowed to die there would be no further bulwark between the world and a universal triumph for Bolshevism.

"No fear!" they told their dejected followers. "The Allies will soon clearly comprehend; only we, the Russians, must get together at once and stop moaning, for though we defended the good cause in the early years of the war, memory among nations is short, and recently in the name of Russia many crimes have been committed! First of all, instead of delegations by districts or by political divisions, there must be one mission, with one policy and program to propose. Russia must present a united front, while the complete eradication of Bolshevism, the utmost liberality toward all races and all parties in the empire, will be our only policy. A clear statement must be offered as to what help is needed, just where and just when it should be given, and as to what payments will be assured the Allies in return. No charity need be asked for, nor could be expected; aid purchased must be recompensed at high rates."

Immediately almost, out of the small discouraged chaos which in Paris represented confusion and anarchy at home only too well, there now emerged groups of experts, with capable leaders at their heads. Four committees were formed to which all questions could be referred, by which they could be decided. In each of these committees the men best prepared for their special work were placed, of whatever political sect they might be.

So the All-Russian Mission was born, with a department for politics, one for military affairs, one for finance, and the last one for provisioning. Into these four frames lawyers, soldiers, diplomats, financiers, sailors, ex-members of autocratic or socialistic cabinets, ex-nihilists, and conservatives fitted themselves, and worked harmoniously, at last, with renewed enthusiasm for the general good. The meetings of the different commissions all ran with surprising smoothness, perfect organization existed, and a newspaper was launched to air the Russian news and views. In this sheet were contributions of prime importance. Coming as they did from the best brains, they were much read. Sometimes a Russian penned the articles, sometimes it was an Ally, big enough in heart to understand, broad enough in sympathy to defend us and advise the other Allies in their own best interest to hear our plea.

When all was ready the leaders of the Russian mission attacked the Peace Conference's head men again. This time with quiet dignity and systematic energy the latter were told of Russia's services in 1914, 1915, and 1916. In thrilling words present danger to the world at large from the Lenin-Trotsky propaganda was recalled. Attention was attracted to the heroic groups making desperate efforts even now against the terror, and to their immediate and pressing needs.

The first answer of the Allies was a hideous blow! It was the grotesque invitation to all Russian parties, including the Bolsheviks, to a conference on the Prince's Islands, where, under the care of two or three guides appointed by the American president, the situation at home was to be discussed in full, and harmony was to be established by mutual concessions![4]

---

[4] See page 66, note 20. The author is obviously sarcastic about President Wilson's effort to solve the Russian situation by negotiation. The two guide/observers designated by the president were noted Midwestern newspaper publisher William Allen White and socialist Edward Herron. The affair reflects some of the frustration among the negotiators in Paris with the Russian situation.

The necessity of replying to this proposition definitely bound all the Russian elements together, for the question on which they were most beautifully unanimous was the very one put to them. Their refusal was so absolutely prompt and universal that the Allies learned for all time there was no use trying to mix Bolsheviks with any other Russian group. This point was settled at once, and no argument or explanation was ever again attempted. By process of elimination the Allies began to take in why it was Russians had come to Paris. And from evil came some good: The Allies fully realized at last there were certain things which we did want, were hoping, waiting, working for, but that a picnic on the Prince's Islands was not among these.[5]

Certain individual Russians, having personal friends among the Allies, were helped by them at this juncture to obtain interviews with the important arbiters. The opportunity was given also to some of the most convincing members of our mission to plead their cause through English and French newspapers and reviews. All this was unofficial, of course, for officially no recognition was yet accorded to the greatest people of the Slav family. However, one strong Russian patriot obtained the Allies' promise—England's and France's—that they would send soldiers to stand behind Denikin's army, holding what ground he gained; the French from Odessa to the Crimean peninsula, inclusively, the English farther east. With certain military points and various ports held as strategic bases behind them, Denikin and Krasnov would be free to make long expeditions with their armies in full force.

These foreign military units were to be upheld and strengthened by fleets of Allied ships anchored along the coast of each one's sphere, besides which an Allied expedition, together with volunteer neutral troops, was to join the movement of Generals Mannerheim and Udenich against Petrograd,[6] these also being strengthened by ships in the Baltic (among which we heard was an American cruiser). American engineers, largely volunteers, were to work on the Murmansk Railroad, which needed repair and care;[7] English volunteers were to be gathered in London for military work round Archangel, to take the place of the American soldiers soon to be withdrawn.

All went well for a time, and these different bargains were being successfully carried out, when a second tragic blow fell: suddenly without warning, the French

---

[5] Nevertheless, the recalcitrant attitude of the Russian mission and its diverse parties did not help their cause.

[6] Nikolai Udenich (1862–1933) was an officer in the Russo-Japanese War who rose to a general in charge of the Caucasian Front in World War I. After the Bolshevik Revolution he commanded White army forces in the Baltic area, leading an abortive offensive against Petrograd in October 1919. Retreating into Estonia, he spent his remaining years in exile in France.

[7] American engineers had helped build the railroad in 1916 to the new Arctic port of Murmansk to open up a new supply route. Hastily built over nearly 1,000 miles of difficult (marshes and lakes) terrain, it was of little use by 1917, with supplies piling up at the rudimentary port.

evacuated every city and every port they held on the Black Sea.[8] Beginning in the north of their zone of occupation, while Denikin—secure in their promise and in the presence of their regiments and crews—was fighting heavy battles far off in the east, the French walked out of Kharkov, Nikolaev, Kherson, Odessa, then abandoned the Perekop Isthmus. All the Crimean peninsula, with great rapidity and without a sign of battle at any point, was also completely evacuated.

Following on the heels of the French came a great wave of civilian refugees. Mad panic reigned, and demoralization was naturally terrible in the complete lack of all protection. After this fleeing multitude came the Bolshevik hordes, burning, pillaging, destroying, killing. The condition of the trustful Russian populace was indescribable. At Odessa, where the evacuation was done pell-mell, refugees so fortunate as to be taken away at all escaped with nothing but their lives. My mother-in-law, a French woman herself, was among those saved in this manner. Letters just come through to us are epic in descriptions and dramatic glimpses of the mad confusion at the embarkation scenes. French soldiers and sailors, with just a few prominent people, escaped, and were taken to Constantinople.

From Crimea several thousand refugees were carried off from the coast towns by British men-of-war and transports. Leaving their harbors farther east, these came to the rescue in the emergency, and organized the saving of our natives, or such at least as could prepare to leave in the short time allowed. The Empress-Mother [Maria Fedorovna] and the Grand Duchess Xenia, with the latter's young children, were put on board an English battleship, together with the old commander in chief of Russia's ancient armies. Its quota embarked, this ship prepared to start. The Grand Duke Nicolas made inquiry whether all the civilians had been taken from the shore: "No, your imperial Highness, they are being evacuated as rapidly as possible, but her Majesty and yourself are of the first ship's load." "Then we must remain here, in harbor, at least until every civilian who wants to come is safely off those docks."

The officer in charge saluted and instinctively obeyed without discussion. The old Grand Duke stood on deck quietly by the fragile dainty figure of the Empress-Mother. They were safe at last, those two, undaunted still, and all their entourage—of British officers and Russian refugees—bear witness to their calm, sad courage, and to the way they thought only of saving and of helping others in the crisis. They stood together looking for the last time, probably, on a Russian scene. Both had loved their country well, and had served it with devotion, refusing to leave till now, and even now they turned their longing gaze to the blue and purple Crimean shore after the ship weighed anchor, carrying them away, until at last the mountains disappeared on the

---

[8] French and colonial forces were unhappy about being cast into an endless and little understood conflict after the war in the West was over, and many mutinied against it, hence their withdrawal.

horizon. After that they retired quietly to their cabins, he and she, who were still very great in their silent misery.[9]

No one seems to know just what occurred to the French troops, or why their departure was decided upon [see note 8 above]. Till the last stage of their soldiers' and sailors' occupation of our shores, the French Cabinet was convinced its garrison in Russia was not thinking of leaving. Even when the news of the evacuation reached Paris, authorities at first contradicted the "false rumors." The truth, however, was soon only too obvious, and there was nothing to be done but to express regret. Meanwhile, thousands of refugees waited five weeks or more under English care—at Constantinople, on the Prince's Islands, in Greece, and at Malta—for permission to enter France.

One of our family [probably a sister-in-law] writes me:

We are in good hands, and our English hosts here in Malta are full of delicacy and kindness, and refuse all payment. But we count the few jewels and rubles we were able to carry off in our haste, and we wonder when they are spent, what will become of us elsewhere? I, who am partly French, hope to get through to Paris soon. The Grand Duke, sad but proud and noble always, went on with his group to land in Italy. The Empress-Mother leaves for England tomorrow. She is marvelous in her courage, refuses to blame any one for her troubles, or to believe that Russia is lost, and her daughter is like her. They think of every one else. All this will put French prestige at low ebb. Perhaps the Allies will explain?

Our mission's good work is most felt, perhaps, in the paragraph of the peace treaty which it is said will grant to Russia—in recognition of her service and sacrifices early in the war—equal rights with the other Allies as soon as she shall have established a secure and popular government. The same men who obtained this concession to justice hope they have obtained, also, the promise of material supplies in quantity— food, implements, raw materials, ammunition, harness, uniforms, clothes, arms, and so on. Of course, all these, if really sold to us, will be at a high price. Arrangements as to man-power are vague; perhaps men are not essentially needed, though, since in spite of her frightful losses—about five millions—through the war, men still seem numerous in Russia. Many are already fighting for liberty as against anarchy; many

---

[9] The real tragedy of refugee evacuation was yet to come, when over 200,000 were evacuated on mainly Russian and American ships in February 1920, after this book was printed. Most of these found relief from the American Red Cross in Constantinople and by League of Nations action in providing five pounds per head for countries to accept them, Yugoslavia to lead them. Subsequently the American Y.M.C.A. was fundamental in providing resettlement assistance, especially in Prague, Berlin, and Paris.

others are returning home, who as volunteers have been on the French front since 1917, or who were scattered by the wind of revolution as exiles all over the earth.

English army units in demobilizing are supplying volunteer recruits, now entering Russian formations through London offices. If I know the sporting spirit and the temper of my own native land there will be adventurous spirits from the United States ready also to lend a hand. For the moment it seems as if German officers and gold were growing somewhat scarce among the Bolsheviks, and without these two reasons the reds are not much good at fighting. Everywhere rabble who meet determined troops either turn and fly, or join the liberating units in great quantities, announcing they are overweary of the Lenin-Trotsky tyranny and lack of bread.

So the Russian mission works on, near the Peace Conference, still not of it, and there has been effective action in spite of many disillusions through the weeks of the long spring. It would seem as if the leaders might well be proud, on the whole, for there are daily reports of Denikin's advances, of the capture of various suburbs of Petrograd, and with startling suddenness from the East Kolchak and his army come forward, sweeping all before them, aiming straight for the "Mother River Volga" and the "Holy City of Moscow."

While he moves into the limelight of history, it seems a good time to look back a little at the past of this remarkable man. Kolchak is still quite young: about forty-five, clean-shaven, with a face striking for its strength and vigor of expression, neither handsome nor ugly otherwise. He is of thin, wiry build, with few but positive gestures, moving quickly. Not much of a talker, what he says commands instant attention; never trying for popularity, he always finds it seemingly. Severe toward what he thinks wrong, he gives complete protection, devoted service to what he thinks is right; always ready to carry responsibility, never mixing in what he considers not his business, a natural leader of men is Alexander Vasilievich Kolchak. [For a photograph of Kolchak, see figure 3 in the gallery of illustrations following p. 110.]

I first heard of him in a rather amusing manner. During the early part of the war the commander of the Black Sea fleet was a fat elderly admiral with a German name [Ebergard], a protégé, it was said, of the occult forces at our court. He had arrived at his high position by seniority promotion and court protections, and he and the fleet under him drifted along comfortably, as accident ordained. The *Goeben* came and attacked, or made feints at attacking our ports at several points, and it was always followed, but never caught, by parties sent after the enemy from Sevastopol's anchorage.[10] Enemy submarines also appeared and disappeared without fear. Meanwhile, whenever the liberal party criticized the commander, or protested that a change would be advantageous, there was a storm at the imperial palace, and it was said that his protectresses

---

[10] Two modern German cruisers, the *Goeben* and the *Breslau*, passed through the Straits into the Black Sea at the beginning of the war and effectively neutralized the much larger Russian Black Sea fleet.

there wept, and said: "Poor old admiral; what will he do? It is so hard on him, and, after all, that fleet won't be needed for battle, and he is so popular in Sevastopol!"

So he stayed on, and the naval officers who came from the south looked grave but remained silent through loyalty. Rumors drifted about, however, of the admiral's conduct being very negligent of duty, to say the least. Tales were told of his fondness for genial society life on shore, of the charming parties given in his honor in attractive homes of the married officers under his command. On the other hand, came talk of spies at work among the sailors, of carelessness and lack of drill, of ships not kept up, of the officer in charge, with his German name, not being in any way what he should be. But Sevastopol was far from Petrograd, not many came from there, and almost none who would have courage to speak against the admiral of the fleet. If the situation gave our liberals food for grave thought it was but usual. Were they not always pretending to be anxious and foretelling evil things?

The social world of the capital was electrified, however, to hear by chance, one day, of an explosion and of the complete destruction and loss of the greatest and newest Russian battleship, *Empress Maria*. An accident, it was said. First the censors suppressed all news, then, ten days after the event, the story leaked out by degrees and was admitted with a great deal of rearranging. Details and accusations flew from mouth to mouth. Spies in our greatest harbor, on our newest, finest ship, the only one fast enough to follow the *Breslau*, just built at wartime prices! The loss was terrible from every point of view! Then followed attacks on the admiral. He was careless, to say the least, and ought to be changed for some one better able to cope with the situation! This time, claims were so insistent against him that the Emperor was finally moved to give a half-hearted consent to the officer's retirement. The consent was not retracted, in spite of tears and pleadings which his Majesty may have had to face in his home circle.

The old admiral found that even in easy-going Russia there was a limit to powers of "protection." He left the service, much discouraged that his good intentions were not recognized sufficiently, though the pension awarded him was so large as to make people gasp. His lady friends in the town of Sevastopol, having gossiped with him before, gossiped about him now over their knitting and their tea, and, making "le roi est mort, vive le roi!" their motto, they quite cheerfully prepared to receive the new commander of the port. He was young, they heard. So much the better; a younger man would be but the more easily flattered by attention. Certainly their husbands' careers would not be neglected for lack of hospitable efforts on the part of society. They wondered how the new chief would appear, and prepared, and waited.

The admiral arrived, or rather, without arriving, as far as the ladies knew, he was simply there. Those who had arranged a reception in his honor were terribly shocked, for one day husbands came home to say they had been on the flag-ship, and had reported to the new commander of the fleet. How did he get here? Why were they not told? What had occurred? And: "When shall we be able to meet and give our reception to this new strange man?" asked the wives.

"He flew here. Yes, literally. Stopping his special train outside the town he took a hydro-airplane and flew out to his flag-ship's side early this morning," the husbands answered. "Did not announce his coming because he wanted to see how things were in their natural state. As to the reception, it never will be given. He sent for us within an hour after he took possession. Met us all quietly without much ceremony; gave us to understand he considered, after looking about, that there was a lot of work to be done to put Sevastopol and the ships in order, that he meant to do it, and that we were to help him. He said that he would tolerate no relaxation from the perfection of discipline and service, especially in these war-times and after what had been reported as occurring here with the blowing up of the *Empress Maria*. Then he gave a few orders, which were to the point, and which showed he had already noticed what was most wrong, and he said there would be further orders soon."

"But when shall we meet him? If he is so young and energetic perhaps he likes to dance. One could arrange a ball in his honor," pursued the anxious women.

But the husbands said no, most positively, and when hard pressed, they added that just at the end of the conversation the admiral had looked at them squarely and had said he came to Sevastopol for work, not play. In these serious times one must be pre-eminently occupied by one's duty, especially when it consisted of a great responsibility such as he carried. As he had never been a society man and went nowhere, people must not feel offended by his refusal of all invitations. He had heard of Sevastopol as being very gay, and of his predecessor as having had great social success. Personally he could not do two things well at once, he found, and he had been sent to command the fleet. He heard also Sevastopol was a gossipy place; possibly, he thought, stories circulated about, whether false or true, had put useful information into the enemy's hands? Perhaps also they had done the former commander harm by making him appear other than he really was?

"I do not mean ever to go about; I have no objection, of course, gentlemen, to your wives and families living here with you in this town and getting what pleasure is possible from its social life, but while I am in charge here and responsible I can tolerate no gossip on any official subject. The fleet and the fortress of Sevastopol are too precious to us to be sacrificed by an idle thought risked or expressed. If I hear, therefore, of any stories whatsoever getting about, I shall be obliged, as a measure of protection, to banish every woman from within the walls to the suburbs. I should never be able to find out which person had been indiscreet, and should not have time to try."

Of course the women were amazed. Then realizing the situation, they resolved to play the game with true patriotism, and became the least talkative group in all Russia. When I reached Eupatoria, a charming resort beyond Sevastopol, in the summer of 1916, Kolchak had just taken command of the Black Sea fleet in the above manner. Except the one story of his exciting entrance on his duties, there was none other which ever passed the walls of the great fortress. The silence was exemplary, and it was said the discipline and the work done were equally so. Now naval officers looked pleased and proud when their branch of the service was mentioned.

In Petrograd I found, when I returned there, people had been rather startled by the new nomination. Kolchak was so young, and what had he ever done? Who in society had ever heard of him? But it turned out that a number of men in positions to know had things to tell of Kolchak, of the brilliant showing he had made in the Japanese War, of the golden sword awarded him for bravery at Port Arthur, of his admirable record since, and the unadvertised but great intelligence and capacity of the man. We would see that within a year the group of men under Kolchak would become the marvel of our service.

The next winter I spent in part on the Crimea's southern coast, about three hours by motor from Sevastopol, which still continued a silent city. Then came the revolution. Though there were wild tales of hideous barbarity from Kronstadt and other Baltic ports, of massacres and mutinies by our sailors, of tragic death and destruction everywhere where ships existed—in the Black Sea fleet the opposite was the case. No one explained the difference except by saying that Kolchak was in command there, and they seemed to consider he was reason enough. No one ever searched for a further one, or worried over what might be happening in the south.

We were cut off from all communications with the capital for several days at the beginning of the revolution, and our excitement and interest, thrown back upon themselves, made us pay special attention to the affairs of our own immediate neighborhood. When the first rumors of events at Petrograd and at the staff reached him, instead of trying to suppress or contradict them, as many leaders elsewhere thought it wise to do, Kolchak published in big print, covering the front page of the main daily newspapers of his town, a proclamation over his signature. It said in effect this (which I quote from memory) to the citizens of Sevastopol and the members of the Black Sea fleet:

The following despatches have reached me:
(Here were inserted the despatches speaking of the uprising by the revolutionaries in Petrograd.)
If I have further news, it will be at once published in full for the benefit of the population. At present I have no confirmation even of these rumors. It is the absolute duty of all citizens and all members of the service to await the future tranquilly, to meet present national occurrences with calm minds, and to devote all their strength and energy to the maintenance of law and order in these days of uncertainty. I fully count on this being done, and with all the strength at my disposal I will see to the keeping of the peace and the protection of life and property here, so that we may be able to act for the best interest of this district and of all Russia.

Kolchak

On the same day orders were given that several of the larger ships should put to sea at once on one of their periodical search parties for the German cruisers *Goeben* and *Breslau*. All these commands were obeyed to the letter; the fortress and the Crimean coast remained perfectly silent and waited without a sign of agitation for further news from the seat of government. The whole province was dominated by the strength of a single master mind, and Kolchak's sailors were too perfectly disciplined to think of rebellion.

Several days later, when telegrams came through, the Emperor's abdication and the establishment of the revolutionary government were accomplished facts, and Kolchak (with his officers and the sailors of the fleet and garrison) immediately and quietly took the oath of allegiance to the provisional revolutionary government. After that event, life went on as smoothly as ever in the established grooves. Of course, "committees" were installed at Sevastopol as elsewhere, but relations between officers and sailors remained excellent, drills and work continued in ordinary routine, and all our part of the country felt safe because of the presence of our sailors and their commander. The very element which everywhere else was considered most unruly, here made for general protection. I never heard what the admiral said of the revolution. He seemed never to have made a communication to any one on the subject, but there was an impression that, having always been a liberal, even when he served his country during the old regime, he must be in sympathy with the revolutionary change. At any rate, his sailors adored him now as before.

When I went north a month after the revolution, I heard in the capital that the Bolshevik sailors at Kronstadt were greatly displeased by the attitude of the Black Sea fleet. They considered the latter was trying to put them to shame, posing to be better than the "protection of the revolution" required. Soon came a rumor that these red sailors of the Baltic, who had murdered their own admiral and many other officers, were going to send a delegation to Sevastopol to instruct the Black Sea fleet committees. One wondered why this was allowed, as the two fleets were quite separate organizations and had never mixed? But the Soviets were already too powerful to be contradicted by the mere government, and the delegation departed on its sinister errand.

At first there was no result whatsoever, and lack of news from Sevastopol led one to believe all was going satisfactorily. Finally, after some weeks, however, came a day when a short dramatic scene on board the flag-ship ended this part of the admiral's career. Numerous additions to that first delegation from the north had by degrees gathered in the Sevastopol fortress, whence Kolchak had no power to expel them, since the "Number One Order" to our troops destroyed his authority in such matters. The red sailors' presence had at last borne fruit, and the committees gathered, asking to speak to their admiral.

He received them on the deck of his flag-ship and listened while they told of the teachings of their brethren from Kronstadt. There was a new law: that the commanders were to be elected by their subordinates and were not to carry arms. Would he therefore surrender his sword to the committee? Kolchak undid his sword quietly with a quick gesture, and holding it still in his hand he made one of his rare speeches, just a few words. His sword had been awarded him for his action in defending the home country at Port Arthur. It had been offered him by the committee of the Order of St. George, and was the Golden Sword given for bravery in battle. It was too fine a thing to be handed to a lot of cowards who were afraid to stand up for the principles of their service and the rights of their own unit, but were being tyrannized by bullies come from outside, into doing things they would later regret. His sword was also the badge of his authority, and without it he would no longer command them, nor any one. He had won it on the sea, and to the sea only he would return it, for those who stood before him were proving themselves at this moment unworthy to touch a Golden Sword of St. George!

Before they got their breath, with a sudden movement he threw the sword he had worn for a dozen years, with its golden hilt and the ribbon of St. George wound round it, far out into the blue water of the harbor. Then he turned his back on the whole group, which stood silent, went to his cabin, had his things packed, ordered his gig and left the flag-ship. The sailors never saw him again, for he took the first train to Petrograd and reported to the provisional government, handing in his official resignation.

He was followed to Petrograd by two groups of sailors: one made up of the Bolshevik delegations, who returned to tell the Kronstadt Soviet that, after many weeks of propaganda, they had at last been successful in dislodging the inconvenient Kolchak; the other, a group representing those sailors of the Black Sea fleet who were still sufficiently devoted to their admiral to bring him excuses and explanations. It was spread about how he received and thanked these latter men for their fidelity to the fine traditions of Russia's navy and for their thought of him, which he would not forget, and how he said good-by, with the hope expressed that some day they might again serve together.

Kolchak after this disappeared from sight. I remember we were a group of parlor patriots one day, speaking of the admiral's work, how fine it had been, how he had never mixed in politics or intrigues, and had disdained catering to court popularity or looking for favors; how he had been a liberal, and had kept the efficiency of his subordinates and their enthusiasm always at such high pitch, and how he had left his great position and thrown his honors into the sea rather than give way in the slightest degree to encroaching Bolshevism or to the temptation to play the demagogue. All this though he had accepted the revolutionary liberty with immediate acquiescence.

"He is the highest type of patriot that we have in Russia, and he is lost to us now when we need him most," said one.

"No, he is only waiting. When the need is greatest and the time is ripe, with sure instinct he will appear again, his hands unsoiled by degenerating compromise with the terror, which must follow these months of weakness as their last and normal result. We shall all see," answered another.

It seemed for a long time as if something might happen to save the provisional government, which was fast degenerating. Kerensky tried, by giving way constantly to the ultra-radical group, to keep his personal popularity, or at least a remnant of his power. Kornilov tried for a return to discipline. Both failed, and soon the Bolsheviks seized the reins, and under German guidance they rode roughshod over all that was left of prosperity, law and order, national honor and personal safety in Russia. Here and there a few held out for right in the great empire. These, if they were in European Russia, were killed, were driven to the little groups round Denikin and Krasnov, or they became refugees in hiding.

On the Asiatic side of the Ural Mountains there was chaos for a long time. The whole population was merely one vast, shifting, disorderly mass. The peasants out there were a conservative, prosperous, scattered element, at least at first, while the cities were soon crowded to overflowing by an immense wave of fleeing humanity from Russia proper, thus about doubling their population overnight. The railroads became completely disorganized by the extraordinary traffic, the confusion of authority, and the wholesale requisitioning of cars to house transient populations.

Bolshevik propaganda had its day of triumph also. Even now, like some legendary dragon it is far from crushed, but it has met in Siberia with definite resistance from various cliques such as roaming groups of Cossacks, foreign colonies, and armed conservative elements, who thought it worth while to put up what fight they could. On the other hand, hundreds of criminals from the government prisons, together with the German, Austrian, and Hungarian prisoners of war, were freed and well armed by the Soviets. They took the Bolshevik's part, of course, with energy, and Siberia became one seething polyglot mass of mad confusion.

It was impossible to those outside even to imagine what was going on in our vast Asiatic territory. One heard of Cossacks under Semenov seizing the power in one place, while Japanese and Chinese under them seemed to take charge elsewhere.[11] One heard also of Germans dominant, with their Bolshevik servants doing their bidding, in many localities. Every known race seemed represented, and the whole of Siberia tossed and rolled and shouted! In the autumn of 1918 the newspapers of foreign countries announced that Admiral Kolchak was at Omsk. He had no party, no soldiers, no politics; he was simply there. Soon one heard of a provisional All-Russian government being organized, in which he held a modest place, and there was a call to the variegated populations to be reassured. There followed orders to elements not

---

[11] Grigory Semenov (1890–1946), a part Buryat native Siberian Cossack, graduated from the Orenburg Military Academy in 1911 and served as an officer on the Eastern Front during World War I, earning the St. George's Cross for bravery. With the collapse of that front, he returned to Siberia and with the support of the Japanese formed his own army in the eastern area between Chita and Vladivostok controlling much of the Trans-Siberian Railroad during the Civil War, thus challenging the authority of Alexander Kolchak and local pro-Bolshevik partisans. He developed a reputation in brutality against opposition and execution of prisoners. At the end of the Civil War he fled to the United States, then back to Manchuria, where he was captured by the Red Army in late 1945 and subsequently executed in Moscow.

Bolshevik, to stop quarreling among themselves and to join in fighting the red terror with its Germano-Austrian supporters.

At first Semenov made difficulties, preferred to lead his Cossacks independently, but he was won over to the government. Then [Ivan] Kalmikov, another Cossack chief, organized a plot for his own aggrandizement, failed to carry it out, and came into the fold gladly. For sundry reasons, not only these men but party after party by degrees grouped themselves about Kolchak, and when the first All-Russian government fell, a new one replaced it, with Kolchak at its head. No one quite knew why, except that the ex-admiral seemed the one man able to inspire confidence in all. Having no party, or personal ambition, he was able to unite every rival interest.

Even so, it has been far from fair-weather sailing for the Omsk government. With almost no money, practically no troops, unreliable transportation, and lack of munitions, the situation seemed well-nigh a hopeless one to face when military action, political molding, and economic reconstruction at one and the same time were needed. But Kolchak the silent found his voice. He communicated with the whole world beyond Siberia in a great cry for aid and understanding, as he undertook his herculean task. Round him he used various methods: persuasion or severity alike were good. He found helpers somehow among the different parties who were there. In exchange for the protection they foresaw might come to them, they worked in the good cause.

The Czechoslovaks, who had painfully reached Vladivostok to embark for the French front, turned back again by the Allies' orders, and faced the rigors of another Russian winter and of great privations to bring Kolchak their succor. They were a group of lions in battle, especially because they had learned to know and hate the Bolsheviks during their long, terrible marches across European and Asiatic Russia. There were Russian volunteers also, mainly ex-officers, who by some miracle had not yet been killed and were refugees. These flocked to Kolchak's banner, organized themselves into an independent unit, all officers, but doing soldiers' work and taking soldiers' rank. There were a few Allied troops as well, especially along the great stretch of the railroad, scattered to guard the government's supplies and precious line of iron communications, from Omsk backward to Pacific ports. Some English did most effective work, while Japanese in quantities were very busy everywhere, and certainly proved themselves most capable.

A commission under Mr. [John F.] Stevens undertook handling the railroad problems, and American engineers, experts and specialists, under this fine man, have done the best sort of work. An American army contingent was ordered from the Philippines, and arrived, full of enthusiasm and energy, for duty all along the road. Ready to uphold the Allies and back the liberal government against the forces of anarchy, these men were frightfully discouraged when, soon after their arrival, they received orders from Washington contradicting their first commands and were instead categorically instructed to keep to a policy of non-interference. The United States troops were even withdrawn to the port of Vladivostok, where they looked on inert, hoping and praying they would be taken away or be sent forward again. It is difficult to sit in a country with idle hands and see so much to do, and every one else doing it, when one is strong and generous by nature.[12]

In February last [1919] Mr. Stevens said: "It is impossible to assure a good railroad system without the backing of American soldiers for the international board of which I am the head." In May a member of the expedition wrote me, saying he hoped we Russians would realize how much every American who had been in Siberia wanted to help in the great work out there, and that they were all being held back only by orders of the strictest kind from Washington. Knowing the value of this time which was being lost, they had again and again protested, and had sent emissaries to Washington, too, but all to no avail, he added.

Mr. Holman, in his brilliant, comprehending article, which will go straight to the hearts of Russians who read it, in *The World's Work* for June, says:

> Cut off from Russia and western Europe by the red battle-line, the Siberian people look mainly to America for immediate assistance. That assistance was promised them, on a large scale, last October, by our War Trade Board, at Vladivostok. Not only were relief measures promised, but also a great loosening up of restrictions on the movement of goods into Siberia. Twenty thousand tons a month of needed commodities were to be sent, according to official telegrams published over the signature of the Vladivostok representative. Deliveries were to begin in November; co-operative associations and reputable trading organizations were to be dealt with fairly. This gave the Siberian population hope, but in February it was impossible to hear of any shipments that had gone to the interior of Manchurian station, except one train of about eight hundred tons of foodstuffs, sent by our government for distribution among needy Russian railroad employees, and a few articles for relief of sick and refugees. Military supplies went westward in increasing quantities, but little or nothing filtered through for the civil population to buy except profiteers' small shipments. Are we to keep our promise?
>
> In the present condition of the country, successful operation of the railroad cannot be assured except by American soldiers garrisoning the principal points. "I cannot assure the people a good railroad system without our soldiers to back me up," said Mr. Stevens to me in February. To turn the railroad back to the Russians to run just now would probably mean a complete breakdown of the whole transportation question. That will lead to the downfall of

---

[12] A clarification is needed here. The American Expeditionary Force never expected to be deployed in battle alongside Kolchak or any other commander far in the interior of Siberia. They were not "withdrawn to Vladivostok" since the units had never gone beyond it as a fighting force. In general, most American soldiers had no wish to be deployed in battle in the chaos that reigned in the region.

Kolchak and the return to power of the Red Guard government. To recall the American soldiers now in Siberia, before the Russians have found themselves, will, in my judgment, be a serious blow to liberalism in that country; it will be an American sanction to murder and anarchy. If it is right to keep our soldiers there, they should be sufficiently strengthened to banish the possibility of even minor uprisings. It is only the smallness of the police forces over there now which makes a single soldier's life unsafe.

In assistance also lie our national interests, for we shall profit in a commercial way by the policy, but for trade alone there could be no legitimate ground for occupation and assistance. It is for the good of the Siberian people, just as much as our policy of occupation and assistance was for the good of the Cuban people, and also is for our own good. It is the law of things that those who do good unto others do good also unto themselves.

On the Asiatic side of "over there" is a new commonwealth longing to be free of Bolshevism, and a people rapidly regaining their stock of common sense. These people will have in time only the friendliest feelings for the Americans who helped them out of their sorrows. That friendliness is of the good-will part of the great international trade that the future has in store for Siberia. That good-will means open opportunities for American railroad builders, constructors of mines, builders of industrial machinery, grain elevators, electric power plants, and many other enterprises. That good-will means ready sale of American export products when needed, such as agricultural implements, woolens, cotton goods, sewing machines, and toilet articles. But if we were not to profit, there is before us the duty of the big brother—a rule of conduct which these days we are applying to Belgium. Why not also to Siberia?[13]

In confirmation of this opinion of Mr. Holman's comes from Paris on May 26 the following telegram: "Advices received here report that Bolshevik strikes are greatly hampering the operations of the Trans-Siberian Railroad, on which Admiral Kolchak is dependent for his supplies. These disorders have been difficult to repress, and the trouble makes the work of the inter-allied railroad commission under John S. [sic] Stevens arduous and unpleasant." This is the American's point, and it is echoed daily in my mail by those who know the case and who appreciate the good and noble cause of the Omsk government, and what it stands for to all humanity.

The Russian point of view is more difficult to get at, for the Russians I have seen and heard are with one accord going out there to offer their services. Not one is coming this way, or has an opinion as yet to express on the American official action. Each and

---

[13] Charles W. Holman, "Hot Siberia Got rid of Bolshevism," *World's Work* 38 (May 1919): 146–47. The map included in this book is adapted from one in the article. Holman was an agricultural specialist traveling through Eastern Siberia and evaluating its potential, including interviews with John F. Stevens.

all speak highly of American private citizens' efforts and their understanding of our situation. The only way to judge of Russia's desires is by the fact that Kolchak begs for aid, and that the Russian mission in Paris is doing likewise for him, daily and with insistence.

In every branch of the Siberian Government there is a systematic effort being made to get things into shape, so that the whole life of the country can be inaugurated. Below the government, and upholding it, the co-operative societies, the merchants, the farmers, and the manufacturers are all wide awake to the fact that they must reorganize themselves and reconstruct a national life from the actual monstrous situation. They are most patriotic and full of good-will, and are flocking to Omsk to get the opinion and instructions of the master mind there. Kolchak, always patient, always strong, and always practical, receives each group and sends it back into its distant province, determined to do its share in the nation's work, and full of faith in the final success of right and justice.

Now the military forces are moving westward steadily. Perm, Ufa, Saratov, Ekaterinburg, Orenburg, the Volga, much of this has been captured already from the terrible red foe, and news reaches us frequently of further success.[14] Kolchak makes flying trips to the fighting front, then in haste returns to Omsk and negotiates with the Allies, or with the various native groups whose demands make his presence there an absolute necessity. He shows himself most liberal towards all parties, with partiality toward none. Even the Jews, who heretofore have not been looked upon with favor by Russian governments, gratefully admit that the ex-admiral's ministry is without prejudice, and they send him large donations in money for the defense of a cause which they feel promises a generous safeguarding of their rights among others. (For a map showing the territory occupied by Kolchak, see opposite.)

As his army advances, the best elements of each conquered province rally round it, and Kolchak presides at conferences of industrials and peasants, or receives delegations of other branches of Russia's people, counseling them to lose no time in helping to set their country in order. He, who was always silent, tells the press nothing of all this, but the contented delegations occasionally give their impressions, and they put on record how the admiral finds time to think of the problem of each class, and how he shows immense capacity in handling these different units so that each will bring its quota of real strength to the general building up.

For thousands of square miles Russia is in a condition of complete devastation, with enforced stagnation of work, famine, and misery, just as is the small area of northern France. A crushed, exhausted, starving, bleeding people at home is straining its last remnant of strength to rise up and to live. Kolchak is pulling his compatriots to their feet, and they try to stand, dazed and tottering. Will the world listen to their cry, and will it hold out a helping hand? Or will it turn its head and pass by on the other side?

---

[14] Much of this westward advance toward the Urals and Moscow was due to an alliance with the Czechoslovak Legion that soon abandoned the area.

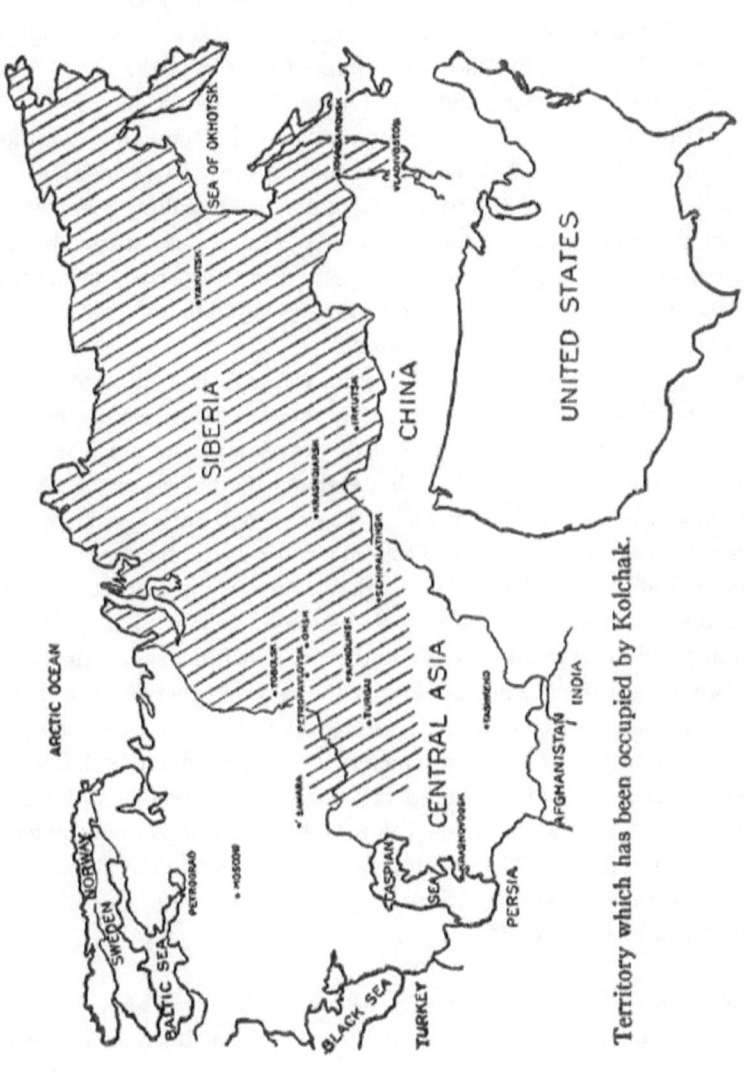

Territory which has been occupied by Kolchak.

In Kolchak's and the Paris mission's voice, all Russians call to the Peace Conference in Paris and to Allies over the whole world. And the latter answer what?[15] They must come to a decision soon, or the Peace Conference will be scattered, leaving half the world at war and wounded still. Their line of action is unguessed [sic] at, after eight months of conversations. Kolchak asks for recognition. Kolchak prays for help, help now, while the giant, which is Russia, is making a noble effort to kill the whole world's enemy, the Bolshevik, and to sweep him from the earth.

There is much argument and talk. One hears it unofficially declared that the "Big Four" in Paris think of answering the call and of recognizing conditionally this rare man's work. Only he, Kolchak, must consent to various conditions—to giving up the power as soon as he has won the victory, also to calling together a constituent assembly to determine the form of Russia's future government. In this case, it is reported, material help will be given to the Omsk All-Russian government, to Denikin and to such other groups as there may be found fighting for the same principles; this help, of course, to be paid for in full.

Kolchak replies that what every Russian wants is the calling of the constituent assembly, promised by the first revolutionary movement, as soon as there is order in the land. He wants it most of all, for he is the weariest patriot of Russia, carrying, as he does, the greatest load of responsibility, doing the heaviest work. And again he begs for help, all possible help in any form the mission in Paris can devise and the pity of nations and individuals can send! Only let it come soon, otherwise the effort to conquer Bolshevism may break down under the strain of waiting and the lack of arms.

The Russian mission in Paris works as one man now. They hope, and pray, and feel inspired to renewed energies, and every exiled Russian heart beats in complete unison with theirs.[16] They are inspired to renewed energy when they hear that Petrograd may fall into the hands of Russia's true sons again, even though they realize that proud city may be almost a cemetery when they enter it, with famine, typhus, and every other human plague rampant! Surely at last the dawn of a great day of consolation is at hand, when Allies who have been indifferent will understand that their interests and their own salvation depend in part upon their charity.

From a member of Russia's mission in Paris a letter comes to me, dated the middle of May, in which the faithful patriot says:

> We have many sad impressions in the present, still, but great hopes for the future. From our Orient our help will come. Behold Kolchak and the mighty

---

[15] The author must have known or guessed the answer. After weeks and months of strained negotiations about four peace treaties, making arrangements for a number of other arrangements, such as a League of Nations, they were tired, exhausted and ready to go home—and not get embroiled in a distant mess that would be difficult to sort out.

[16] The author is apparently responding to criticism that the Russian parties at the conference were badly divided in their quest for allied support.

fighters round him, how they move forward as surely as the sun, and the Bolsheviks, perhaps no longer commanded by German officers, or paid with German gold, go down at last before the onslaught of our men. Or else in masses the pseudo-reds even join Kolchak's armies, and turn their guns against their own comrades-in-wickedness of a few hours before. Ex oriente lux![17]

So on to Moscow the patriots move, and when they reach our ancient capital, most holy of all Russia's cities, they will find many among its populace ready to weep with joy and waiting to kneel upon its streets with icons as the crusaders pass. These, mounting on up toward the great Kremlin's gate, open again the fortress palace to the whole populace. The latter has been banished outside its walls ever since it was used for barracks by Trotsky's red guardsmen, or as the hoarding place for stolen provisions and treasures, which these ruffians seized, but at last real Russians will be at home again, upon the ground they always owned, where even autocratic Czars had made them welcome.

I can see in imagination the weird beauty of the splendid edifice, and feel the thrill of the crowd on its great square. The doors of the cathedral once more swing wide as of old, and perhaps the Patriarch Tikhon will appear upon its steps to welcome his children, come home at last.[18] That day, with his devout people upon their knees, the venerable head of the church will intone a "te Deum" such as the world has rarely heard! While the prayers of a whole race shall rise in one vast volume there will be certain sons of Russia to whom the nation's thoughts must turn in gratitude.

First among these are the martyrs who defended Russia's honor early against the red terror's dastardly attacks and give their lives in the good cause when help and hope were not forthcoming. Then, the brave little groups who kept the faith of a great race, and who fought on against the peril to the death, as did Denikin's army, or Krasnov's. Also those patriots merit praise who by thought, and act, and word have upheld Russian interests in the face of indifferent friend, or of intriguing foe, on the outskirts of the Peace Congress, who through long months of waiting and discouragement kept up our hopes, and whose energy never once has failed our nation. Last, but not least, will the thanks of our whole race be due to the group which in

---

[17] Actually the downfall of the Kolchak regime was caused mainly by desertion of the Czechoslovak Legion and the rise of Siberian partisan groups that were opposed to Kolchak's rule.

[18] Patriarch Tikhon (born Vasily Bellavin, 1865–1925), studied at the Pskov Theological Seminary and graduated from the St. Petersburg Theological Academy in 1888. Much of his service was in the United States, where in 1898 he became bishop of the Aleutians and Alaska, reorganized as the diocese of the Aleutians and North America with a new St. Nicholas cathedral in New York. He returned to Russia in 1907 as Metropolitan of Yaroslavl. He was elected patriarch in June 1917 upon that title's restoration. Tikhon valiantly but vainly opposed the Bolshevik actions against the church after the revolution. He was canonized in the 1980s in recognition of his sacrifices.

Siberia, facing a thousand problems, raised up the sad and tattered banner of Russia and brought it home in triumph to the mother city, Moscow. Their strength gives the final blow to down the treacherous enemy, and at their head the modest figure of their leader stands out as the best type of his people—sailor, soldier, statesman, and patriot above all—Alexander Vasilevich Kolchak.

VIII
Siberian Impressions

"Refugee reserve officers in the United States are ordered to report to the military attaché of the Russian embassy at Washington for duty at the front," said the American newspaper one morning in May 1919.

We read this with dawning hope of things doing again at home. It meant that the battle was to be renewed on a large scale, evidently, since till now the various groups fighting had been but bands of volunteers—around Kolchak, Denikin, and other heroes—who, struggling against terrific odds, had tried to break up the Bolshevik armies. Now, since it was thought necessary to bring back the men (who for one or another reason had gone across the seas), one could consider it certain that new armies were being raised and trained for service, and that this call was to get back all the valuable material which Bolshevism and its persecutions had scattered broadcast over the whole world.

Rapidly the officers gathered into little groups, reported for their orders, and then turned their steps either toward Siberia, toward the Black Sea, or to the north of Russia. Wives were brave over the partings and looked for work, which would support them in exile, or else, braver still, they prepared to go out to the home country again and take up their share of the husbands' burdens. It was a difficult choice for many women—either way the risks and responsibilities were heavy, and the future was impossible to foresee. Sad faces and weighted hearts were the rule in the Russian colony.

My own husband, though outside the classes recalled to service because of his age, and supposedly out of commission because of his old wound (which still greatly and frequently troubled him), became so interested in the movement and the possibility of being useful that he decided to volunteer again. His first application was to the Russian mission in Paris for information as to where the experts there would consider it best for him to go, and at once he received an answer begging him to give his effort to the Siberian side, where there were many soldiers to be put in shape and few officers to do it, whereas on other fronts there were plenty of good officers already. So it came about that a letter was written to Kolchak, giving Cantacuzène's past history and asking if the supreme commander of the "All-Russian provisional government" would accept my husband's services in any capacity, civil or military. In about six weeks an answer came from Omsk, laconic and to the point: "Come at once."[1] Two

---

[1] Admiral Kolchak had established his military headquarters and the provisional government of Siberia in Omsk, a city in Western Siberia and key point on the Trans-Siberian Railroad of about 50,000 population at the time. It is now over one million, the largest city east of the Ural Mountains, and near the border of the Russian Federation with Kazakhstan.

or three weeks for the making of an outfit, and the necessary time wasted in trying to get accommodations on the earliest possible ship, then finally all was ready. Goodbyes as little sad as possible to the children, and we moved westward. On the shores of Lake Michigan a last quiet week of sunny days and of nights soft still with the final warmth of the summer's flame was spent, a gentle time when the soul could get its balance and grow stronger to face new dangers—of which one knew no detail yet but only felt the weight.

Days difficult to live, for we forgot the perils just ahead and laughed sometimes, and then suddenly the vision of what threatened left us with a sudden sob, caught in the throat and stopped. The last day and the last hour, and each played up for the other—striving for self-possession and summoning a smile to meet a traveler's last look backward. Then for the officer the long trip westward, the three or four days' wait at Vancouver for his ship's departure. Finally the heterogeneous baggage thrown on board, sorted and put in safety for the long sea trip.

Telegrams of adieus, bells and whistles and shouted orders, and the vessel was off, separating our fighter more and more from the shore, which for some time past has been a safe refuge. The long trip across the ocean is intensely monotonous and very wearing, especially for the nerves of those going into the maelstrom of the Siberian struggle. There are many long hours in which to wonder over the fate awaiting such as are brave enough to offer their service and perhaps their lives on the altar of patriotism.

The rough sea, high wind, and creaking ship are not conducive to a cheerful outlook, and those on board were seasick and easily discouraged. Seventeen weary days were thus lived through, while one was tossing uncomfortably and straining for a mental glimpse of the future. English officers, Canadian tradesmen, Japanese and Chinese merchants, also a very few Americans, with a half-dozen or so Russians going back to serve—such made up the company on board. The Russian and the English officers naturally drew together soon after the ship sailed, and formed a little circle to themselves during the trip, where conversation ranged on political or on military matters, and advice was offered back and forth as to conditions which had to be met and precautions which had to be taken against dangers of every kind, from Siberian cold and lack of food to political intrigue among allies and Bolshevik murder and torture.

The ship *Empress of Japan* at last drew near to Yokohama's harbor, and piles of nondescript luggage appeared on deck: saddles, canned food, string bags, smart officers' khaki-colored trunks and bags of leather for the Britishers, of patched canvas or wood for the poorer Russians. Japan, usually renowned for flowers and sunshine, seemed as gloomy as the travelers' hearts. It was drizzling, cold, slippery; altogether disagreeable—and the small group of wayfarers were chilled to the bone while they fought to get their baggage off the ship and through the custom-house.

The hotel was pleasanter: good beds and food made one forget the worst sides of the errand one had come on, while a steady floor and dry clothes helped to better impressions of the future and surroundings. The town proved to be unattractive, so at least my husband felt as he wandered over the stone pavements and peered about: a small, dark, greasy-looking people in dirty kimonos came and went in an endless crowd, perched high on wooden sandals which clapped, clapped with a staccato note on the stones. The noise of their walking pervaded the air, and one couldn't escape it night or day—and the queer, pungent smell of the Orient helped to make up an impression of a strange new world. The flimsy houses seemed unattractive, overcrowded, dirty; and the conveyances uncomfortable. Altogether discouragement grew as time progressed. Only one thing seemed consoling and that only if one was fond of shopping. The silk shops were a delight. Color, quality, beauty of design, all splendid, as the material fell into graceful folds, iridescent almost, with the richness of their glossy sheen. One hesitated what to choose; one wanted everything; and one ended by buying twice as much as planned, because the polite shop man, anxious to please and to tempt, bewildered his victim into dumb acquiescence.

The dull, damp chill continued in the air and ate into the vitals, or perhaps it was the feeling that one was moving farther away from those one cared for and from a warm fireplace which was next best to home, going out into a world of misery on a crusade, led by a lone hope and a single purpose—duty. Patriotism in such a case seemed a dull principle and required a great effort.

Our officers knew a thrill in entering East Prussia, or Galicia and Hungary, in 1914, and they still felt it when they and their men slowly moved back again in 1915, contesting every inch of the ground they were defending. It took enthusiasm also in 1916 to hold the lines straight and even take an offensive against the enemy's full strength. In the months of revolutionary times officers still tried to rally their soldiers, and when the latter obeyed it was only for love of leaders who gallantly continued to fight the Germans before them, the indiscipline about them, and the propagandists behind them. Now it required a new building up of their brave spirit to go in cold blood back into the fight after months of exile and soft living—the mere thought of the sights and troubles of Siberia made them shiver in painful anticipations.

A trip to Tokyo for papers and passports, of which apparently one never has enough, and which are never sufficiently vised. There Cantacuzène saw a quantity of interesting people—some stationary, some the driftwood carried hither and thither on the current of travel. Every one had news to tell—the most varied, exciting, contradictory news. Always positive of the truth of each announcement, the authors, if doubted, but repeated it the more emphatically and the louder. What the head of every government in the world ought to do, what each of these would not do, and what each would, was told by the ambassadors and secretaries of the others. Then there were the impressions of all the floating population of travelers, those going to Siberia and those coming out. Every man saw things differently, and the most amazing part of it was how little each had seen or knew really of the country for which he was so positively recommending policies.

Unfortunately, Russia was not represented at its best by the Russian group in Tokyo. Adventurers, deserters, refugees, vague, frightened diplomats, who had not been able to hold their own. The entire mass lacked cohesion and a head. On the other hand, there were warm friends to Russia to be found—men and women who were helping and guiding, or trying to work up the world's sympathy. Mr. Roland Morris, the American ambassador, was one of the leaders in this.[2] Amiable, hospitable, and giving the impression of reliability, he gladly received such people as came to him for some small passport services. My husband saw him thus, and, having letters from mutual friends besides and many interests in common, the two men sat talking lengthily. Cantacuzène stayed on to lunch, glad to get points from this man who so recently had gone into Siberia quite anti-Kolchak, and had returned, after untrammeled investigations covering many weeks, to report to President Wilson that the "All-Russian" government should be recognized at once, also supported and upheld in every possible manner. A pleasant message, this, to Russian ears, even if it had borne no fruit.

The good opinion of Kolchak was unanimous in the East among those who watched him; and the splendid fight he had put up against Bolshevism was universally admired, as was the way he had handled the complications made for him by conflicting political groups in Omsk, the intriguing personalities in his staff and government, and the troubles brought on by the hesitations and rivalries of our allies, each of whom had given small help but much advice. As one approached, the personality of this remarkable man dominated the horizon more and more, and commanded a respect, esteem, and admiration which seem universal. Curiosity augmented and when the embarkation for Vladivostok occurred there was excitement mixed with fears and doubts. The sun came out just then. A good sign this!

As the ship steamed into Vladivostok's harbor every one went on deck, firstly to get a glimpse of the homeland for which one was hungry after eighteen months of expatriation. However much they feared to find it changed, to see the poverty and misery of these sad times, still it was good to think of hearing our language, of seeing the familiar types again. Even to eat a "borsh" or "shchee" with a salted cucumber and black bread will seem an act of patriotism. None of the party of officers on board had ever been this side of the empire before. All had done their fighting on the European front, so curiosity was keen, and with wide-awake eyes they took in the impressive beauty of the great harbor they were entering. It appeared more beautiful than that of Vancouver, higher mountains rising out of the sea, and the stretch of water much broader. The towering banks are arid and have a severer type of beauty,

---

[2] Roland Sletor Morris (1874–1945) was a Philadelphia attorney and Democratic politician who served as U.S. ambassador to Japan from 1917 to 1920, his only diplomatic assignment.

but the proportions and lines are altogether splendid, and the coloring that day was brilliant with azure, russet, and gold, the light over it all intense.

Suddenly from the inner harbor came a boat to meet the one carrying our men; a Russian Government boat, looking trim and smart and flying at its stern the "flag of St. Andrew." It brought one's heart into one's mouth to see the Russian colors once more in their place! Eighteen months ago we had left Petrograd draped with torn and soiled red banners. This now really seemed to my husband a promise of new strength; would the impression last? The pretty craft came up close and our officers crowded to the side of their own steamer to watch the welcomers' maneuvers. Both ships stopped and officials from the smaller one climbed on board the larger to ask questions of each traveler, to examine papers, search for a reported Bolshevik (who naturally was not forthcoming), finally to approve of everything and take themselves off again.

The dock was reached soon afterward.[3] With shouts, excitement, good-natured confusion, a hundred orders, and little obedience, but endless intelligent emergency work, a landing was made. Every one was ready to lend a hand to strangers. Chaos apparently, but results that were unexpectedly quick and satisfactory in spite of it. Paradox everywhere—Russia, in short, with its old nature, and ways and mystery, untouched by the experiences of the past two years. And one felt warm and at home somehow. It was said there were no "izvoshchiki" (cabbies); then one was immediately found. It was said there were no rooms, but a man to whom one came recommended, offered hospitality. A cozy small room it was, with clean bed and dry bedclothes—the possibility of sleeping, washing, smoking, and of drinking with him his morning tea was offered Cantacuzène.

The other meals he took out—paying forty-five rubles for a light lunch and seventy-five rubles for one dish in the evening! He was sustaining his second shock—having been given the first when cabby asked one hundred and fifty rubles for driving him from the dock to the house and expected to get it! People had told our men of the terrible prices, but it was hard to believe such tales—now they began to digest the unpleasant idea that money had no value and that they would probably be forced to buy a flour-sack and stuff it full of bills, which would be handed out rapidly. And the variety of the money! Every kind of foreign note and coin—then paper of several sorts: old-regime and Kérensky money, besides all the kinds used in Siberia. One is easily "money poor" instead of "land poor" in such a place.

They lunched and dined in a tumble-down, small, and expensive restaurant; they sat and smoked and thought, listening to the strains of a marvelous string orchestra made up of Hungarians. Ex-prisoners of war, these were now freed, but had no means nor hope of going anywhere. They could only earn a little and life cost much; exchange was prohibitive, and the distance to their home was vast. So, stranded here in a Far-Eastern cabaret, this band of ex-prisoners played out its sufferings and its

---

[3] The date of landing in Siberia is probably late June 1919.

longings to an appreciative and enthusiastic audience of sad, understanding Slavs, who would gladly aid the poor artists if they could.

For a day or two Cantacuzène sat about, waiting to get passage by the occasional train leaving for the front. He tried to readjust himself and get the atmosphere; he listened to the gossip which flowed toward him in never-ending volumes. Vladivostok teemed with foreigners, mostly Allies who had been sitting miserably about for months waiting for orders to do something worth while. Meantime they were trying to kill time. The weary hours lagged dreadfully while they sat and looked on, forbidden to lend a hand! Mischief was rife, of course, and Vladivostok, since the Allies' occupation, vies with Port Said in its unsavory reputation—mixed races, bad morals—the worst of the East and the West—and in such an atmosphere every one degenerated. Queer tales of misery and of crime were told.

The only name unsullied by rumor was Kolchak's own. No one but admitted his honesty, loyalty, devotion, patriotism. Unambitious for any recompense, either in money or position, anxious only to down Bolshevism, then retire somewhere and rest; at his post, above all intrigue and all smallness, strong and brave he is always. As for the foreigners, one heard a lot against them, strangely enough more especially against the Americans, who only ten months ago were landed here, and were received with open arms as saviors and friends. One was filled with wonder that it should be so, for in old days Americans and Russians have always fraternized and understood each other. Then, listening carefully and sifting down the many detailed stories, one found the gist to be about as follows.

Nearly a year ago, with many promises, great show of friendship, and fair official words, came the American soldiers.[4] They were received with simple faith in their message and intentions, and they started toward the front "to help." At once almost the counter-order came to them, and back to Vladivostok they were obliged to retire, to settle down and cross their arms. Since then, whenever they were asked to act in any matter, they have replied that their strict orders were "not to interfere."[5]

---

[4] Perhaps more expectations than promises?

[5] There indeed was confusion about the mission of the American force, which numbered no more than 9,000, much of it in non-combatant units: quartermaster, intelligence, etc. A few officers visited Omsk to confer with Kolchak, but the main goal was to assist in the departure of the Czechoslovak army; a secondary motive was to guard against a permanent Japanese presence in the area. And it is not quite true that the Americans never responded to a call by local officials, since a detachment was sent to Souchon, 50 miles east of Vladivostok, to quell unrest among coal miners. It suffered the only American battle casualties, about 20, from an ambush by a pro-Bolshevik force. For a thorough account, see Betty Miller Unterberger, *America's Siberian Expedition, 1918–1920: A Study of National Policy* (Durham, NC: Duke University Press, 1956). Blaming the United States for its failure to turn the tide on the Siberian front with a much larger intervention force is Ilya Somin's *Stillborn Crusade: The Tragic Failure of Western Intervention in the Russian Civil War, 1918–1920* (New Brunswick, NJ: Transaction Publishers, 1996), but he does not take into consideration the state of transportation, the large Japanese

His own situation riled the dough-boy, humiliated the American officer, too; some tried to explain what they themselves couldn't understand: the contradictory policy of Washington and their own obligatory inertia; others tried to cover their shame with peevishness or arrogance, and hurt the natives' feelings doing it.

The American salary in dollars, of course, would outbuy poor Russian rubles every time. Whether of girls or clothes or food, the best went to the Americans, while the Russians were disdained, till pride rose in rebellion. High words followed and sometimes blows, and hard feeling became a settled fact. The situation in its new form was encouraged by third parties, especially by the Japanese, and nothing was done to soften matters by any one. American onlookers as well as Russians told that many of General G——'s [Graves] words and deeds seemed unfortunate, and that his Chief-of-Staff, ——, took apparently every occasion to do the wrong thing and to add insult to injury.[6] Various Britishers confirmed this view with their testimony.

Through all the growing discord, however, even now, the American Red Cross personnel has acted in a way to win universal love, gratitude, and admiration from the wounded, the ill, and the poor refugees. The officials, doctors, and nurses have gone about like ministering angels, saving Russians from death and misery as much as possible; doing every other person's work, raising hope, sustaining life, trying to bring back health and a smile to vague, emaciated bodies and wan faces. The testimony was universal, enthusiasm never failed whenever this name of the American Red Cross was mentioned.[7] For some unknown reason the Y.M.C.A. agents are not spoken of in the same tone. It is said many of these were engaged by the society which

---

army, nor the general confusion caused by economic breakdown and the presence of over five million refugees.

It is also important to note that the American presence was supplemented by two cruisers of the Pacific Squadron under Rear Admiral Austin Knight that dominated the port of Vladivostok during this period.

[6] Major General William S. Graves (1865–1940) also received much criticism in the press at home. He defended his actions in his *America's Siberian Adventure, 1918–1920* (New York: Jonathan Cape & Harrison Smith, 1931). Most American officials had a very low opinion of Kolchak. After a visit to Omsk in July 1919, Ambassador Morris wrote Secretary of State Robert Lansing, "Admiral Kolchak is, in my judgment, an honest and courageous man of very limited experience in public affairs, of narrow views and small administrative ability. He is a dictator in name but exercises little influence [...] He has no military knowledge or experience." Morris was also annoyed to be presented with a "laundry list" of essential requirements that included 600,000 pairs of boots, 400,000 rifles, 500 million cartridges and many other items at a cost of over $250,000,000 (Saul, *War and Revolution*, 396–97).

[7] Two successful ventures of the American Red Cross in Siberia received much publicity: the organization and staffing in Manchuria of a white-painted "typhus train" that made visits along the Trans-Siberian road, and the care and shelter provided to the "Petrograd Children's Colony" that was rescued by the Czechoslovak Legion and turned over to the Red Cross. After temporary lodging in the vicinity of Vladivostok, the children were repatriated on a refitted Japanese freighter by way of the United States through Finland to their homes in 1921.

they represented among Siberians of the worst classes, and that mainly they wore German names and sported German manners. Several people told my husband it was largely this group who had created the prejudice against the American Allies by their pretensions and brutalities, which real Americans were deploring or trying to fight.[8]

Now and again one heard wild talk among the Russians in Vladivostok, of the possibility of an uprising and the massacre of all foreigners, except the Japanese, who were obsequious and smooth, always vastly polite, and who behaved toward the Russians with circumspection and tact amounting to genius.

After two days in Vladivostok my husband left for the front, and as he was starting he had occasion to test the temper of the people. A Polish military doctor pushed into the line of people who were waiting for tickets in the station, and took the place ahead of Cantacuzène. The latter at once protested energetically, and after some language the man stepped out of the way, only to shove himself into the line again just behind my husband. This was not tolerated of course by the crowd who, roused by the second attempt at usurping a good place, battered the culprit about a bit. He humbly consented to go down to the end of the line, whereupon patience returned as if by magic to the little group of Russians who had been waiting for their tickets so quietly before the incident.

The train was delayed two days in Vladivostok after it was loaded, by what were announced as "bandit disorders ahead." No one seemed to be able to offer a clearer explanation of the immobility, and, with an indifference characteristic of the times and place, the passengers tolerated waiting without much protest. Rumors announced Omsk was being evacuated; but no one believed it. It had been too frequently said before to be treated as serious news. They started at last. As far as Irkutsk the Trans-Siberian road was well guarded, and quite well ordered. It ran through Semenov's province, and one had glimpses of capable discipline everywhere in the country commanded by him.[9] It seems he exacted respect for his army, and that the church should be honored, too, and through all this large tract the villages looked fairly prosperous and the prices of necessities were comparatively lower than elsewhere. There were rich pastures, and on them cattle, sometimes rather unexpectedly fine animals were to be seen, and one heard there were rich mines of coal and metals in this province, even gold in large quantities.

For a somewhat romanticized account, see Jane Swan, *The Lost Children: A Russian Odyssey* (Carlisle, PA: South Mountain Press, 1989).

[8] Other sources are much more favorable to the Y. Its mission was primarily to support and assist the American Expeditionary Force and the Czechoslovak Legion. See, for example, Edward T. Heald, *Witness to Revolution: Letters from Russia 1916–1919*, edited by James B. Gidney (Kent, OH: Kent University Press, 1972).

[9] The author is basing her account on her husband's personal impressions on the scene. Semenov's discipline was produced at a price, much loss of life. Heald describes a scene of Bolshevik captives locked in box cars and starved to death by Semenov. Ibid., 252.

While on the road, among other savory bits of gossip, it was said that the Czech General Gajda had been paid 75,000 francs to leave the country, as he was giving much trouble. He had accepted the proposition, left Omsk for Vladivostok, and, reaching the latter city, decided to remain on his train and bargain further. He wasn't very successful at it, and (from "pique" perhaps) he then headed the upheaval which shook political conditions at the port, and which puzzled those who looked on from far away. When our officers reached Irkutsk they were told officially of the evacuation of Omsk, and there the train passengers were sorted out. Only people actually going forward on government or army business were allowed to continue their travel; the others were kept at Irkutsk. From this city to Omsk was another week on the train.

The cities seemed large and rich through this district in ordinary times. Now they were overcrowded, and gave the impression of possessing quantities of inhabitants who, living in box cars all along the railroad, and around the stations, had only such comfort of fuel, food, and clothing as they could manage to gather by their own means, fair or foul. The cities' ancient commerce was being strangled—clothes, provisions, and transportation were frightfully needed. Often there were thirty or more people living in one car, and the small stove in the center burned those who were near and left such as were out of range to freeze. The car inhabitants ran out for wood, and brought back in triumph whatever was handy: ties from the roadbed, broken boards from the snow-shields put up to protect the line, rough, broken bits of cars or houses, also.

Food was accidental and very short always. Anything eatable could command fabulous prices. The trains moved with difficulty on the congested rails, where complications were vastly increased by the constant changing of the commands along the road. The seizing of locomotives by a powerful factor was terrible [sic?]; and the Czechoslovaks had made holding up the outgoing army trains, and also the retreating refugee trains, one of their chief occupations and sports.[10] They had constantly hindered the possible rapidity with which our troops could be carried forward and the efficiency with which evacuation of the civilian population could be accomplished. There is much illness among the city inhabitants, and especially illness reigns in these floating crowds along the Trans-Siberian road.

The train on which my husband was seemed clean, however, and possessed a fair supply of food sold at fabulous prices. It was a train used by the foreign missions usually, and was the best to be found. The management of this train and of the road

---

[10] Though receiving some assistance from the Japanese and American forces, the Czechoslovak Legion, some 60,000 strong, was scattered along the Trans-Siberian and left much to its own devices. All the legion wanted to do was get out of Siberia, hence taking control of transportation whenever it could. Evacuation began in August 1918 but consisted only of a hospital ship with sick and wounded, and was completed two years later. It is often referred to as the Czech Legion since all but about 10% were Czech, the rest Slovak and German. See David Bullock, *The Czech Legion, 1914–20* (New York: Oxford Osprey Press, 2009). Other, smaller units served on the Western and Italian Fronts.

seemed fair, but the occupants were kept constantly excited by the reports of there being bandits ahead, who would probably stop further progress.

Approaching Omsk one met many a train of poor, hopeless, helpless refugees; who, with pinched, sad faces and emaciated bodies, moved in a great stream from their small homes at Omsk backward toward Irkutsk.[11] It had been long days, and weeks, and months, since these people had known the taste of good food or had felt real comfort; and as one saw misery in so many pairs of eyes, one registered a vow to help them with all one's possibilities. In vain trying, however, unless one goes beyond the frontiers for the help. Siberia is too worn out. Presently, when Omsk was reached, came "official" news of the evacuation taking place, and the English officers talked of the dangers which all would soon be running in Omsk and its environs—let alone those of the firing line.

At Omsk no food, no comforts; complete congestion, while the price of living was so appalling one bought nothing. And there was nothing to be found, really, in the shops. The single track of the Trans-Siberian road had often in its history played tricks on us Russians. Now in the dire need of evacuation time, everybody did his best, but the Czechs were more experienced, better armed, and stronger and they carried out terrible raids on trains and travelers. Immediately on his arrival Cantacuzène reported to Kolchak. An appointment was made for early the following morning—and the evening was free to unpack, settle, and look around. The hotel was horrid—could give only an ill-kept room ten by twelve feet with almost no furniture, and that broken and dirty. The whole on the "Grasnaia ulitza" (dirty street) a most becoming appropriate name. One hoped and prayed not to stay long in Omsk!

The interview with Kolchak made a great impression on my husband. The admiral was finishing his coffee, while looking out of the window, and he put Cantacuzène down opposite him. He was uncommonly nice to one whom he felt to be understanding, perhaps, of his habits and life. He complained of the Allies, also of the Bolsheviks, who were fighting with extra "punch" just then.

The reds had put their Chinese mercenary troops in the front lines of the Bolshevik army, had promised to let them rush through our loyal lines, and then give them a rest and some recreation among their own people. All this was a great incentive, naturally, to move forward. The looting, the murders, and torturing counted for little therefore as compared with the asset of pushing out of Siberia and carrying the madness into the Chinese Republic. If this policy succeeds—God knows what may occur! Kolchak said he wished to appeal to America, that by his clamorings he had hoped to bring help in material forms at least: food, clothes, medicines, ammunitions, and arms. "It will help the Americans themselves to aid us," he announced, "for Bolshevism is the whole world's enemy; and especially that of a democracy such as

---

[11] The main rail points on the Trans-Siberian behind (east of) Omsk and Kolchak's headquarters were, in order, Irkutsk, Chita, Harbin, and Vladivostok, all under different and varying control.

the American Government is. The necessity of the civilized world hanging together as against red doctrines is obvious."

Kolchak soon had another caller come for orders, and my husband had time to look about. The Admiral lived in a tiny house, quite unpretentious in its arrangements, and only the two sentinels at the door marked it, or suggested his rank. The "supreme commander" had no visible servants besides his "striker," who waited on him without the least ceremony or formality. Not a sign of any luxury. His work hours were from 10 A.M. to 4 the next morning, and all day long he bore the intense strain of people constantly coming and going for orders or consultation. Never a moment to himself did he take. He lived quietly with his aides-de-camp, of whom he had several on duty.

Personally he gave an impression of enormous strength as one met him, or as he sat talking at his desk, leaning forward slightly in his intensity. The rather large square head, face, and shoulders impressed one with the man's complete reliability. The eyes and hands were remarkably fine. Though impulsive and quick in manner and articulation, he could be very silent, and was so while listening. He had great magnetism—all the qualities and defects, in fact, of a man who is *very* big: honest, loyal, patriotic, with not the least desire to save himself from trouble, danger, or responsibility. Always ready to die, and asking nothing but to go on fighting Bolsheviks until the end—either his own end or theirs. It was his one ambition and policy.

The men around Kolchak were those whom he had found on the spot, or those chosen and sent to him by others. They also were willing to go and join in his effort, living in danger and discomfort. There were six of these men more or less prominent, who were Vologodsky, Smirnov, Sukin, Gandzhin, Pepelaiev, Tretiakov.[12] The first of these held the title of President of the Council of Ministers, was a "social-revolutionary" Siberian, an ex-lawyer of Tomsk, aged about fifty and was considered honest. He had the disadvantage of being more of a talker and less efficient than would be desirable in times like these. Sukin, who was the representative of Sazonov near Kolchak and Acting Foreign Minister, was clever, though somewhat too arrogant to be popular: and he was also accused by many of being unscrupulous. He was very pro-American.

Smirnov, Minister of Marine, was an honest man, a professional seaman, loyally devoted to Kolchak, with no interest in politics at all and no special following. Gandzhin, Minister of War, had not been a success as commander of an army, and seemed a vague but amiable quantity who left those under him to do as they pleased. Tretiakov [?], a product of civilized life in Moscow and Paris, as Minister of Commerce, played an effaced role, but was considered to have brilliant possibilities for the future. He was handsome, accomplished, and aged but thirty years or so. Pepelaiev, also a Siberian, was fairly popular and represented a very liberal element

---

[12] Judging by available sources, none of these had any reputation for administrative competence, nor much of a following. Tretiakov, "prime minster," had the distinction of being executed, along with Kolchak, in February 1920.

in the Cabinet. He seemed intelligent and to trust Kolchak sincerely, also to be a man of strength and honesty of purpose, though of small experience in governing. He had had good training, however, in the old Siberian "chamber" or Zemstvos, and he impressed one as a man capable of development.

Around these principals were large groups of people, intriguing, advising, gambling in sensational news. Most of them had little to do, and as time hung on their hands they got into all sorts of mischief. It was hard to tell who was with and who was against the government in this crowd, and one saw about each foreign mission a small group of ne'er-do-wells, who watched rivals and reported or advised, always disadvantageously, both the foreigners and the Russian Ministers. Every one was hard put to it for the wherewithal to live in those times when prices soared, and there were many makeshifts, some of which were rather tragic to watch. The ever-present feeling of the morrow's fate being impossible to foresee gave a devil-may-care attitude to the general mentality, and among Russians and foreigners moral standards were low, and any form of excitement or distraction was very welcome. There were constant parties in society where men and women played petits chevaux or other games till dawn, because they could not walk home in the dark for fear of attack and theft, or murder even. Every one had faced the emergency of flight or of death frequently, every one might do so again at any moment. Great courage was shown, but meantime: "What can we do but try to forget our troubles and live as best we can?"

After a few such evenings one wearied of their empty noise, and even a dirty hotel room of a size less comfortable than was known elsewhere seemed a haven of rest and independence. On the bed a sleeping bag made for the front seemed a refuge, since it was uninhabited by any of the vermin found in the bed, and was warm and cozy besides—qualities greatly to be appreciated.

Admiral Kolchak was altogether wonderful. Quite fearless and unselfish, he spent frequently a few days at the front, inspiring the troops and helping the officers and men with advice and example, always simple and utterly brave. Then he returned to Omsk, and patiently worked through the heavy length of days and nights, explaining or devising the solution of each new puzzle which came up. He was faithful and patient in the face of deceptive Allies, who now and then revived his hopes by a promise flung across the seas, but who always followed these by long silences with no action whatever. Kolchak stood between the devil Bolshevism, on the one hand, and the deep sea of rising discouragement and misery about him, on the other. He fought intrigues and poverty, famine and propaganda, reactionaries and radicals, while hoping against hope for recognition and relief from without and for calm about him. Recognition by his "allies" would have meant a new strength to fight the contradictory elements at home, relief would have minimized the sufferings of the needy refugees and population, stamped out illness and dismal misery, aiding the general morale, and thus giving him arguments with which to quiet complaints.[13]

But nothing came—save smooth words from missions sent to investigate, and one or two promises in writing, which, having warmed the brave man's heart, fell to dust and emptiness, like the ashes of a fire burnt out. The smooth and gentle Japanese; the noisy Cossacks shouting for an arrogant stand; the radicals fearing but resisting these, all threatened periodically to upset the government. Then the needs of Chinese and other mercenaries pressing on us, well-fed and officered largely by Germans, committing worse crimes, leaving worse and more complete destruction, than did "Attila of Hundom." When he went forward there was all the misery of nakedness and famine to repair; when he moved back, all the frightful complications of caring for thousands of refugees, who retreated with the army in terror of tortures unprintable.

Holding all the reins, making the whole effort, he faced representatives of Allies who knew his difficulties, yet made no signs of stretching out a hand. Small wonder the man was worn to a point where those who watched and felt his greatness noted with anxiety how ill he looked, and how strained his nerves were becoming.

An uprising led by a Czech in Vladivostok was Allies' work; troubles between "non-interfering" American armies and rebel Cossack brigands, who were supposedly in the pay of a second ally, occurred. Impossible situations and complaints were due to a fourth ally's pretensions. There was lack of ammunition while trains of arms and food were held up by the Czechs, who wanted locomotives to hasten their own retreat toward the Eastern port of embarkation; train-loads of civilian refugees were held up also in the Omsk evacuation. A general massacre was feared since the Czechs seized locomotives to double the speed of their own departure. It was hideous, inhuman! Yet, instead of the deep fury most men have felt, this eminent hero, in making a short public speech, had said quietly one day, with a wan smile: "The Allies' representatives are kind to me, and we get on excellently together. I hope this is a sign that the Allies themselves like us, and mean to stand with us." That occurred some time ago, and things have gone from bad to worse; but there was no record of bitter utterances by Admiral Kolchak. Even in desperate straits he went on fighting, too busy to talk, but showing undiminished courage, and he inspired enthusiasm in those who saw him act.

My husband received an order to travel in a car belonging to the train of the Minister of War. There was talk of not evacuating the government from Omsk almost to the last moment before its departure, and the civilians and the military were in a real panic over their danger. Kolchak himself was perfectly calm. He didn't want to leave, but there was no chance of defending Omsk successfully, and he gave way to the situation's exigencies. Around Kolchak Janin from France wanted to occupy himself exclusively with the Czechs and Poles, while Knox of England wanted to mix into and direct all our Admiral's orders, and because he was not obeyed he suddenly left

---

[13] The Kolchak government was recognized by France and Great Britain.

in hasty annoyance.[14] There was no American momentarily in the entourage of the leader. The little Japanese envoy stayed till the very last, and had been most efficient and helpful, with an excellent, respectful attitude toward Kolchak.

Once their compatriots' trains had passed, the Czechs refused to guard the railroads. They had also stolen most of the material we Russians had. They were comparatively well armed, while their uniforms had taken the last supplies of Russian cloth; also our final reserves of equipment, guns, and horses has gone to them. No wonder they had made our people hate them for their selfishness and treachery! Semenov, who was headstrong and with no thought of what his acts might lead to, was so furious with their actions he had stopped the Czech troop trains, one after another, as they went through the province under his command and held them up until all stolen goods were handed over to him. He even turned one whole battery of artillery back to Irkutsk.

In leaving Omsk it was almost impossible to find a place in which to travel, primarily because nearly all first- and second-class cars were seized by the Czechs for their own use, while only the third-class and the boxcars were left for our Russians. Even the hospitals found it impossible to get good cars, or to transport their wounded because of this arbitrary action on the Czechs' part. The wounded and the typhus patients were largely left behind in the wards for lack of transportation, but as many as possible of the doctors and nurses were removed, because the Bolsheviks were known to show special cruelty in torturing and martyrizing [sic] these, while it was supposed the sick and wounded might be spared. This turned out not to be the case, however, and soon news came to the retreating army that all the poor ill and wounded had been frightfully ill-treated first and then murdered. Officers found by the Bolsheviks wounded on the battlefields were also invariably subjected to terrible tortures and then killed.

For days, the Omsk people were packing and being moved eastward with the best of order, rapidity, and a show of discipline quite remarkable under the circumstances. On the last day a panic began, and grew, and then things became more difficult to handle. Confusion reigned. It was impossible to find the car places indicated; every train was congested, and instead of a berth with the Janin party, my husband

---

[14] General Maurice Janin (1862–1946) was mainly in charge of advising the Czechoslovak Legion of over 60,000 and in securing its removal from Siberia to fight on the Western Front. By September 1919, however, that mission shifted from activity in the war to being the main army of the new Czechoslovak republic and part of the French strategy of developing along with Poland a "cordon sanitaire between Soviet Russia and Germany. Naturally he was anxious to get the legion out of Siberia as soon as possible. By this time the forces directly under Kolchak's control numbered less than 50,000.

"Knox" is Major General Alfred Knox (1870–1964) who served as chief of the British military mission in Russia during the war and revolution but had left that position by 1918. He subsequently was a long-time Tory member of the House of Commons (1924–45) and known for his efforts to build up the British army vis-a-vis either Germany or Russia in the 1930s.

found himself, after various troubles, assigned to a car which was being arranged for some foreigners.

Just before they left Omsk an airplane fell, disabled, containing a Bolshevik "commissioner" and a young aviator; both living. They were at once surrounded and the "commissioner" was shot. The aviator was questioned as to what was happening in the red country. He said that all officers who, like himself, had been left in Bolshevik country had been forcibly mobilized at the point of the bayonet. Those with families saw their wives and children taken as hostages and shot on the first sign of the husbands' or fathers' abandoning the Bolsheviks' firing line. Those who, like himself, had no relations left, saw fifteen of their comrades locked up every time they flew, and in case of an accident which, like the present one, meant he would not return, all those fifteen prisoners would be shot or tortured.

The case of General R. was one which confirmed this young man's tale. R. had been made chief-of-staff on one of the Bolshevik fronts soon after he was seized in Moscow, while his wife and daughter were put in the hands of a young Hungarian war-prisoner Bolshevist commissioner in a small town near the capital. After some months of service R. decided that not even to save the lives of his dear ones should he go on fighting with the Bolsheviks, and that he must do his duty and make an attempt to get across to Kolchak's lines. He found a faithful messenger to carry a warning to his wife advising her to try to escape also and join him. By good chance the Hungarian commissioner was in love with R.'s daughter, so discipline had been somewhat slackened around the women. They did manage to escape, in old peasant garments, just before the sentence passed on them could be executed, because the infatuated Hungarian had removed the guard from around their quarters. Making their way first on foot, then by springless peasant carts, they traveled from Moscow till they found General R. back of Kolchak's lines. There were hundreds of poor officers less fortunate than the general was, who were obliged to leave their friends back beyond the Bolshevik frontiers, from where no sign had come to them for a year or more. Certainly it was a dreadful situation!

Leaving Omsk a Monday morning about eighteen hours late on the schedule of departure, my husband's heavy train moved back toward Irkutsk. The trip took a week, though the foreigners' train had right of way. From everybody complaints were heard (beginning with the head manager of the road and running down to the last small train official) of the Czechs' arrogance, selfish pretensions, and brutality.

Warned of the probable attacks on trains by robbers and brigands with Bolshevik tendencies, our men were considerably bothered by anxiety. As this load was of foreign Allies an armored train was run ahead for parts of the trip, to protect the guests. In the province of Krasnoyarsk a Bolshevik proclamation fell into the hands of the secret service and was shown to my husband. In view of the pretensions of the friends of Bolshevism in the United States (who claim the reds are a popular and democratic party) it may be interesting to quote. This paper appealed to the people to stop fighting, and in proclaiming the anti-Bolshevik leaders traitors to their country it said that there had just been an election of the old Grand Duke Nikolai Nikolaevich in Moscow, who was consequently now the actual Emperor of Russia with Lenin as his Prime Minister and Trotsky at the Imperial war office; also that all those who were loyal Russians must attack the trains of troops belonging to Kolchak the democrat. The men who were distributing this document among the peasants carried about with them the imperial standard (or flag) and sang the imperial anthem. They said the new Emperor had all his ancient powers and privileges again!

The news also came by telegram, that the Bolsheviks had attacked Omsk with their Chinese mercenaries in the first line, these being promised ten thousand rubles apiece for taking the city, and the hope being held out to them that they were on the last lap of their campaigning and would be allowed to go home to China once Siberia was won for the reds. It was really enough to make decent men tremble. Imagine the yellow races gone mad with Sovietist theories![15]

On their arrival at Irkutsk the group Cantacuzène was with found everything up in the air. News of the uprising under the Czech General Gajda at Vladivostok had just arrived, and in Irkutsk itself a new outbreak of the "social revolutionaries" was just stopped by the arrest of the disorderly men who instigated it. The Czechs added to the confusion by handing in an ultimatum saying that they would like to be transported to their own home, or else the Kolchak regime must be overthrown and a social-revolutionary government be established in its place, under their supervision and protection! The transportation of the Czechs was not in Kolchak's hands, as the whole question of the duty and comfort of these Allies was in the hands of General Janin, high commissioner for France, and the rest of his foreign colleagues.

One had an impression through all the noise and agitation of imminent changes. It seemed impossible for any man, whatever his genius, to handle the situation of a serious retreat, with no provisions of arms and munitions, food or clothing, and with refugees crowding the land in waves. Various political parties were in opposition, too, and all the foreigners were intriguing and struggling each for supremacy. Some even used treacherous methods to seize the power. With disorder on the one railroad, occasioned by the strain of evacuating an army plus the civilian populations, with the arbitrary commandeering of trains by the Czechs for those in whom they felt interested, and adding to all this typhus, famine, cold, and cutthroat prices—one can present to one's imagination the tableau of the trip from Omsk to Irkutsk in early December 1919.

My husband personally helped to bury eighteen bodies drawn from a refugees' boxcar near his own on the road, and he had occasion to see what the horrors of life were for the women and children, crowded promiscuously into these cars, thirty or forty in each. They were without fuel, though forests all around were plentiful, but

---

[15] There is no evidence to support the substantial Bolshevik use of Chinese mercenaries in Siberia; perhaps Tatars?

beyond reach for poor refugees, the snow being more than six feet deep and impassable along the Trans-Siberian. Cars were so dirty, and filled with vermin, that disinfection and burning could be the only remedy. Nevertheless, the people lived in them, minus everything and with no possibility of either cleaning or airing their quarters. Soap and medicines were totally lacking, and there was no straw to sleep on. The latter was nowhere to be found, even at the price of its weight in gold, had gold been producible. Scenes one must see to believe in their full extent of misery, and which were very strange in this century of comfort, were being enacted everywhere.

From Irkutsk to Vladivostok was a much easier trip. One was farther from the front and minus the refugees, whose trains were slower than the train my husband had taken. One was struck by the extremely good discipline of troops seen everywhere under the rule of Ataman Semenov, head of the Cossacks. The line itself was guarded by Japanese and American troops posted alternately along the route. My husband had met Semenov on the western front in 1915, when the latter was there as a very young officer, and Cantacuzène was greatly interested in the visible signs of his development. He sent his uncle (also General Semenov, and old schoolmate of my husband) to meet the train at the station of Chita (capital of Zabaikal province, and residence of the Ataman). The general said that his nephew's position was difficult politically, but that they meant to fight to the last extremity, and to help Kolchak beat the Bolsheviks. He asked too for aid from the Americans, through my husband's mission, to keep our people alive. On the road between Harbin and Vladivostok was an American engineer, Major C———, who having his private car, gave Cantacuzène the first good meal eaten by him in six weeks. The host was one of John S. [sic] Stevens's engineers and a member of the splendid company of Americans doing all possible to help run the Trans-Siberian under great difficulties.[16] Really an admirable and helpful work, carried out in the finest spirit!

Arrival in Vladivostok at 5 a.m. The station had been bombarded and was pretty well battered and knocked to pieces, during the Gajda insurrection, a few days before my husband reached the city.[17] In Vladivostok Cantacuzène heard the following

---

[16] John F. Stevens (1853–1933) was a noted American railroad builder, best known for his supervision of the construction of the Panama Canal. In 1917 he headed an American railroad inspection mission to Russia, a complementary delegation to that of Elihu Root's. He returned in 1918 to direct the Russian Railway Service Corps (1918–23), mainly in Manchuria along the Chinese Eastern Railway, the "short cut" line of the Trans Siberian across that region of China.

[17] Born as Rudolf Geidl in the Dalmatian province of Austria-Hungary, Radola Gajda (1892–1948) served in the Balkan Wars and World War I in the Austro-Hungarian army and was taken prisoner by the Russians in 1915. He joined the Czechoslovak Legion in January 1917, distinguishing himself in the capture of Perm in December 1918 before leading the unsuccessful revolt in November 1919 in Vladivostok against Kolchak. Subsequently, he left Siberia and was a general in the Czechoslovak army in the 1920s and became involved in pro-fascist but anti-Nazi politics as an advocate of war over Sudetenland. In the 1940s he suffered under Soviet arrest and imprisonment and died soon after his release.

details of this bloody intrigue of the Czech adventurer, who had been honored by a command and a military title in our All-Russian army and had turned traitor to his benefactor, Kolchak.

A proclamation was posted by Czechs on November 16, declaring the regime of Kolchak intolerable, and asking that the Czechs be immediately repatriated to Czechoslovakia, or receive full powers to act in Siberia. This proclamation was posted widely in Vladivostok; also it was published in whole, or in part, by the Vladivostok newspapers. Active recruiting by General Gajda—social-revolutionary elements of soldiers offered to join his cause in an armed uprising against the Kolchak government... He was upheld by about two thousand five hundred men. The Czechs did not rally around their leader, who postponed action for twenty-four hours because of a thunderstorm.

A Siberian constituent directorate was formed, with Yakushov, prominent in the pre-Kolchak regime, as a leader, with General Gajda as the active military commander. A zemstvo flag (green, red, and white) was hoisted over Gajda's train in the railway yards, about a quarter of a mile from the railway station. General Gajda opened recruiting stations near his train, and attempted enrolling both soldiers and civilians. Taking the oath, the recruits were given a rifle and an overcoat; also epaulets of ribbons of green and white. Major [Benjamin] Johnson, commanding the International Military Police, visited the scene, and at that time no bloodshed was expected by Gajda's forces. It was believed that such a response would come to the raising of the "banner of revolution" that overwhelming forces would occupy the railway station, also that throughout the city there would be an uprising of workmen.

On Monday there was a short sharp burst of rifle-firing in the railway yards, between the station and a group of trains which included Gajda's own special and luxurious one, but nothing occurred yet. The story of who fired the first shot is rather vague, but the tale most credited was about two Czech officers, who, with a few men from Gajda's train, had started toward the railway station to look over the ground with a view to bringing a body of men to replace those the All-Russian government kept there for public safety.

After this first struggle the whole thing crystalized at once. General firing began, coupled with rushes of small bodies of soldiers to occupy points of vantage. Severe fighting followed, and continued until after nightfall. At nightfall the government forces held possession of the station, but Gajda's men drove them out and occupied the station finally, holding it till Tuesday morning. Gajda's chief-of-staff stated that six men were killed and twenty were wounded in taking the station.

Tuesday morning Gajda's chief-of-staff was quoted as saying to an officer who had gone into the station to get some women away from the danger: "The game is up and we'll take our medicine." Six men were sent from the railway station by Gajda to go to Czech headquarters and ask that Czech forces come to his assistance. (This story was told by one of Gajda's men, wounded and being given medical treatment by the Canadian Red Cross.) The Czech troops held aloof, however, and did not go to the assistance of Gajda.

Some time between two and five o'clock on Tuesday morning Gajda left the railway station. He was captured about five, on the hill above the yards, was marched on foot from the point of capture, up Aleutskaya Street, to the Russian Staff headquarters under armed guard. He had been wounded in the foot, but not seriously. His chief-of-staff was also captured and taken to Russian headquarters. General Gajda had been given three days to leave, and it was reported he would leave by steamer that week. He had been turned over by the Russians to the custody of the Czech staff.

A certain number of deserters from the government army who joined Gajda were shot in the railway station and vicinity, on being captured by loyal troops, and their fate was an excellent example to others of their type.[18] By dawn Tuesday morning the fighting was virtually ended and government forces were in entire control of the city, so that there was no difficulty in bringing the wounded from the station and yards. This work continued all day. Indications on Tuesday night were that Vladivostok would be normal Wednesday and that banks and business houses would be opened. All banks and virtually all business houses in Vladivostok had been closed since Monday—the streets unusually quiet. There were no signs of disorder, and the police reported there had been no accidents, no lootings, and no murders during the last three eventful days.

Embarking again at Vladivostok seemed a tragedy, and to leave all the danger behind one, and go back to comfort and safety, a crime. So many came to ask some slight service of the departing group—would some man going toward plenty sell a suit of clothes, a leather vest, or a pair of boots? Were there any underclothes or old handkerchiefs to be had for the hospitals—where people died for lack of everything? Almost all the travelers gave of their slender stores to the still poorer creatures who remained behind. Letters were sent by hand to many a friend or relation living in safe countries, with appeals for help—food, provisions, warm clothes, everything so frightfully needed. Sailing brought a lump into one's throat—to leave one's country (even to help it) in the depths of misery made one heart-sick; yet there was a mission to be accomplished, possible aid to be obtained, and my husband was the chosen messenger.

His trip back was interrupted for a few days in Japan—waiting for a steamer and getting the usual papers viséd. It was there the news reached Cantacuzène of the change of government and of the new ministry, created on more radical lines with Pepelaiev at its head. The Japanese papers announced with an innocent air: It is reported from authentic sources that all the misunderstandings which were brought about by the Czechoslovak memorandum are considered at an end, and that the most friendly relations exist between the Russian people and the Czechoslovak representatives.

---

[18] Unfortunately, this was a common occurrence during the Russian Civil War in Siberia.

Two weeks later, having landed in New York, the tragic appeal of Kolchak (perhaps his last to the Allies?) appeared in the daily papers. It said that the Czechoslovaks had held up his ammunition trains, sacrificing his last chance of standing against the Bolsheviks before Irkutsk, also that the same group of Allies had held up the troop trains and those with refugees, in their retreat, until one hundred and twenty sections of our army's transportation (one hundred and twenty thousand soldiers with their poor arms and baggage) had been lost to us; captured and victimized by their hideous opponents. The brave admiral still uttered no invectives against either the Bolsheviks or the dastardly ally who was throwing him into the enemy's hands. He merely stated the facts and called on the Allied nations to remonstrate with the Czechs—putting their treachery on record for the world to judge.

By the irony of fate, or perhaps with evil intent, this message occupied only a corner of the newspapers and was in small print, while in large type and with vivid head-lines stood out the bitter facts of the army and its commander cut off from their base—Kolchak the brave caught in a trap, and in a situation where it would seem he and the heroes of his army must have been surrounded and crushed. No further news for days, and the silence causes deep mourning in every loyal Russian heart. If these men escape, it will be a very miracle of providential succor. Heaven looking down on such courage and such patience might show pity where humanity has remained cold. Not all humanity, however; for among the letters brought to me by my husband from Siberia is one from a phlegmatic British officer, Colonel Y——, and he said:

> The situation is most serious, owing to the appalling increase of refugees—men, women, and children from Ekaterinburg, Ufa, Perm, the Ural, and now from Omsk—thousands with hardly a stitch on, and in nearly every case what garments exist are made of cotton—with the severe weather already set in! They come in trains, on top of trains, in carts, and on foot, destitute, without money or food. People living in warm houses can't possibly realize what this winter will be for the poor people of this country (Siberia). Remember there is nothing to buy in the way of clothing, and besides the ruble has dropped till it is three hundred and fifty to the dollar. It isn't so bad for the person who has dollars to buy rubles with, but you must understand what it means to the Russian, who, being paid in rubles at the old rate, yet has to buy food and fuel with prices sky high, or who lacks money altogether.
>
> On top of this, disease is rife and there are no medicines. The great heart-rending cry is "Oh, for some warm clothing"—for soldiers, warm underclothes and shirts and socks. For women, outer garments, underclothes, in fact everything; children, too, anything to warm freezing bodies. Thousands of lives depend on these, so please do what you can for the sake of humanity! No other form of propaganda can do so much for the prestige of cilization as this. Send wools, flannels. Any materials sent can be made up

in our workrooms. We will have the women make their garments, sewing or knitting. It would do your heart goos to see how grateful these Russians can be, and are, for what has been done! Russia moans and cries out to the world. She is a living body, and her tortures cannot be looked upon in cold blood as extraordinary. Never before has the world witnessed such an experience in social evolution. Russia is living and every pore in her body is shedding blood.

In spite of this suffering, our people are so numerous, our land has such possibilities of recuperation, our Slav race is so powerful, that Russia is far from conquered. Heroic men are fighting, and will go on fighting; and one may still count on the future, however black the present is. Russia has been overrun with Tatars and with Turks, with Swedes and Frenchmen before, yet it was our people who defeated Mustapha and the brilliant Charles, even as they did Napoleon. Last August Kolchak called on his allies for help, saying if arms and ammunition did not come, he must retreat. He stood at the Volga then. Now at Irkutsk he stands. The Bolsheviks are already shouting their victory over the world at large. Kolchak, knowing no one will hear, has ceased to call. But he hasn't ceased fighting; and neither have some others. Our driven armies have turned and won before in history; always they have won alone against great odds. So it will be now; one must have faith and hope and even charity, all of which are Russian qualities. With our national patience and insurmountable courage we have sometimes worked miracles in the world's history. Today Russia's friends, for whom she has offered her life, seem to have deserted her and all is dark. We must believe that Russia's crucifixion will save the world, and her resurrection, following soon, shall prove that her great sacrifice was not in vain!

IX
Daughters of Russia

Down through the centuries the Russian woman's life has always been in part an Oriental one. The country has been a meeting ground of East and West, and until great Peter's time, our women's role was mainly in the "terem," and they took no part in outside or social life. There were exceptions to the rule, of course. Olga, grandmother of St. Vladimir of Kiev, about the year 955 A.D., went on a trip to Byzantium and brought back to her home country its first knowledge of Christianity, which she had accepted. Later in 1469, a Byzantine Princess came to Moscow as wife of Czar Ivan III, and she brought with her scholars, scientists, and artists. This Czarina Sophia was the center of Russia's intellectual life while her husband's reign lasted. Martha of Novgorod led a rebellion against Ivan the Terrible during this same reign.

A few other feminine names appear in Russian history, but generally speaking all women lived tranquilly, behind closed doors and trellised windows, till the end of the seventeenth century. In the Kremlin palace at Moscow, the ancient Czarinas' apartment still exists—unless the Bolsheviks have destroyed it—arranged as it was in olden times. The rooms are low and vaulted, with deep, small windows placed high in the walls, from which one can look down on the great square below. There are vast colored stoves of valuable faience, and great splendor of decoration on lines recalling the Far East. The walls are colored much as Persian carpets usually are, with dark, brilliant contrasts. Dull gold and silver keep up this impression, as the eye wanders to heavy, wrought-metal chandeliers, candle-sticks, and icons, and to the nail-studded chests for jewels and for clothes which stand about.

One can visualize with little imagination the rich beauties of ancient days, dressed in heavy velvets and brocades, and in soft silks and cashmeres brought from India and China, sitting about at embroidery-frames, or doing other fragile work with lazy fingers, to pass the long hours away. They had slaves to do their bidding, also dancers, minstrels, and dwarfs to keep them amused, and the Great White Czar frequently visited them; but even so there must have been many a day when bondage weighed heavily, and they all faded young. Some women intrigued in politics through their influence over a powerful husband or a son, but in most respects the wives of great boyars—nobles—resembled our Czarinas in their futility.

Peter the Great changed this, as he did much else in Russia. He ordered the women out of their retirement and from national dress into French clothes. He gave

Western fêtes at court, and he made every one take part in his own boisterous fun. His wife, Catherine, a daughter of the people, was made his constant companion; went with him to his wars, and took a share in the work and play of his stirring life at home. When he died it was to her he left his crown, and she reigned for some years, Russia's first Empress in fact as well as in name. After her there was a series of them: Anna, the daughter of Peter's older brother, who was fat and vague, left no impression on our history;[1] Elizabeth, Peter's own daughter, followed and showed much of her father's temperament, doing a great deal that was fine and constructive in spite of her dissolute life.[2]

Last, but not least, greatest and most magnificent of all our sovereigns, the second Catherine reigned and was called "Emperor." Intellectual, virile, friend of half the philosophers of her epoch, her own letters unconsciously testify to her high instruction, broad cultivation, as well as to the vast range of her interests. Past master of diplomacy, she kept all Europe amazed at her feet, and by her military campaigns she added province after province to her domains. She led in her court's gaiety, invited artists, writers, players, soldiers, architects, musicians, and scientists to her capital. She gave Russia its finest collections, palaces, and public buildings; decorated its towns with monuments and parks; founded industries, planned cities, made a code of laws which were a wonder of the times.[3]

She created a university which is still the greatest in Russia and founded the Academy of Fine Arts, which even recently, until the revolution, ranked among the first in Europe. She chose for her ministers, admirals, and generals the most brilliant men of her empire, whether they were princes or peasants, and kept them in their places if she thought they served the country well, even when they dared to cross her own autocratic will. Her wars and her voyages, her fêtes and her loves, were many, and in her one existence she lived, twenty times over, the works, deeds, and emotions of an ordinary man. She reconstructed Russia and put it in touch with the outside world, and, in spite of certain vices, her brains and her high aims, with her glory, filled her own contemporaries—as they have posterity since—with admiration. One

---

[1] Empress Anna (1693–1740) was the daughter of Peter the Great's half-brother and co-ruler for the early part of his reign as Ivan V. Anna's reign was noted for the rise of German influence and the domination of her lover, Ernst Johann von Biron, but she continued to fund the Russian Academy of Sciences and other institutions founded by Peter the Great.

[2] Elizabeth Petrovna, who ruled from 1741 to 1761, is noted for reviving the Western momentum of her father, Peter the Great, engaging more in European wars, and continuing the legacy of aristocratic supremacy, as well as introducing into Russia the future Catherine the Great as the wife of her nephew, Peter III.

[3] Catherine the Great was a German princess with no blood relationship to previous rulers. She adapted well to her role as the wife of Peter III, was implicated in his murder, and became one of the most notable rulers of Europe during her long reign, 1763–96. She was also distinguished by her espousal of Enlightenment ideas and for the number of her lovers.

traveled over Russia a hundred years or more after she died, and one still found traces of this great personality in the farthest corners of its provinces. The two capitals, Moscow and St. Petersburg, bore her impress in all the best they held. One was forced to admit she was a superwoman, and that her country owed her memory deep gratitude for the work she expended on it and the love she gave her people, whom she truly understood. [See the portrait of Catherine the Great, figure 4 in the gallery of illustrations following p. 110.]

Catherine died in 1796, and since her time Russia's national life has changed little. Our women only needed to hold the place and powers this Empress had made for them, and society, in and around the court at least, remained most brilliant throughout the nineteenth century. The peasant woman's life, on the other hand, was narrow to the extremest limit, small and sad. She worked always, and had many children and much misery as her regular portion—this even after the emancipation of the serfs in 1863.

In the upper classes, on the contrary, there was an elite of women highly cultivated and most attractive. All through the last five reigns of the Romanovs St. Petersburg ranked high for its salons. There were also Russian women who made a great mark for themselves in art, in science, or in politics, while many cut creditable figures as secret diplomat agents, serving their government well in foreign capitals. Between these two extremes of aristocrat and peasant there were the "intelligentsia" and the "bourgeoisie." The first supplied brains of the best quality, which contributed to the country's development, but also from their group came our nihilists and other underfed and over-excited types. Those of the second category lived quiet, sheltered lives, on the contrary, and did little except to care for homes and families, read romances, eat sweets, and talk. It was they who kept the tradition of the "terem" alive to a certain extent. They grew fat early in life, and had neither ambition nor energy to shine. Whether in society or in their round of home duties they seemed always gentle, placid, and quite uninterested in what occurred outside. Mentally, morally, and materially they depended on their men to keep them going.[4]

When I reached Russia, in 1899, I found the life in St. Petersburg absorbing, and the women about me very new and strange in type, and exceedingly interesting. In my husband's family every one was most cosmopolitan, and I had no typical impressions there at all. My mother-in-law was French, and underscored the value of her own race on all occasions. She spent much of her time in Paris, and kept her frame of life on foreign lines. She had brought up her only daughter at home, and had then taken her to Paris with a French governess for the last polishing of instruction. I necessarily turned elsewhere than to our family circle for real Russian experiences.

I noticed at once the extreme vim and intense capacity for pleasure of St. Petersburg society, where the extraordinary wit and quickness of repartee, the immense culture, the knowledge of numerous languages, and the large variety of subjects discussed

---

[4] This passage is reminiscent of Ivan Goncharov's depiction of "superfluous men" of Russian society in his novel *Oblomov* (1858)—only these are "superfluous women."

were most striking. Conversations betrayed all this unconsciously, for there was not the slightest pose. There was a kindliness, too, not usually seen in social gatherings elsewhere, with a generosity toward one another and to a stranger in their midst which never failed. The most beautiful—and there were many handsome women—lacked the attitude of professional beauties.

Those who were rich wore Paris clothes with fine jewels, and had palaces where they gave balls and other splendid entertainments. They brought carloads of fresh flowers from the south of France for their cotillions, and fruits from the Caucasus for their supper tables, in spite of thermometers at thirty below zero. On the other hand, those who were poor were dressed by a seamstress at home, wore no ornaments, and lived in a flat, but they asked their friends to quiet evenings of music or of bridge, simply offering them a cup of tea with dignity.

Yet never was a difference made between the rich hostess and the poor; each could have and keep her success and her friends. All society would gladly go to the first one's party, then to that of the other, showing an equal pleasure. It seemed as if nothing counted to hold a place in St. Petersburg's charmed circle save intelligence, breeding, good taste, and a generally agreeable tone, with beauty as a secondary advantage. If good luck befell any one of the small smart set all her clan rejoiced, while if a sorrow came they wept and prayed together in simplest good feeling, each taking part in the other's trouble.

In general, these women seemed to me quite different from any I had known before, both in mentality and in looks. At first I could judge only their superficial aspects, but I was struck immediately by their easy-going unhurried ways. No fuss was made in welcoming a stranger. They had no "party manners," but went on quietly with the general conversation, letting me sit back or join in, whenever I felt like it. Rather casual they were, and some foreigners called them indifferent, but it was hardly that. It seemed to me only a sort of frankness. One began to feel at home while the chat progressed, as if they took one's personality and antecedents for granted. One was soon cordially accepted, and then gradually brought into an intimacy unknown elsewhere, made of close camaraderie and comprehension, with a complete lack of criticism.

Once I had indicated that I held certain broad principles in common with them, wide latitude was shown toward individual tastes and ways. No concession was ever demanded from my opinions, which were listened to with amiability and ready interest. About a dinner-table I found there were always so many varying views held on each subject which came up that the talk was most original and animated, and generally very amusing. During the season night after night we all sat up till morning for balls worthy of the name never ended till five or six o'clock, and seven or eight was the more frequent bedtime hour; yet no one looked fagged, or seemed dull, or ever wanted to go home. A very marked fact struck me: no two hostesses ever gave parties the same evening. There was always a little talk and arranging so every one could enjoy each pleasure as it came, and there were no apparent rivalries or feuds.

The court balls were wonderful—six or more given in the season, with the most magnificent palace in all Europe for their background. It was only Russian Czars who could place a party of three thousand people in a ballroom without crowding their guests, and who could seat this many at supper in another single hall. The imperial hothouses supplied flowers and huge palms, while the food, the music, and the uniforms were all so perfect they were impossible to outdo. The women managed to shine, however, in all the light and splendor of the scene. I discovered no one marked type of looks among them. Blondes with Scandinavian blood, whose ancestors had come into the country with Rurik and his Viking brothers; brunettes with Oriental blood, handed down by Tatar ancestors; tall and short, fat and thin they were. Well made, as a rule, they looked healthy but not athletic. Rarely noisy, but generally most cheerful company, I found my new compatriots especially interesting and attractive in facial expression. It was as if with a top layer of simplicity there burned beneath the surface vast possibilities of temperament and emotion, of strength and energy, and of serious brain power as well. They never had had to do anything yet, as they came down developing through the ages; but were it necessary, one felt these souls could and would make good.[5]

There was a world of sympathy and passion, with a capacity for joy and suffering which was intense, and which lurked always in the quiet, charming faces of Russia's upper-class women. By degrees, as I became more used to them, I noticed all this less; but whenever occasion presented itself the traits above mentioned came to the surface at once and played their part in our life. Through the years my admiration for these women grew, as each new turn in our fortunes showed them in a new light. I have never seen greater dignity than my Russian sisters showed, when occasionally they were under the stress of strong emotion. Whether in happiness or sorrow, their great sincerity of heart, intensity and brave directness, brought them up to the sublime; and always they escaped being awkward or melodramatic. One could approve the course they took or not, but one could not help being carried along with them in feeling, whether one wished it or whether one struggled against the current. No Westerner can realize till he has been among them the latent power of the Slav; neither can any Westerner resist the marvel of these rich natures, which are so soft, so strong, and always fresh and new, with their treasures of deep sentiment. This overflows in the music, art, and literature of our land.

If Russian parties are attractive, Russian life gets into the blood and makes all else seem tame, and I have yet to meet a foreigner who, having been for a time in the great empire, was not full of regret at leaving, and did not long to return.

At court functions, especially those where national dress was worn, the mere sight of the women was unforgettable. They looked like their own icons, with their

---

[5] This is a good portrait of Russia's prerevolutionary aristocratic society, apparently oblivious to the growing presence of a rapidly growing, poor and exploited working class in St. Petersburg, the center of this society, as it became the largest industrial center in the country.

high diadem-like "kakoshniki" of seed-pearls, set with great, barbarous, scintillating colored stones. Long lace veils hanging from the "kakoshniki," priceless heirlooms for the most part, covered the top and back of head and shoulders, so none of the hair showed, a remnant of the Orient, perhaps. An underdress of white satin, hanging straight, embroidered with seed-pearls or rich gold and silver, showed down the front of the figure; while the overdress of Renaissance brocade or embroidered velvet, though décolleté quite off the shoulders in court fashion, had heavy sleeves which hung in panels to the ground, making a straight sweeping line from the top. The train belonging to this overdress was always so long as to be quite hopelessly unmanageable as it swung out upon the floor. Usually heavily trimmed with fur (sable predominating in the room), these trains were embroidered exquisitely by the patient fingers of our cloistered nuns.

Old India or Persia furnished patterns. One, I remember, of pale rose velvet, was covered with great sheaves of Easter lilies in natural size and color, seemingly bound together with diamond chains; another chef d'oeuvre, of soft gray, had a complete peacock represented in all its glory, tail spread out upon the train, with the bird's narrow, graceful head and body climbing up the wearer's slender waist. The dowagers usually wore rich, plain velvets which, though made in Russia, resembled much those of the palmy days of Venice and Genoa in the early fifteenth century.

One rubbed one's eyes, weary from the riot of color and the flash of precious gems. They seemed a dream of fairy-land, those fêtes at court, and the classic beauty of the young Empress made her a perfect central figure in the gorgeous grouping round her. She had such height and carriage as fitted her for the splendid things she wore, and she loved to deck herself in cloth of gold or silver, studded and trimmed with jewels. She wore more of these than could any one else, yet she never seemed weighted down or overdressed. Physically she was the ideal sovereign, moving with great majesty or standing in statuesque pose among us. The beauty of her features and coloring was unmarred by the tragic expression which always lurked both in the large blue eyes and in the severe but well-drawn mouth. She rarely spoke, and always looked bored and intensely sad, but merely for its decorative quality her presence was beyond all praise, and one thinks of her as part of the historic tableaux now forever past and gone.[6]

In their homes the Russian women seemed to me at their best. On their country estates they led, till 1914, an active life, for the owner's wife always took charge of certain parts of the administration, besides attending to the vast household with its numerous departments—smoking the meats, preserving the vegetables and fruits, and making the native wines being the least of these duties. The woman managed the hothouses, the vegetable, fruit, and flower gardens; she attended to the barnyard, the dairy, and the splendid poultry, and had the lace and carpet factories, the carpenter

---

[6] This description of Empress Alexandra, the wife of Nicholas II, matches with that in Robert Massie's classic *Nicholas and Alexandra*.

shops, and so on, under her complete control. Often when the husband did not care for farming, or was engaged in some outside military or civil career, his aristocratic lady even handled all the business of estates, and showed herself an expert in agriculture, the breeding of stock, and everything connected with running from fifty to a hundred thousand acres, upon the income of which whole families must live. All this was taken as a matter of course, and there was no fuss made over it, nor any looking for praise from outside.

The charities handled by our women, the industrial schools, and all the thousand and one occupations which came from the effort to develop their people kept these female landowners immensely busy, yet I scarcely know of any one of them who struck me as being rushed or too preoccupied to sit down for a friendly chat. Those who did not read all the good publications coming out in three or four languages could be counted on one's fingers, and every one had as a matter of course read and digested the classics of standard literature from many countries. I found the older American writers were well known, and the most varied moderns—from Mark Twain and Jack London to William James—were digested and appreciated, remembered and quoted. It is not surprising such women were attractive companions, or that home life was delightful.

"The mother" was always the center of the home, and spent much time in apparent freedom from care, sitting behind her tea-table, knitting, while, with an air of its being casual, at certain hours of each day husband, children, and the intimate friends who had grown into the household, found opportunities to bring to her their problems, their troubles, or their joys, certain of sympathy and understanding. One had invariably a feeling of warmth and hospitality, however modest was the lodging, however simple the fare, and one wise old lady told me once gently: "I don't like it abroad, because there no one has what we have—that is, time for friendship."

I fancied that my Slav compatriots could love more, and better, and longer than do other races of women, because they had more time and had better learned the science of life and the enjoyment of quite simple things. No other people whom I had ever seen gave their lives such a full, rich note of meaning, or got so much out of it as did our upper class until the war. Nowhere either have I observed women grow old with such smiling contentment.

A clever Italian once said after he had spent a season in St. Petersburg, when I asked him what he had most liked: "The old women without a doubt; they are so comprehending and so fresh at heart. They mellow into age—like fine old wine, which gives one strength and courage to go on oneself toward time. There is no dryness, no bitterness, and they are clever and in the movement, and unaffectedly interested in everything. I find them quite adorable! No wonder they keep large groups of relations, friends, and devoted servitors about them. They have gathered these through long lives. They are your most wonderful feature, for it is not difficult to be attractive when one is young and beautiful, but to attract at sixty or seventy, and hold admiration without a sign of effort or of aid from dress—one cannot quite seize the art! It is an innate national trait to be like this, I believe."

I found this to be so, and by degrees I decided it was the sincere, deep sympathy they had towards all humanity and all work and effort. They loved their neighbors as themselves, and kept a ready hand outstretched; and they truly forgave others as they hoped to be forgiven what sins lay on their consciences. Not many these, and none which came from meanness. There seemed very little straining at life's harness, somehow. In Russia "marriages of convenience" were never much the fashion, so young couples started out with a fair chance for happiness at home; divorce was difficult and much frowned upon until the war, so if the hearth was unhappy the pair either tried to swallow their situation and make no moan, or else one heard vaguely of left-hand romances which lasted through the years and turned with time into softened tender friendships. Sometimes I noticed, on the contrary, that such alliances ended in renunciation and sacrifice to duties of hearth and home.

The light-headed, cold-hearted flirtations for amusement, and from boredom, such as one sees almost universally in other gay societies, seemed almost totally lacking, or at any rate were rare exceptions, and, though occasionally things really went wrong, I can think of no single case where deep sentiment was lacking. There always seemed a serious excuse for the lapses from law and convention. Strangely, also, society was generally very tolerant to such culprits as there were in its midst, and showed them more sympathy than blame. Pity for the woman was expressed, and understanding help was ready and was given invariably. This trait seemed to me one of the most winning qualities to be found among my compatriots.

The war demolished the old severities completely and divorce then became an easy thing, with the church's consent, but the high-bred group had largely scattered by that time, and what social units renascent Russia will show, or what will be her accepted standards, it is difficult to surmise.

In our lower classes, who were always quite uneducated and had lived for generations in the dark, the women seemed fully to do their share in carrying the general burden. They kept home and children, got on well habitually with the good-natured giants they married, and worked hard under their mothers-in-law's orders, in patriarchal fashion. Generally each woman obeyed both parents and husband, and loved and reared a large family until she faded, very young, as the Orientals do. But I found they became transformed creatures if brought into a better atmosphere. Such girls as came into our household as maids and nurses, or in other positions for service, showed intelligence, devotion, and touching gratitude. One wanted to give them aid, one felt, and not only to them, but to all their kind. However, it was not possible for any small group to bring about the immense changes in our laws that would have been necessary to develop the peasantry, so when we gave our village people personal care and work to do, or when we helped them through a bad year now and again, we reached the limit of our possibilities. It was very striking to see them so grateful for little things they received, and their unbelievable quickness to respond to any advantage offered was winning and encouraging.

When the war came, in one great wave the women rose to meet the situation. Without exception they gave their men, for the mobilization was general: fathers, sons, lovers, brothers, husbands—all were leaving, and yet the work of these men, whether in village or on estate, must go on or national production would come to a standstill, and armies and population would both lack food. Every woman in Russia realized the government could supply nothing to our armies but the bare necessities of war. There were neither nurses, nor doctors, nor medicines, nor Red Cross supplies of any kind; there were no warm clothes for the soldiers and refugees, no underclothes or overcoats, not even enough boots to go round among the troops. Misery and suffering beyond all calculation stared the people and the fighters in the face, and the powers above were swamped by demands they could not meet.

The women rose then to their full height, and carried through individually and collectively real miracles of organization. No labor was too heavy, no strain too great. The lazy manner of old was replaced by one of suppressed fire, as brains and bodies, which till then had known but pleasant things, worked twenty hours in the twenty-four. Everywhere there was rapid preparation, sudden efficiency. Within a month flying columns of first-aid units were on the firing line, while back of it at every château and in every city palace a hospital was improvised and offered gratis to the local administration, with volunteer nurses and doctors waiting in their places.

In St. Petersburg, as in the country, every motor was given and used in Red Cross work, and homes too small to use as storehouses or hospitals were turned into shops producing clothes and bandages. Sewn and knitted comfort lay piled up in every salon, rows of hospital beds and furniture stretched across ballrooms; sewing machines—whether one of fifty of them—hummed in every house. Conversation was reduced to the news, military and political, and to the discussion of ways and means to treat problems which cropped up. To face these was not easy, for there were few able to teach or lead. Almost no one knew anything; largely we had to feel our way, and it was hard to judge what thing was most needed, when so much was being called for. All one had was given without counting and without stint; jewels were pawned to pay for Red Cross trains and other practical small things. Faces went white and strained; and the passion in the eyes, dormant of old, was all alight. It took the outward form of exalted sacrifice.

I read here once on a begging poster: "Give till it hurts!" and I thought of the Russian women in those early days of the great war—and for three long years afterward—when they gave and gave, and pared down their own lives, but never seemed to feel it even, as time and money, hearts and souls, went into the great movement. In the largest houses meals were cut down to one dish or two; dresses were not renewed, and every one walked in the snowy streets—those who before had owned rich motors. One sitting-room only was generally kept heated, and great reception halls became mere warehouses; or if all these were warm, it was because the wounded and convalescent were living there. Every one responded to the calls, to the extreme limit of his or her possibilities. Perhaps this great over-straining was one reason why, when deeper troubles came, the population was no longer able to hold out against them and broke down.

The war went on for weeks, and months, and years; some women physically suffered a collapse, others mentally or morally could not stand the strain, with the constant wear of work, the intense anxiety as to home conditions, and the agony of slow retreats and frightful losses at the front. Yet most of these patriots went on mechanically with their duties, though their figures wore to shadows of what they had been before.

After about a year of war a new type of woman appeared among us: Amazons who did men's work in field and stable, farmyard and street, and who did it well, making men's wages easily. In the country these developed rapidly, and handled many duties never thought of before in their connection; and the new phase promised much for the future of woman's power in the land. Many daughters of the soil also tried soldiering, even early in the war, especially those from our mountain districts who possessed magnificent physiques. I was in the Caucasus in the summer of 1916, and I found the small town where I spent two months had sent a contingent of fifty women to the front, who were fighting as volunteers, while another unit, equally large, was preparing to leave.[7]

They usually engaged themselves as men, and often their sex was not recognized during long service. One case like this came to my notice, which seemed especially striking. Several wounded soldiers from a single regiment were brought into a hospital back of the firing line one day. Among them a tall, slim young chap was discovered by nurses and doctors to be a woman. Badly wounded she was, and her comrades whom the surgeon questioned seemed greatly surprised to learn the secret of her sex, which she had guarded perfectly through much hard fighting and several months of life in camp or in the trenches. They said she had never shown the least fatigue or the slightest tremor of fear; had been always the first to volunteer for any dangerous duty, and was the fiercest warrior in the regiment when the battle was on. They could hardly believe the news.

When she was well enough to speak herself, she told the head sister her story. Young and strong, a Caucasian tribes woman, she had remained at home at first and let her men go out to war. The Germans had killed her father, her husband, and her three brothers in the first six months. Then she felt she must kill Germans to revenge

---

[7] Women in combat was an especially unique Russian phenomenon in World War I. For more on this, see Laurie Stoff, *They Fought for the Motherland: Russia's Women Soldiers in World War I and the Revolution* (Lawrence: University Press of Kansas, 2006); and an even broader military role is analyzed in her *Russia's Sisters of Mercy and the Great War: More than Binding Men's Wounds* (Lawrence: University Press of Kansas, 2015).

her own family thus wiped out, so she had gone to the nearest recruiting station, given a false name, and as they were in a hurry drafting the new men they made no physical examination of any one who looked as strong as she. The tale she told that she had lost her identification passport was accepted and she was given a soldier's paper without question. She went forward to the training station. "After that it was smooth enough sailing, for I had always handled a gun, and could ride and walk and shoot with the best, and was used to our rough mountain life and camping. Only, sister, I must get well now quickly, and return to my duty to revenge my dead and shoot more of the enemy."

There were a lot of such girls and women in the ranks—sometimes thirsting for revenge, sometimes following a husband or a lover. The general testimony was to their splendid pluck and endurance. I never heard any criticism of their conduct, nor could fault be found with the discipline they showed.

Aside from these female soldiers there were many women in more normal roles, living constantly, during three years, out of the firing line. Great ladies stayed with the troops and turned their newly hardened, blackened hands to doing chores; risking their lives daily to bring the wounded back toward home and help. They established long lines of first-aid motor cars, and were generally supporting these machines from their own purses. Aristocrats were ably seconded by their sisters from every walk of life, as they all struggled shoulder to shoulder in the great cause. Ex-beauties of the court and their own maids were wearing the same khaki, doing the same fine work saving mankind, and among the groups scattered up and down the front one saw artists, courtesans, peasants, or bourgeoises, with the nobility, giving faithful service in nurses' dress. They all did without beds or sufficient food, and they worked night and day to feed and clothe the soldiers before battle, and to gather, transport, and care for the wounded afterward.

Hundreds of these sisters won medals of St. George, and some had several successive grades awarded them for repeated gallant services. One, the head of a flying column, whom I had known well in Petrograd's gay days, as a fragile belle at many a ball, seized an enemy's boat moored to a river bank and ferried it back and forth for two long days and nights under German fire, carrying provisions and munitions going and the wounded on her return trips.

Another Red Cross sister, who had been attached for some time to a certain unit of troops on the Polish front, volunteered and went into battle with a company of infantry sent forward to capture some trenches. The fight was especially deadly; every officer in the small band was shot before the last trench was reached. The sister and her stretcher-bearers, with the young student doctor attached, had helped all those they could. The officers had been stretched out, and when possible made comfortable, but not one of them was able to stand or to give orders, and still there remained that last trench to take. In the emergency this woman, seizing a sword, rushed to the head of the small waiting band of soldiers and, shouting the order to charge, with her veil and skirt flying, she led the way!

Of course every man followed her. With tremendous enthusiasm the trench was captured, and the little Red Cross sister had time to realize the victory was won before she dropped dead, her heart pierced by a German bullet. With deep reverence the men carried her body back to safety. Later she was given a military funeral, and because she had already received the whole series of decorations given to women she was now awarded a man's decoration for her man's work, the Officers' Cross of the Order of St. George, which was laid upon her coffin by the committee of that order. I was told at the time her honors were unique, as much so as her actions meriting them had been.

Back of the lines all over Russia, each in her quiet corner, other women worked and prayed, and worked again, and perhaps their patience and the way they faced the gathering difficulties through those hard months of 1914, 1915, and 1916 were no less fine than the action of their sisters who accompanied our armies.

I was always hearing of their courage in the field and their power of making a little go a long way to help the men; also of the inspiration which the women gave. It was all the soldiers ever received in the way of care and comfort, for from first to last the government could do nothing in this line at all. There was never even a question of making trenches livable, or of the possibility of giving proper uniforms, and, of course, no one thought of offering a pleasure or distraction to either the officers or soldiers who, during three years, strove to hold our frontiers in the common cause. They had no vacations from the firing line, even, save ten days once in each three months, and that was only thought of in the second year of war! All the money we women could scrape together went for absolute necessities which the authorities could not provide; and the latter felt they had every reason to be proud if they managed to supply just munitions and black bread in sufficient quantities to keep such huge armies as were needed on a battle-line two thousand miles in length! The government was not successful always in giving even so much to its sons, and misery was always great. No wonder German propaganda sowed its seeds on fertile ground!

When the revolution came every woman rejoiced, for high and low, in each stratum of the nation, its daughters had been discouraged by the complete helplessness of the autocratic regime in facing war problems. To every fireside the new theories brought fresh hope and courage. Those farthest from the capital kept these longest, but, after the third or fourth month of liberty had passed, illusions faded out all over Russia. The women began to wonder what their duties could be in the conditions of growing disorder. Some soon faced a business crisis, with the wrecking of homes, the arrest, martyrdom, and murder of their sons, husbands, brothers, and fathers, while they heard insults never-ending addressed to all they held most dear.

In the upper classes the women leaders of the revolution preached true liberty and against blind tyranny with all their strength. The venerable Catherine Breshko-Breshkovsky forgot her age and her thirty years of prison, and traveled about calling to arms in the crusade against anarchy. Then she went to live near Kérensky at the Winter Palace, of which he had taken possession, doubtless hoping to uphold that demagogue's failing will. Many other women worked and spoke, hoped and believed, to the eleventh hour, loath to give up their fair ideals born of the revolution.

The action of Maria Bochkarova was, perhaps, the most marvelous of all. A peasant, with a cruel life behind her, a soldier in the front ranks since the war began, she realized in the early months of the revolution how the monster anarchy was threatening Russia's safety and honor. Without hesitation she acted, and by her own personal effort alone she created, drilled, and conducted into battle that wonderful organization, the "Women's Death Battalion." The members of it took an oath to save our national honor or to die. They made it their business to be such an example as men might well be proud to follow. To me this group collectively stands in our history on a par with that single heroine of France, Joan of Arc. They suffered for the lack of all material things, but never complained; they withstood the test of ridicule and all temptations, as they did also the taunts of prejudiced onlookers.

First they fought against the Germans at the front, and were killed like flies because the regiments on each side broke and fled, leaving these women to face a bloody fate. Their ranks were reformed at once then, and companies were filled out with fresh volunteers. Again they threw themselves into the melée. Against terrific odds they stayed there, fighting, dying, till they were called away for a still rougher and more tragic duty. Kérensky, the people's idol once, could no longer, after October 1917, trust his own guardians about the Winter Palace, so he ordered back the women from the battle front to protect him. And they did so faithfully until the end.

The crash came, and the mob of Bolshevik soldiers attacked the palace of the ancient Czars, become Kérensky's home and offices under the new regime.[8] The troop of women stood their ground there firmly. Hour after hour, day after day, through that time of chaos and of blood, they defended the last citadel of law and order. The fight continued till nearly all were sacrificed and they were too few to cover more than one entrance to the great building. Long since, Kérensky the dictator had fled, leaving his defenders to their destiny, while the other ministers, braver than he, remained, only to be arrested in the council hall. Still Botchkarova's company rallied again and again. At last but a few women were left, and they had nothing more to hold, for the mob had seized the palaces's rear doors and entered it. All was over, and the Bolsheviks took up the government in triumph.

The leaders of the first March revolution have long been exiles abroad, begging Allies for their assistance in the great cause of Russia's liberty, and waiting in patience for the rebirth of our land. Such women as were the "femmes des halles" in Paris,

---

[8] Obviously the author exaggerated the situation around the Winter Palace, and the "palace of the ancient Czars" would be in the Kremlin in Moscow.

or the Rosa Luxemburgs of Berlin, are conspicuous by their absence in our country throughout the present reign of terror.[9]

Undoubtedly, like others, Russian people have many faults, but throughout their history, and as I have known them, our women seem soft and gentle creatures, utterly feminine. Orient's heat and northern snows, the vague broad steeps and the closed-in forests, low Baltic marshes and high pinnacles of Caucasian rock—each is reflected in the Slav's great mystery, each has contributed something to her nature. When her present trials are over, and she comes at last into her own, it will be seen what late experiences have done to mold the riches of her nature. She has learned only from suffering and sacrifice throughout the centuries, and yet has labored on and has accomplished much. How she will blossom when at last the sunlight shines upon her, is a question for the future to prove.

---

[9] She apparently is unaware of the Bolshevik Alexandra Kollontai nor the Left Socialist Revolutionary, Maria Spiridonova, among others.

Index

Academy of Fine Arts 158
Academy of Sciences 158n1
Ai-todor 85–86
Aksent′ev, agricultural specialist at Bouromka 33–34, 41, 44–45
Alexander I xi
Alexander III 55, 85n11
Alexandra, Empress xviii n30, 161, 162n6
Alexis, Tsarevich 87n12
Allies xviii, 63, 65, 72, 80–81, 83, 88, 108–13, 117–19, 129–32, 141, 155, 169
All-Russian Congress of Soviets xv
All-Russian Government, Kolchak's 136, 139. *See also* Omsk.
All-Russian Mission 118
American Central Committee for Russian Relief xvi–xv
American Civil War x, xviii
American Expeditionary Force (AEF), Siberia 130, 130n12, 141–42, 141n5
American Legion xviii
American Red Cross 121n9, 142, 142n7
American Relief Administration (ARA) xvii, xvii n29
American Y.M.C.A. xvi, 121n9, 142–43
Americans in Siberia 141–42
Anastasia 85n11
Anna, Empress 158, 158n1
Anna-Vladimirova (husband's former nurse) 7, 43, 46
Archangel 64, 66, 115, 119; soviet in 116n2
Astor, John Jacob III xi n7
Austria-Hungary x, 101, 152n17
Austrian prisoners 17, 34, 46

Bakhchisarai 78n5
Baltic Fleet xiii, 38n4, 55n5, 126
Baltic Germans xx, 57n6, 57n7
Baltic Sea 88, 119
Baltic States 78
Bar Harbor, Maine xix
Bark, Petr 81, 81n7
Beaulieu xi
Belgium 131
Bellavin, Vasily. *See* Tikhon, Patriarch.
Berlin 121n9, 169
Bessarabia 78
Biblikov, veterinarian 44
Big Four, at Paris 66n20
Biron, Ernst Johann von 158n1
Black Sea xiii, 77, 109, 120, 122–24, 136
Black Sea Fleet 81, 87–88, 122–23, 122n10; Kolchak in command of 124–26
Bochkareva, Maria 169
Bolshevik Revolution xvi, xviii, xx, 41n7, 45n8
Bolsheviks, mentioned 47, 54, 66, 72–74, 80, 80n6, 83, 87, 101, 103, 105, 122, 128–29, 146, 150, 169
Bolshevism 54, 81, 106–07, 109, 113, 115, 117–18, 127, 136, 139, 141,147, 150
Bonaparte, Napoleon 38n3, 156
Borodino, Battle of 84–85, 85n10
Bouromka, Cantacuzene estate, frontispiece viii, xii–xiv, 7–9; destruction of xx; description of 8–9, 25, 29–30; little news from 49; peasant emancipation at 32–33; threatened 37, 42–45, 56–57

Bouromka village 12–15; Austrian prisoners in 18; Bolshevik control 43; improvements in 14–18, 31–33; priest in 18–19, 29, 37, 37n2, 40, 50–52; soldiers from 37–39; vodka in 17, 26, 36–37, 37n2, 43

Breshko-Breshkovsky 168–69

Breslau 122n10, 123, 126

Brest-Litovsk, Treaty of, negotiations 62–63, 63n15, 63n16, 77–78

British navy 120

Bronstein. *See* Trotsky, Leon.

Brusilov, Aleksei 82

Buchanan, Sir George (British ambassador to Russia) 75

Byzantium 157

Canadian Red Cross 154

Cantacuzene, Boris (brother-in-law of Julia Cantacazene) xiii, 15

Cantacuzene, Elizabeth (mother-in-law) 14, 18–19, 26, 29–33, 120, 159. *See also* Sicard, Elizabeth.

Cantacuzene, Julia Grant xii–xvii; arrival in Russia 12–13; at Bouromka 17–20; knowledge of languages 23; train trip to Bouromka 22–25

Cantacuzene, Marie Alexandrovna (grandmother of Mikhail Mikhailovich, granddaughter of Mikhail Speransky) 30–33

Cantacuzene, Mikhail Mikhailovich (husband) x–xiv, xvi, xviii–xix, 15, 19, 40, 55–56, 99n3; departure from Omsk 149–51; with Kolchak in Siberia 136–56

Cantacuzene, Mikhail Mikhailovich (son) xii–xiii, xix

Cantacuzene, Mikhail Rodionovich (father of Mikhail Mikhailovich) 31–32

Cantacuzene, Radu (Rodion) xi

Cantacuzene, Rodion (grandson) xii

Cantacuzene, Varvara (Bertha; daughter) xii–xiii, xix n34, 29

Cantacuzene, Zenaida (Ida; daughter) xii, xix n34

Catherine I 158

Catherine II, the Great 158–59, 158n3

Caucasus 115, 166

Caucasian Front 119n6

Chaikovsky, Nikolai 115, 115n2

Chechens 78

Cherkass 23

Chicago x, x n3, xviii–xix

Chicherin, Georgy 64, 64n18, 66n21, 69

China 145–46, 151–52, 157

Chinese Eastern Railway 152n16

Chita 128n11, 153

Christmas 1915 7, 12

Clemenceau, George 72–73

Cleveland, Grover x

Congress of the Country and Municipal District Councils, Crimean 82, 106–07

Constantinople 54n1, 72, 120–21

Constituent Assembly xiv, 80n6

Constitutional Democratic Party (Kadets) 54n1, 80

Coolidge, Calvin xix n34

Cossacks 15, 29, 32, 49, 83, 98–99, 115, 115n1, 128, 147–49

Crimea xvi, 71, 76; in Russian Civil War 82–84, 89–91, 107; provisional government of 76–81; suffering of 87–89

Crimean Peninsula 77–78, 85, 115, 119–20, 125

Crimean War 85, 85n10

Curtis, Clarissa xix n34

Czechoslovak Legion 132n14, 141n5, 142n7, 144, 148–49, 149n14, 151, 152n17

Czechoslovakia 149n14, 153

Czechoslovaks 129, 144, 148–49, 154–55

INDEX

Denikin, Anton xvii; army of 75, 82–85 82n9, 89–91, 109–10, 110n8, 113, 115–16, 120, 128
Denmark 85n11
Diet, Crimean 82
Dimenti (coachman) 8
Dmitry (prosperous peasant at Bouromka) 36, 39
Don Region 115n1
Don River 109
Draper, Jeanette xviii
Dresden 9
Dukhonin, Nikolai, General 56
Duma 23, 35, 71, 76n2, 80
Durnovo, Petr 98n3

East Prussia 33, 138
Easter 1916 28–30
Eastern Front xv
Ebergard, Admiral 122–24
Elene (author's maid) xvi, 7, 20–21
Eichhorn, Herman von 47, 49, 77–78, 78n3, 104, 106
Ekaterinburg 55n4, 132, 155
Ekaterinodar 83–84
Eliot, Charles xvii
Elizabeth, Empress 158, 158n2
Empress Maria (Russian battleship) 123–24
Empress of Japan 137
England 119, 121
Episcopal Church xi
Estonia 119n6
Evpatoria 76, 124
Evropeiskii (Hotel Europe) xiv–xv

Faberge workshop xvi
"Feast of Three Kings" 19
February Revolution xviii
Finland 116n3, 142n7
Finland Station 55n3
Finns 116

First World War. *See* World War I.
Florida viii–xix
Food Brigades 62n14
Food Decree 47n9, 69n22
France 27, 52, 87n13, 115n1, 119–21, 132, 148, 148n13, 151
Francis, David, Ambassador xv, 63–64, 64n17, 115

Gajda, Radola 144, 151–54, 152n17; revolt in Vladivostok 152–55
Galicia 12, 33, 107, 138
George VI xix
Georgia 78
German clique at court xiv
German conspiracy theory xv–xvii, xx n39, 40
German gold 55–56, 55n5
Germany xvi, xviii, 47, 52, 55, 59, 65, 78, 84–85, 109, 115n1, 149n14
Goeben (German Cruiser) 122, 122n10, 126
Gogol, Nikolai 11
Golden Sword of St. George 127
Goncharov, Ivan 159n4
Goremykin, Ivan 23
Gough-Calthorpe, Somerset Arthur, Vice Admiral 76
Grant, Frederick Dent (father) x
Grant, Ida Honore (mother) x–xii
Grant, Julia Dent x–xii
Grant, Ulysses S. (grandfather) x, xix
Grant, Ulysses S. III (brother) xi
Grant's Tomb xix
Graves, William S. 142, 142n6
Great Britain 81n7, 148n13
Great Russia 65, 107
Greece 121

Hanbury-Williams, Sir John xix n34
Harbin 145n11, 152
Harrison, Benjamin x

Harvard University xvii
Herron, Edward 118n4
Holman, Charles S. 130–32, 131n13
"Holy Russia" 17, 27
Honore, Henry xi
Hoover, Herbert xvii
Hungarians 136, 140
Hungary 107, 110, 138
Huns 65, 79, 104

Iassy 108–09
Imperial Alexandrine Lycee xi, xiv
India 162
International Military Police 153
Irkutsk 143–45, 146n11, 150–55
Italy 31, 52
Ivan III 157
Ivan IV 157
Ivan V 158n1

James, William 163
Janin, Maurice, General 148–50, 149n14, 151
Japan 137, 139n2, 154
Japanese 128, 141n5, 142–43, 145n10, 147
Jerome (chef) xii
Jews 7, 20, 37, 103n5, 132
Joan of Arc 75
John VI, Byzantine emperor xi
Johnson, Benjamin, 153
"July Crisis" xv, 58n9

Kalmikov, Ivan 129
Kandalaksha 64
Kanin, Admiral 81
Kansas 118n2
Kantakuzen, Grigory xi
Kennan, George F. 64n17
Kerch 77
"Kerensky Offensive" xiv, 39n5
Kerensky, Alexander xv, xviii, 54, 140;
  as minister of war 54n1; as minister
  president 59, 59n11, 98n3,111, 128; in
  Winter Palace 169
Kerensky money 140
Kharkov 85, 108–09, 120
Kherson 120
Kiev xii, xiv, 7, 19, 36, 44, 73; bank in
  48, 104; bloodshed in 102–05, 103n5;
  Germans in 47, 54, 99; new Ukrainian
  government 47, 78; revolution in 92–96,
  98, 109
Knight, Admiral Austin 142n5
Knox, Sir Alfred, General 148, 149n14
Kollontai, Alexandra 170n9
Kolchak, Alexander xvi–xviii; described
  122, 141, 142n6; Cantacuzene interview
  with 145–46; defeat of 154–56; Omsk
  headquarters 128–29, 128n11, 130n12,
  134–36; praise for 146–48
Kornilov Affair xv, 128
Kornilov, Lavr 82, 82n9, 128
Krasnov, Petr 70, 70n23, 84, 115, 115n1, 128,
  134
Krasnoyarsk 150
Kremlin 63, 68, 134, 157
Kronstadt 71, 125–26
Krivoshein, Alexander 16
Kshesinskaia, Matylda 55, 55n3, 59

Lake Michigan 137
Lang, General Pavel Karlovich 11
Lansing, Robert 142n6
League of Nations 117, 133n15
Left Socialist Revolutionary 63n15, 72n26;
  Party of 78
Lenin, Vladimir xiv n17, xv, 54, 54n2, 60,
  118, 151; aid to Germans 58n10
Lenin–Trotsky tyranny 122
Lewiston, Maine xix
Liberals 117
Lithuania 78
Litvinov, Maxim 66n20

Little Russia (Ukraine) 26, 28, 31, 36 100, 104. *See also* Ukraine.
Livadia 77
Lloyd George, David 72–73, 75
London 119
London, Jack 163
Lubny, Ukraine xii,7, 19
Lucas (Lukantchik) servant on estate, 7
Luxemburg, Rosa 170
Lvov, Georgy 111

Malta 121
Manchuria 128n11, 130, 152n16
Mannerheim, Carl Gustav Emil 116, 116n3, 119
Maria Fedorovna, Grand Duchess xiv, 79, 85–87, 85n11, 90, 120–21
Marie-Alexandrovna 29–31, 44. *See also* Cantacuzene, Marie Alexandrovna.
Marne 84
Marshall Field's x
Martov, Iulii 54n2
Marx, Karl 59
Marxism 45n8
Massie, Robert 162n6
McCormick, Cyrus, Jr. xvi–xvii
Mensheviks 54n2
Michael-Petrovich (servant at Bouromka) 29, 36, 42–44
Mikhail Nikolaevich, Grand Duke 11
Miliukov, Paul 54, 54n1
Mirbach, Count Wilhelm von 63, 63n15, 78, 78n3
Mobilization 14–15
Moghilev 56
Morris, Roland 139, 139n2, 142n6
Moscow 69, 106, 112, 128n11, 146, 151; advance on 115, 122, 134; Bolshevik government in 63–64, 78n3
Moses-Kouzmich (senior servant) 9, 31, 43–44, 46

Mott, John R. xvi
Murmansk 119, 119n7

Nabokov, Konstantin 80, 80n6
Nabokov, Vladimir 80n6
Nevskii Prospect xv
New York xii, xviii–xix; East Side 60, 134n18, 155
Newport, Rhode Island xi–xii
Nicholas I 87n13
Nicholas II 13–15, 23, 34, 38, 41n7, 43, 53, 55n3, 55n4, 85n85, 87
Nikolaev 120
Nikolai Mikhailovich, Grand Duke xiv
Nikolai Nikolaevich, Grand Duke xii, 22–23, 34, 37–38, 77, 79, 87, 87n13, 120–21, 151
Nikonov 80
North Russia 74
Novocherkassk 84

Odessa xi, 31, 109–10, 119–20
Olga, acceptance of Christianity 157
Olga-Ivanovna (village doctor) 16
Omsk 128–29, 139; Bolshevik attack on 151; Siberian government 132–33, 136, 141n5, 143–50
Order Number One, Petrograd Soviet 57–58, 126
Order of St. George 127, 129
Orient 134, 138–39, 161–62
Ottoman Turks xi

Page Corps xi, 98n3, 99
Palmer Bank xviii
Palmer, Bertha Honore x–xi, xviii
Palmer House x
Palmer Mansion x n3
Palmer, Potter x, xix n34
Palmer, Potter IV x, xix n36
Palmyra 20, 22, 24–25, 40
Panama Canal 152n16

Paris xvii, 66, 75, 83n9, 111–13, 116n2, 116–17, 121n9, 131, 146, 159–60; Russian mission in 133–34, 136, 169–70
Paris Peace Conference 111–13, 115, 118–19, 119n4, 122, 132–33
Patriarch, Russian Orthodox Church 67. *See also* Tikhon.
Pasteur Institute 16
Pavlovsk Military Academy 115
Peace Conference. *See* Paris Peace Conference.
Peoples' Commissars 66; Council of 73
Perm 85, 132, 153n17, 155
Peter and Paul Fortress 55
Peter the Great 157–58, 158n1, 158n2
Peter Ivanovich (factory manager, Kiev) 92–98
Peter III 158n2, 158n3
Petliura, Symon 99n3, 102n4, 103n5, 106–10, 110n8
Petrograd ix, xiv n18, 34, 43, 54–55, 63, 66, 71–73, 106, 123, 140; advance on 122; author in 125
Petrograd Soviet 38, 58n9
Phanariot Greeks xii
Philadelphia 139n2
Philippines xi, 129
Plehve, Viacheslav xviii
Poland xvii, 20, 33, 103n5, 107, 149n14
Poles 51
Poltava, city 36, 85; province xi, 16, 98n3
Port Arthur 125
Port Said 141
Potter, Bishop xi
Prague 121n9
Prince's Island 66, 66n20, 118, 121
Prinkipo 69n22
Prinkipo Proposal 66
Prisoners of War 128
Prohibition of Alcohol 40, 40n7

Provisional Government (1917) xiii–xiv, 38n4, 45n8, 54n1, 55n5, 58n9, 76–77, 98n3, 100–01, 111

Rabinowich (village userer) 13, 37
Radek, Karl 63, 63n16
Raffalovich, Arthur 111–12
Rasputin, Grigory xviii, xviii n30, 87, 87n12
Red Army 115, 128n11
"Red Guard" 62, 65, 85, 90, 131
Reed, John ix
Revolution of 1905 xiii, 26
Revolutionary Days ix, ix n1, xvii, 39n6
Riga, Treaty of 103n5
Robespierre 61, 100
Rodzianko, Mikhail 58
Rome x
Roosevelt, Franklin D. xix
Rumania 72, 78, 110
Russia, future of 52–53, 113–15, 121, 155–56
Russian Civil War ix, xvii, xx, 70n23, 82n9, 128n11, 129, 150–55
Russian Nationalities xx
Russian Orthodox Church ix
Russian People ix, xiii, xvi–xvii
Russian Railway Service Corps, American 152n16
Russian Red Cross 7, 26, 59–60, 165–68
Russian Refugees 120, 121n9
Russian Social Democratic Workers' Party 54n2
Russo-Japanese War xii–xiii, 13–15, 47n10, 98n3, 99, 119n6, 125
Russo-Turkish War xi

Sarasota, Florida xvii–xviii; Chamber of Commerce of xix
Saratov 57n7, 71, 132
Sazonov, Sergei 81, 81n8, 146
Saturday Evening Post x

INDEX

Semenov, Grigory, Ataman 128–29, 128n11, 143, 149, 152
Sevastopol 72, 78, 80, 83, 108, 122–25; Battle of 85
Siberia xx, 33, 89, 128–32, 136–37, 145, 149n14, 152–55
Sicard, Elizabeth (mother-in-law) xi, 9–10, 12–15. *See also* Cantacuzene, Elizabeth
Simferopol 76–78, 83
Skoropadsky, Pavel (Pavlo) 47–49, 47n10, 48n10, 49n11, 98n3, 107; as hetman of Ukraine 78, 98–105; critical view of 102–06
Smith, Douglas 87n14
Smolny 69
Social Democrats 116
Social-Revolutionaries 116
Somme 84
Sophia 157
Souchon, American casualties at 141n5
Southwestern Front xiv, 39n5, 58n9
Soviet Russia 149n14
Spanish-American War xi
Speransky, Mikhail xi, 9, 30–31
St. George's Cross 70
St. Nicholas Cathdral 134n18
St. Petersburg xi–xii, xiv n18, xvi, 8, 44, 80; author's impressions of 159–64; rising opposition in 161n5. *See also* Petrograd.
St. Petersburg Theological Academy 134n18
Stevens, John F. 129–31, 131n13, 152, 152n16
Stolypin, Petr xiii, 16
Sturmer, Boris 23
Sudetenland 152n17
Sukin 146
Sulgrave Club (Washington) xx
Sulkevich, Khan 79–80
Switzerland 54

Tarnopol 38–39

Tatars 51, 75, 78–79, 78n5, 151n15, 156, 161
Tchaikovsky. *See* Chaikovsky, Nikolai
Tchair 77
Tikhon, Patriarch 134, 134n18
Tikhon's manifesto 67–69
Tobolsk 85
Tokyo 138–39
Tolstoy, Leo 53
Tomsk 146
Torneo xvi
Trans-Siberian Railroad xv, 63, 128n11, 131, 142n7, 143–45, 144n10, 150–53
Tretiakov, Pavel 112
Trotsky, Leon xv, 54n2, 55n5, 62, 69, 73, 78; as Red Army commander 64n18, 134, 151; description of 60–61
Trotsky-Lenin government, subservient to Germany 62–63, 151
Tsushima, Battle of xiii
Turkey 78
Twain, Mark 163

Udenich, Nikolai 119, 119m6
Ufa 132, 155
Ukraine xi–xii, xv, xvii; as source of German relief 48–49, 48n10; conditions in 1918, 50, 50n12, 79; German agents in 55; independence of 45n8, 100–03
Ukrainian Democratic Republic 103
Ukrainian Rada 100–10
United States xiii, xv, xvii, 53, 107, 116n2, 122, 134n18, 136, 142n7, 146, 150
Ural Mountains 128, 132n14
Uritsky, Moisei 72, 72n26

Vancouver 137, 139
Venice 163
Verdun 113
Vienna x
Vinaver, Maksim 76, 76n2, 80
Vladimir, Grand Prince 71

Vladivostok 128n11, 129–30, 139–41, 141n5, 142n7, 145n11, 148, 151, 154
Vodka 12, 47
Volga Germans 57n7
Volga 132
Vologda xiv n18; diplomatic missions in 63–64
Volunteer Army 84, 88–90
"War Communism" 69n22
War Trade Board, Vladivostok 130
Washington Post xviii
Washington, D.C. x, xviii–xix, xix n34, 107, 129–30; Russian embassy in 136
Western Front 144n10, 149n14
White, William Allen 118n4
White Sea 89
White House x, ix
Wilhelm, Kaiser 35, 99
Wilson, Woodrow 66, 66n20, 72–73, 118, 118n4
Winter Palace 41n7, 169

Witte, Sergei xviii
Women's Death Battalion 169
Women's National Republican Club xix
World War I xii–xiv, 38n3, 47n10, 70n23, 98n3, 99, 128n11; strain of 166; women in combat 166n7
World War II 70n23, 115n1
World's Work 130–31

Xenia Aleksandrovna, Grand Duchess 87n13, 120

Yalta 77, 87–88
Yaroslavl 134n18
Y.M.C.A. *See* American Y.M.C.A.
Yokohama 137
Yugoslavia 115n1, 121n9

Zinoviev, Grigory 65, 65n19, 66, 69

Figure 1. Nikita and Lisa, valet and maid at Bouromka

Figure 2. Lieutenant-General Denikin, Commander-in-Chief of the South Russian Armies

Figure 3. Admiral Kolchak

Figure 4. Catherine the Great

Figure 5. Catherine Breshkovsky

www.ingramcontent.com/pod-product-compliance
Lightning Source LLC
Chambersburg PA
CBHW032024230426
43671CB00005B/199